Sellout

Sellout
The Giveaway
of Canada's
Energy Resources
Philip Sykes

Hurtig Publishers, Edmonton

Hurtig Publishers
10560 105 Street
Edmonton, Alberta

Hardcover ISBN 0-88830-075-1
Paperback ISBN 0-88830-076-X

Designed, typeset, printed and bound in Canada

Contents

For my wife Toby,
our children Rosalind, Megan and Adam,
and all their contemporaries.

The resource map of the continent has been re-drawn, exclusively on north-south lines.

Introduction

I met them at a sherry party. In that courtly Haligonian ritual at Dalhousie University's Faculty of Law, where they all work and where they had gathered to unveil the portrait of a former dean, the four scholars who prompted this book were at home. It was an occasion with a certain formality, yet modest and comfortable, like the winding paths around the campus where professors jog in track suits, like Canadian National's Nova Scotian Hotel, where a derelict can sleep warm until breakfast time on the carpet inside the foyer's glass doors.

Here they came together in the summer of 1972. Only R. St. J. Macdonald, the upright, steel-haired dean of the Faculty of Law, was a native Nova Scotian. The others had chosen to come here, drawn perhaps by the salt air, the unpredictable shoreline and the sense of neighbourly well-being that still animates cities built on a human scale. Douglas M. Johnston, the thoughtful marine law specialist, was from Scotland and Rowland J. H. Harrison, who had trained in Alberta in oil and gas law, from Australia. Ian McDougall was a tall, lean British Columbian with a national reputation in environmental law and an intense patriotism that may first have burgeoned when, through the long nights of his boyhood, he read with fascination the private papers of his distinguished grandfather, the late General Andrew McNaughton. Never, ever, will McDougall mention this relationship now. Austerely academic, he distrusts the intrusion of the emotional element into any discussion of public policy. Yet the relationship, with its hint of a dynastic continuity in the struggle to preserve Canada's integrity, is not without historical intrigue.

The professors talked that summer of the quickening of pace in Halifax that came with a wave of resource development, of the one hundred oil companies drilling offshore without regulation, New Brunswick's power sale to the state of Maine, the Mobil exploration on bleak Sable Island, that oversized sand bar held together by a meagre cover of coarse grass. They worried about the arrogance and secrecy in which these and other projects were conceived and effected, about the New Brunswick Power Commission's denial of a public impact statement, the rumoured $2 billion nuclear plant on Stoddard's Island and Premier Gerald Regan's unpublished "studies" on the economic benefits of offshore petroleum.

Even in Halifax, they sensed, development was starting to distort the human scale. The professors decided to pool their expertise in a brief about the protection of the public and the environment that would, they thought, provoke a discussion alerting Maritimers to the shattering impact large-scale petroleum development could have upon a region so dependent on the tourist's dollar. They were disappointed. When they presented the brief, entitled *Economic Development with Environmental Security*, to the retired company vice-president representing the Canadian Council of Resource and Environment Ministers in Halifax, there was no reaction at all. Inquiring weeks later, McDougall was promised only that the document would be "looked at" by an official sifting "input" for the council's big conference planned for November, 1973.

Their brief presented a careful program of environmental protection for the Atlantic region, which, they feared, was about to "accept a really bad deal." They felt that, as McDougall put it, "it doesn't occur to the governments that they can't be hurt by delay, that it might be better to hold off development until they could ensure a return that would aggrandize the Maritimes rather than the United States." Because they knew some environmental damage was inevitable they wanted to be sure that the benefits would more than compensate. "An oil spill here," McDougall argued, "is an economic disaster as well as an environmental one, since it destroys recreational areas in one of North America's best tourist regions, on the doorstep of 100 million people. Scenery has greater economic value here than elsewhere. We stand in danger of losing our coastline."

11

To show there were solid historical grounds for these apprehensions, the scholars we shall call the Dalhousie Four scrutinized the case histories of five proposals for the development of energy resources in other parts of Canada. They looked at the Columbia River treaty of 1964 which sold the control of the Canadian part of the Columbia basin to the United States; the fifteen-year fire sale of Alberta's best natural gas; the Alberta plan to transfer the flow of the province's rivers from the north to the south (shelved in 1972 by the new Conservative government); Manitoba Hydro's plan to increase power capacity by destroying the Churchill River; and Quebec's $6 billion scheme to remould the river basins east of James Bay to keep the lights burning in New York State.

It was then, having examined disparate resource deals from the standpoint of Canada's national interest, having compared the pressures for development at work in British Columbia, Alberta, Manitoba and Quebec, having weighed the claims of costs and benefits, that the four professors reached general conclusions that would bring attention from far beyond the Atlantic region.

Those conclusions were of obvious national significance. Canada, said the Dalhousie Four, is almost always the loser in big energy deals, which are generally undertaken for short-term ends and with get-rich-quick motivation. They are often launched on provincial initiative without serious consideration of the environmental costs or the damage to the national economy. The usual purpose is to service industry in the United States. The involvement of the federal government, the professors found, is "consistently unimposing," even when the constitution provides a clear mandate for action by Ottawa.

The Dalhousie Four claimed no blinding originality in all this. The findings, singly considered, were not new. The thesis, for instance, that resource development is undertaken to service multinational corporations would surprise no reader of James Laxer's *Energy Poker Game*. Ottawa's dereliction in questions of economic planning were painfully apparent to all who had followed the speeches of the former Liberal cabinet ministers Walter Gordon and Eric Kierans. (Kierans, with his customary flair for crisp definition, was to term the Dalhousie brief "the record of a nation on the way to being a colony.")

12

But Laxer, Gordon and Kierans were, or had been, politicians, urging a "case" for particular political doctrines. What was new about the Dalhousie brief was the authority of the legal scholar's method, investing the critique of the resources sellout with new coherence and conviction. Here were four respected specialists, working in the spirit and method of scholarly inquiry, setting out initially to formulate only a protective code for the environment of their region. Almost incidentally, they had thrown into relief the apparent incapacity of the central government, over more than a decade, to husband Canada's non-renewable resources.

Out of Dalhousie had come a startlingly clear picture of what had happened to Canadian development in the fifties and sixties and clearly what could happen through the seventies. The high-pressure promotion of the Mackenzie Valley natural gas pipeline and the widening realization of the tightening price squeeze that could be exerted upon Canadians by the near-monopolistic oil industry in the wake of the United States' energy crisis would serve only to highlight the national implications of the Dalhousie study.

Kierans by now was exhorting Canadians to "keep the gas in the ground until we need it." British Columbia Premier Dave Barrett was proclaiming that his province had been "skinned" by the Columbia River treaty. The connections between the melancholy resource projects launched under provincial auspices in the recent past and the even more dangerous undertakings now being promoted under federal sponsorship were very clear. McDougall had been speaking of offshore exploration when he said that "if we cared about getting rewards for this region instead of the United States, exploration might not start for thirty years," but that was becoming a general view of the energy problem among a significant number of Canadians.

It was with this national relevance in mind that publisher Mel Hurtig decided the work of the Dalhousie professors warranted popularization in a journalistic treatment that might reach larger numbers of Canadians than a formal brief to an official body could hope to do. Popular history, after all, has had little to say about the Canadian sellout in energy resources, which has been going on at least since the fortyish politicians who are now provincial premiers were kids in high school. Popular history in our country has focussed almost obsessively on our politicians, their exits and entrances, their triumphs and pratfalls. And popular historians, wrapt in speculative probings into the psyche of Joey, Wacky, Dief or the inevitable Trudeau, have not recounted adequately the alienation of Canada's natural wealth. They offer tantalizing vignettes of Wacky Bennett's mischief; we glimpse him chortling in delight after having snubbed Ottawa's E. Davie Fulton. Or they spotlight the histrionics of Robert Bourassa, promising "economic liberation" to Quebeckers from the darkened stage of the Coliseum. But they rarely show the consequences of such capers—the damage to the Athabasca Delta, or the dead sturgeon floating down the polluted La Grande.

The work of the Dalhousie Four, in contrast, was entirely concerned with the consequences of political acts. Their interest lay not in anecdotes but in sketching in bold, gaunt outlines a special picture of Canada in the historical period of large-scale resource development. This book, built around their outlines, is an effort to round out their picture. It is not a neutral effort; I accepted from the outset the central ideas of the Dalhousie Four—ideas that had confirmed and added meaning to my own findings as a journalist in the environmental field.

Two notions, widely accepted among the scholars of resource development, have yet to enter the popular histories. One notion is that in our time, in the waning decades of the Age of Fossil Fuels, part of the accounting of the nation's economic health must be reckoned not in dollars but in natural resources—in billions of barrels of crude oil, trillions of cubic feet of natural gas, millions of acre feet of water and billions of kilowatt hours of electrical energy. The second notion is that in many of Canada's least-known regions—in the Mackenzie Delta and the Arctic Islands, in northwest Quebec and northern Manitoba—complex natural life systems are threatened by sudden, drastic and irreversible changes that will be neither controlled nor even understood by Canadians at large.

For the scholars of resource development, the contemporary threats to Canada's survival appear immediate and tangible. National survival, for the resource scholar, is no abstraction. "We're not really interested," says Ian McDougall, "in transferring the remnants of a Canadian economy from Wall Street's control to Bay Street's. Canada is losing shorelines and valleys —its tangible physical assets. If we don't establish Canadian controls over the economic and environmental rules of development, there'll be nothing left worth transferring." The flow of rivers, the very rocks and trees, are part of the question of survival.

This view is increasingly shared by resources scholars across Canada—as much by McGill's Dr. John Spence and the University of Manitoba's Dr. Robert W. Newbury as by the Dalhousie Four. Scientists are working in many disciplines— in anthropology, biology, engineering, economics and law, geology, petrochemicals, geography and sociology, land use and native rights—to preserve peoples and regions that have always been popularly undervalued in the border strip of urban Canada.

For these men, the twenty-year history of big energy deals is at last clearly framed. They have a picture of a period, a period in which Canadians sold too much of the nation's irreplaceable store of energy resources too cheaply; Canadians exported energy that could have powered new industry and employment here; Canadians paid the social and environmental costs of producing energy others would use; Canadians failed to realize the "economic rents" of resource exploitation in Canada; Canadians permitted the alienation of the most valuable and accessible reserves still in the ground; Canadians lost control of the prices they must pay as consumers of their own resources.

Now the pace of development is faster, and its dimensions broader. Canadians stand in danger of losing control on an unprecedented scale. Mammoth developments are in motion, their timing, their financing and ownership, their pricing and market decisions largely determined outside Canada's borders. Secret diplomacy between government departments and energy corporations has effectively precluded democratic decision-making for years. And now the accelerating depletion of domestic resources in the United States quickens the pace of Canadian sellout. Five eastern premiers get together with the governors of the New England states to promote superports and refineries that will plug the economies of the Canadian provinces into the profitable petroleum scarcity of the eastern U.S. Pipeline lobbyists invest the prospect of selling massive quantities of Canada's northern gas to the United States with the spurious glamour of another "northern boom." A reorganized energy industry led by the huge petroleum corporations sprawls acquisitively into new fields of resource development.

Here, then, is the sombre picture that was sketched for us all by those quiet scholars at Dalhousie—a picture of twenty years of selling out.

Chapter One

The Jackpot Question

"Would it make sense for Canada to allow these foreign-controlled corporations to develop the enormous potential reserves in the Canadian North and to grow even more fabulously wealthy in the process? To me, it would not."

— Walter Gordon, former Liberal cabinet minister.

With this statement, Walter Gordon has put the jackpot question. It is a question that troubles countless thoughtful Canadians. They may not have posed it, even to themselves, with quite the precision that Gordon commands. They may not even have conceived it in the same context of the Mackenzie Valley natural gas pipeline, relevant as that is to any consideration of a Canadian future. No, the disquiet they feel, though faithfully mirrored in Gordon's rhetorical question, is less easily defined, more fragmented and also more general. The tangible national unease over the North, resource development and foreign control is compounded, in truth, by more than one troubling question. For example, are we headed into a catastrophic energy crisis with gasoline rationing, power breakdowns and factory closures? Is Canada losing control of development in the Arctic? Are native peoples, the original Canadians, paying the price for projects of colossal destructiveness? Doesn't the record show that Canadians get "taken" when corporate promoters are licensed to exploit our resource wealth?

This study will deal with all those questions and explore the connections between them. The connections, really, are what it is all about. It was suggested, in the first place, by the work of the four legal scholars at Dalhousie University who had them-selves traced the common lessons to be drawn from five major resource projects proposed or undertaken in widely separated regions of Canada over a period of fifteen years. Their work, important in itself because it specified how Canadians were "taken" in these schemes and how the national interest was placed second to short-term local gains, was invested with new urgency by the developments of 1972 and 1973—the rising controversy over the Mackenzie pipeline and the American panic over petroleum scarcity. It seemed important to trace the connecting threads between the resource blunders of recent history and the even more grandiose proposals placed before the nation today. Through much of 1974 and 1975 it seems likely that the hearings of the National Energy Board will pro-vide a forum for one of the decisive debates in Canadian history as a consortium of twenty-six corporations pleads for national approval of a $6 billion pipeline that would carry natural gas from the Arctic to markets in the United States and eastern Canada. In those same years it is certain that both federal and provincial governments will face hardening pressures to make other resource deals with U.S. interests. Some of the same pres-sures, the same priorities and the same continental and cor-porate forces were at work in the deals examined by the Dalhousie Four. Their examination provides valuable clues to the forces and pressures at work in the pipeline application, the international trade talks and the managed inflation of petroleum pricing.

Walter Gordon, it will be suggested, gave the right answer to his own question; we shall be better equipped to see why he was right when we have looked at the broad critique of Cana-dian resource sellouts that was mounted by the Dalhousie Four. As specialists in international, marine, resource and environ-mental law, the four Dalhousie men—Dean R. St. J. Macdonald and Professors Douglas M. Johnston, Rowland J. H. Harrison and Ian McDougall—were well-qualified to assess the regional resource blunders, and the author, though supplementing their findings with his own research across the nation, has not had occasion to introduce significant variation into their conclusions.

Do you remember Jean-Luc Pepin? He was, as recently as October, 1972, Canada's minister of Trade and Commerce.

Shortly before the Dalhousie Four professors completed their brief, *Economic Development with Environmental Security,* Pepin argued that Canada would be crazy to "sit on" its reserves of natural gas and oil. "In maybe twenty-five to fifty years," he said, "we'll be heating ourselves from the rays of the sun and then we'll kick ourselves in the pants for not capitalizing on what we had when gas and oil were current commodities." His remark, uttered at a time when the imminence of an American supply crisis in petroleum was becoming apparent, reveals the state of mind in Ottawa that permitted Canadian self-sufficiency to be jeopardized. By the time the Dalhousie brief appeared Pepin's statement looked incredibly dated.

No one, by the spring of 1973, was questioning the reality of the U.S. energy crisis. "Circumstances in the United States," reported an energy task force under Dr. John J. Deutsch to the government of Ontario, "will bring about a continuing upward pressure on energy prices . . . the effects of the energy crisis in the United States will 'spill over' into Canada. This 'spill over' has already begun and is having a pronounced effect on Canadian energy developments . . . . Increases in costs to consumers will be substantial, especially for gas and other clean and convenient fuels."

The initial impact of the crisis upon Canada, it soon became clear, would be an impact upon the price of petroleum supplies which would ripple through manufacturing industry in the form of higher production costs. By imposing a more than one hundred percent increase in the wellhead price of Alberta natural gas, which provided ninety-four percent of Ontario's supply, Premier Peter Lougheed had geared Canadian gas prices to the levels obtainable in the sellers' market of the United States where the dearer gas would be mixed in with larger quantities of cheaper supplies before reaching the consumer. In Canada, outside Alberta, the increase would be passed on directly to utilities and factories, boosting the costs of production by an estimated $52 billion over thirty years and reducing the competitiveness of the manufacturing sector. Canada imposed controls on crude oil exports to the United States in March, 1973, and, after a brief parliamentary flurry in May over the "bootlegging" of huge quantities of gasoline from Canadian refineries to U.S. retail outlets, it became apparent, even to the Liberal government, that the volume of gasoline exports had to be controlled from Ottawa.

In the case of crude and refined petroleum, the market was already substantially under the control of the eight corporations of the world oil cartel which negotiated the price of supplies from Middle East and Venezuela producers, controlled the Alberta producers, the Canadian refineries, the tanker traffic and the retail gasoline outlets. The corporations could use their control of supply and price to force out independent retailers who had undercut their pricing. Oil corporations, with totally integrated operations, were ideally placed to exploit the threat of scarcity by forcing up prices and eliminating competition. The Deutsch committee also noted "the surprising degree of horizontal integration by energy companies . . . . The long-term implications of this trend," it warned, "could be significant for energy prices."

For Canadians outside Alberta then the short-term energy crisis was to be not a famine in supplies but an escalating price squeeze in the form of higher hydro and heating bills, dearer gasoline, higher manufacturing costs with reduced competitiveness in the American market, and curtailed expansion.

The corporations jacking up the prices of oil and gasoline to Canadian consumers were also engaged in a sustained lobby for the Mackenzie Valley pipeline, which would plug high-priced natural gas from the Mackenzie Delta into the profitable American market. Imperial Oil, the Canadian subsidiary of Standard Oil of New Jersey, the world's largest energy corporation, had already contracted to export the first gas found in the Delta. Imperial, Shell, Gulf, Texaco and the other oil cartel giants wanted quick approval for the 2,500-mile pipeline because Alberta's huge gas reserves were in decline, more than one-third of the best and most accessible gas produced in the province having been sold in the United States at fire sale prices by the same corporations and their affiliates. In addition to its pressure for the pipeline, intended primarily to service the American markets, the industry was urging expanded exports of the remaining gas in Alberta.

The international petroleum corporations had another motive for wanting quick Canadian approval of the Mackenzie gas line. They were sitting on a huge pool of oil and gas under

20

Prudhoe Bay on Alaska's north slope. Once they had overcome the rulings of the American courts, they would fling an 800-mile oil pipeline south across Alaska to the ice-free port of Valdez, where giant tankers would carry the oil to U.S. west coast ports— jeopardizing, in the process, the coastal waters of British Columbia. But tankers could not carry the natural gas unless it was first liquefied—a costly process. Only the Mackenzie Valley gas line, serving as a "land bridge" between Alaska and the lower forty-eight states, could carry cheaply the gas they had "corked" under the permafrost of Prudhoe Bay. The giant corporations, therefore, pressed for the Mackenzie Valley gas line as persistently as they pressed for the Trans-Alaska Pipeline that would carry their oil to the south.

In promoting the pipeline, corporation propagandists and their allies in the Liberal government establishment emphasized the huge "potential" in oil and gas they claimed was lying under the permafrost; they minimized the enormous production difficulties, the lack of success in striking oil, the very high cost of Arctic gas and the social disintegration they were bringing to northern communities. Their campaign encouraged the popular misconception that there might conceivably be enough petroleum in the Canadian North to "solve" the U.S. crisis and, in the process, trigger a boom in Canadian development.

It was fantasy, spun out perhaps to distract attention from the serious and accelerating depletion of fossil fuel reserves in the world, the United States and even Canada. In the ten years between 1970 and 1980 the world will consume 200 billion barrels of oil, as much oil as man used in all history before 1970. That 200 billion barrels is forty percent of all the oil proven to exist. The life index—reserves divided by annual production—of the world's conventional oil is thirty-eight years; by 1980 it will be about twenty years. Sixty-seven percent of today's known conventional reserves are in the Middle East, fifteen percent in Latin America, seven percent in the United States and two percent in Canada. Their life indexes are sixty-nine years for the Middle East, fourteen for Latin America, twenty-three years for Canada and ten for the United States. American reserves are declining so fast that the U.S. will have to import an estimated 10 million barrels a day by 1980; that is more than eight times Alberta's output now, and production there may be declining by 1980! Though Canada sells about half its oil and gas production to the United States, this represents less than five percent of U.S. requirements in both commodities. Exporting larger quantities of these resources will certainly be a profitable exercise for the foreign-owned energy corporations, but it will never begin to solve the American supply crisis; indeed, the signs are that Canada may have its own deficit of conventional oil supply to worry about in the 1980s. Increased exports from Canada will never be of more than marginal importance to the huge U.S. economy, but could be crucial for the development of manufacturing industry in Canada.

Exploration and seismic crews from the major corporations, in the brash tradition of ill-considered resource development in Canada, have intruded disruptively into the subsistence economy of native people in the Mackenzie Delta and the Arctic Islands. It is not the first time massive projects have been launched without prior thought for native communities that might be disrupted or destroyed, or for environmental damage. This, the Dalhousie Four found, was one of the common features of ill-considered resource projects during the past fifteen years.

The destructive impact of these current and planned undertakings will fall most heavily on some of the best, least dependent native communities in Canada, such as the relatively prosperous fishing village of South Indian Lake, threatened by the diversion of the Churchill River at Missi Falls, and the self-reliant Cree of northwest Quebec whose subsistence economy is being shattered by the $6 billion James Bay hydro project. The social tensions created by the pipeline scheme have been embittered by Ottawa's procrastination in moving openly towards a settlement of native land claims before encouraging the corporate promoters to buy up cheap exploration permits, a lamentable contrast with the Alaska Native Land Claims Settlement, which flowed from free negotiation in the years following the Atlantic Richfield oil strike at Prudhoe Bay.

Unlike the Mackenzie project, which is under the tight control of a federal-corporate alliance, the proposals and developments discussed in the Dalhousie study were undertaken on provincial initiative, generally for short-term gain and to service the United States. These projects account for a significant fraction of the $70 billion Canada is expected to require for capital-intensive resource development in the present decade, a requirement that critics argue will distort the nation's economy, raise the value of the Canadian dollar and help to price our goods out of foreign markets. Though Energy Minister Donald Macdonald says the country can handle all this and get back to high employment, his former cabinet colleague Eric Kierans calls the emphasis on resource development a prescription for industrial suicide.

The provincial projects, considered together, make the theory of a continental pool of resources a tangible reality.

The Columbia River, the greatest single potential hydro resource in North America, has been plugged in to the industrial system of the U.S. Pacific Northwest; the twenty-eight percent of its flow that is within Canada has been sold by treaty to be controlled, as if by a master tap, by the Bonneville Power Administration in the state of Washington. The Canadians who signed that treaty broke fifty years of tradition in the special diplomacy governing boundary water questions, and flashed across the border the message that Canadian waters could be purchased. It was bad enough that the power from the river's fall in the British Columbia mountains was harnessed to enhance per capita incomes in Washington and Montana instead of creating jobs for Canadians. What was worse was that the Americans saw it as an invitation to promote engineering plans for turning around the Canadian rivers they considered "wasted" in the North. There is evidence to suggest that ideas of such mammoth river engineering have even yet not been laid to rest.

As with water, so with gas. The twenty-year boom in Alberta's natural gas, exploited to the hilt by the great petroleum corporations, resulted not in the establishment of a diversified industrial base in the Canadian West but in the creation of jobs in the United States. In a series of cut-price transactions between interrelated corporations, Canadian consumers found themselves subsidizing development south of the border. The irony was that when the advocates of Alberta industrialization gained power at last under Conservative Premier Peter Lougheed, the result was to be a $200 million windfall for the foreign corporations and a decision to penalize, through doubled prices, the eastern Canadian consumers whose planning had already been jeopardized by the massive export contracts.

As with water in British Columbia and gas in Alberta, hydro potential in Quebec and Manitoba, harnessed through the most destructive manipulations of river systems ever contemplated in Canada, must be turned over to service U.S. industry. New Brunswick Hydro will export to Maine from its Lorneville plant near Saint John. Next, huge foreign-owned refineries and perilous superports in the Maritimes will service the eastern seaboard of the United States.

Almost unchallenged by Canadians, the economy of their country has been reordered and the resource map of the entire continent redrawn, exclusively on north-south lines. The Columbia's power, Alberta's gas, hydro from Manitoba, Quebec and New Brunswick, refined petroleum from Nova Scotia and perhaps a St. Lawrence superport all are designed to flow from north to south, as will the oil and gas from the Mackenzie Delta, the Arctic Islands and the Atlantic offshore, synthetic crude from the Athabasca tar sands and, before long, the uranium the U.S. nuclear industry will be demanding in impossible volumes in the 1980s. In the face of all this, the federal leaders in Ottawa have feigned rejection of the continental pool of resources. If this is a rejection, what would acceptance mean?

If U.S. corporations continue to scoop up the resources belonging to Canada and to assume control of services and infra-structure provided by Canadian taxpayers, the life index of Canada as a nation surely will be conspicuously shorter than that of its rarest natural resource. In the light of this record, created with the help of tax concessions, depletion allowances, federal grants, cut-price leases and laughable royalty rates, one can hardly blame American political leaders for assuming that everything Canadian is for sale. Irritating as it may be to hear Senator Frank Moss demanding control of our rivers, or Senator Henry Jackson or George Shultz speculating on the future of our fossil fuels, they are scarcely to be blamed when W. A. C. Bennett, Robert Bourassa, Gerald Regan, Jean-Luc Pepin and Donald Macdonald so persistently flashed the invitation, as Eric Kierans puns it, to "come and gut us."

In a careful study of rulings by the National Energy Board, ostensible watchdog over Canadian needs in natural gas, Dalhousie's Ian McDougall cited the approval of a pipeline to the United States that represented more than $300 million in investment. The pipe had the capacity to carry more gas than its owners had contracts to transmit. Not unnaturally, they hustled around for more business. When they got it, the board felt obliged to let them export as much as the pipe could carry because of the huge investment, even though its ruling showed it was not happy with the contracts. There is an awesome permanence about even thirty-six-inch pipes carrying Alberta gas to the U.S. They are said to be good for eighty years. By the logic of the energy board's decision, they will be full of gas for as long as there is gas to draw from the well. In another decision where the price did not seem to be right, the board reluctantly approved an export because refusal would cause inconvenience to customers in the American West who had become accustomed to being serviced with cheap Canadian gas. The export would have to be approved, the board decided, out of respect for the "amity and comity" that prevailed between the nations in matters of natural gas!

Apply that rationale to the Mackenzie Valley pipeline, designed to carry more than four billion cubic feet per day. Assume that the necessary $6 billion has all been committed, that the pipeline promoted by twenty-six powerful corporations is under the tundra and the gas is flowing. The companies producing gas have export contracts with their corporate relations and everybody, for the moment, is happy. Now, let's imagine, the National Energy Board, having reassessed the nation's reserves, finds the necessary twenty-five-year protection for Canadian needs cannot be met. What then? Is there to be interference with a contract, or rejection of an export bid from one of the pipeline promoters? Such an action, as the Carleton geologist F. K. North has pointed out, would be "tantamount to an act of war." Once the pipeline is plugged in, it will become, in the context of the tightening energy crisis, an American lifeline. No consideration of Canadian needs will unplug it. The resource wealth of the Arctic, for as long as it lasts, will flow to the industrial heartlands of the United States and the Kierans concept of Canadian growth based on increasingly sophisticated manufacturing will be a faded dream.

It is, as North has said, the U.S. energy crisis and the foreign-owned corporations that create the demand for a pipeline now. Canadians do not need it. Canadians are not ready for it.

Some of the most highly qualified specialists on the northern ecology say we need a decade of study before we can be sure it would not be ruinous to ram a million tons of steel through the permafrost. The scientists are not ready. The native people are not ready—they want a freeze on development that will provide time to research their land claims and negotiate a settlement that will provide a measure of self-sufficiency through land, cash and royalties and a role in land use planning. The tax laws and leasing regulations are not ready—they could be revised to provide decent revenues for Canada from exploration, discovery and exploitation. Once the export element is laid aside, the corporate pressure and propaganda ignored, the breathless hurry to build a pipeline to the Arctic appears rather foolish. It may be that by the middle of the 1980s the depletion of Canadian reserves will demand a pipeline, or a railway, or even service by improved supertankers, to bring northern gas to Canadian industrial centres, and a publicly-owned national utility might be created to perform the service, charging commercial rates to the producers and refineries. Because the possibility exists that Canadian industry may need Arctic gas by the mid-1980s, Ottawa should be starting its research programs into the various prospects now.

In their after-dinner speeches, pipeline promoters invariably compare their project with the building of the Canadian Pacific Railway. It is a false analogy. The CPR ran east to west and helped to bind Canada. Like the river routes of the fur traders a century before, and the radio and television of the Canadian Broadcasting Corporation, it was a nation-building project.

As presently conceived, the Mackenzie Valley pipeline is an alien thing. It is not something Canada needs. Like the ill-considered projects of the Dalhousie critique, its purpose is to service the United States in the period of its energy crisis. Legalistic formulae to provide fifty-one percent Canadian ownership, or to shuffle the chess players in the consortium boardroom, will hardly alter the case. If Canadians do not need this pipeline, all the rest is irrelevant.

The worldwide energy corporations described in later chapters of this book already control an awesome slice of Canada's economic life. It is time to curb their expansion. If they are not stopped now they could take the jackpot.

Chapter Two

Energy Crisis: True or False?

"It doesn't make sense for Canada to permit a foreign country to export its energy crisis here when, considering our own resources and requirements, we need not have an energy crisis at all. It doesn't make sense for us to export, along with our resources, our economic strength and our productive capacity."

— Bruce F. Willson, President, Union Gas Ltd., Chatham, Ontario.

On May 26, 1973, the Saturday of the Memorial Day weekend in the United States, Henry Craigs crumpled and died. He fell beside his gas pump with two shotgun bullets in his stomach and his death was reported in every North American newspaper worth the name because he was the first recorded victim of the increasingly controversial energy crisis.

When a man in his forties had driven up to the pumps and ordered his tank filled, Henry Craigs had said no. His employers at the service station had told him supplies were tight and customers were to be served "on a ration basis." This customer had bought a tankful, Henry Craigs remembered, only the day before. When Craigs told him that, the man drove away. When he came back, he took a double-barrelled shotgun from the trunk of his car and fired at point-blank range into Henry Craig's stomach.

The killing in Oakland, California, provided American news agencies with the lead paragraphs of their holiday roundup stories. "The shooting," reported Associated Press, "was the most serious incident involving demands for gasoline as millions of U.S. residents took to the highways on Memorial Day holiday weekend." The reports told of motorists across the country getting edgy about gas. If by a crisis we mean the point in time at which an already serious problem thrusts itself inescapably into the consciousness of hitherto uncaring millions, then perhaps the slaying of Henry Craigs on Memorial Day weekend will mark the start of the energy crisis of the seventies.

It is, like most such tricks of history, a rough marker; but it is apt. Gasoline is the right gauge. The despair and fury of the man with the double-barrelled shotgun is the ultimate in a frustration that millions who live by or with the automobile will share in some measure. For more than thirty years we have had in North America a car-driving, car-owning, car-loving, car-craving and car-earning society and never, until the spring and summer of 1973, have we really thought about gasoline, its uses and its price, its ownership and control and its manifold implications for the way we live. If energy resources, their finite nature and their accelerating depletion, have been a concept too big to get our minds around, the prospect of being deprived of the gasoline that keeps us mobile, commerce humming and the highways crowded is too close to our lives to be ignored.

That prospect loomed in the spring of 1973. In the United States, anxiety was general and a worldly official of California's Office of Emergency Services had concluded that "frankly, I think any motorist who lets his tank get below half full . . . is foolish." Texaco, slashing heating oil supplies to four eastern states, had introduced the first rationing in any commodity since World War II. Maine was importing "emergency" kerosene from Canada. In Washington, the Office of Emergency Preparedness reported that 342 gas stations, mostly independents, had closed shop. In a later report the Federal Trade Commission said 1,200 independents had been forced to close.

The "crisis" mood was catching hold. Framing an energy conservation act, the influential Democratic Senator Henry Jackson snapped that "we can certainly get along with a lot less horsepower than has been coming out of Detroit," and urged a "substantial" tax on large horsepower cars. Incongruously, the magazine *U.S. News and World Report*, mandatory reading for the corporate organization man, offered advice on "Twelve Tips on Stretching Gas Mileage: Warm up engine . . . ."

At the same time it was becoming clear that the "crisis" was being manipulated by the huge international oil corporations. These corporations planned to open large new service stations in places where supply-starved independents were being forced out of business. "Big oil is bigger than the United States government," Connecticut's attorney-general, Robert Killian, told a Senate anti-trust hearing. He and his colleagues from other states, having investigated the anti-competitive practices of the major distributors in their states, were urging that the big integrated petroleum corporations should be broken up. Producers of oil should not be allowed to refine and market it as well. Nothing less than a break-up, said Florida Attorney-General Daniel Dearing, would end their total control of the market; he called the industry a "unitary structure—more than a monopoly, more than an oligopoly." The federal Justice Department later charged Texaco Inc. and an independent refiner with entering an agreement to restrain sales of gasoline to independent retailers.

In Canada, meanwhile, American buyers were trucking out thousands of gallons a day from eastern Canadian refineries. New Democrat Tommy Douglas startled the Commons and caught Energy Minister Donald Macdonald off guard with the revelation that gasoline exports had been skyrocketing all spring. The exports, less than 30,000 barrels a month during January and February, had shot up to 360,000 in March and to more than half a million in April. Exports for the first four months of 1973, totalling 872,000 barrels, were fifty times greater than those of 1972! April's figure alone was greater than the total of 1972's gasoline exports.

Macdonald, reluctant to control the outflow, appealed to his friends in the major corporations to make voluntary reductions in the exports. One of them turned him down flat; the others grumbled and groaned. Finally, at midnight on June 15, exports of gasoline and heating fuel oil were controlled by a federal decree that would, Macdonald said, bring gasoline exports "basically right down to zero." The Trudeau cabinet had earlier ruled that propane, a liquid form of natural gas, would not have to meet the "surplus to Canadian requirements" test imposed on natural gas. Ottawa licensed an immediate doubling to 82,462,000 barrels in the annual propane exports of three giant oil corporations. Propane, cleanest of motor fuels, is ideal for the virtually pollution-free operation of vehicle fleets used on short city runs.

"This crisis," a Toronto gasoline wholesaler serving independent service station operators not franchised by the giant corporations had said, "has dropped right into the lap of 'the majors'. They can sell all they can get their hands on at top rates. The independents were once of some use to the major refineries in that they helped get rid of surplus gasoline, but they are soon sacrificed when Uncle Sam calls. The majors are now in a position to put the independents right out."

For three weeks in May the Toronto wholesaler had canvassed the large, foreign-owned refineries for supplies, "but I don't have a gallon and they won't promise me a gallon on a contract basis." All he could get was what the refineries would spare him on a day-to-day basis. "Don't mention my name," he urged, "or the majors will ruin me."

In addition to supply, the corporations controlled price. The Toronto wholesaler explained that the two price quotations he had to hand, which varied by only one tenth of one cent, were above the *retail* prices charged by the cut-rate operators he traditionally supplied. Even if those operators could secure gasoline at the new refinery prices they would find themselves undersold by stations run by the major corporations. "The refineries have put their prices up six times in the last three years," the wholesaler said. "Their hike at the end of May was a real whopper. And what was interesting was that they justified it in a different way. All the other times, they just said that higher prices for crude oil had made necessary a higher-priced refined product. This time, though, they justified it by referring to prices in the United States market! Of course, it's costing the Ontario motorist millions of dollars. I've come to the conclusion that a government takeover of the business is the only answer, but with the majors and the Liberals being so thick, you can be damned sure that's not going to happen!"

Scarcity, in fact, was enabling the foreign-owned major corporations to rationalize the process of gas retailing to their advantage. For several years they had been losing ground in Ontario because of their high prices. Independent operators using supplies purchased from medium-sized oil companies in

Quebec had increased their share of the market, causing a failure rate of one in four among service station operators franchised by the majors. The corporations responded with "off-brand" gas bars, selling their product at discount prices and under unfamiliar names—Shell's gas becoming "Beaver" and Esso's "Econo" and "Gain"— and presenting the observant motorist with a curious three-price structure in retail gasoline. The brand names were available at more than fifty cents per gallon, the off-brands at about forty-five cents and the cut-rate operators sold at about thirty-nine cents.

The tide turned after the majors successfully lobbied the Liberal government for new regulations that would prevent Ontario retailers securing any gasoline from east of the Ottawa Valley. Suppliers such as Caloil of Montreal were forced out of the Ontario market and prices began to escalate. The medium-sized companies, dependent on the major corporations for the supplies carried from overseas and shut out of part of the Ontario market, were caught in a double squeeze. By the spring of 1973 Caloil faced prices at the refinery gate that would have translated into pump prices of seventy cents a gallon for regular gasoline in Montreal. That company promptly scrapped plans for fifteen new outlets, Gasex abandoned five, Premium Oil, three and, in Ottawa, Capital City Gas and Fuel announced it would close eighteen or twenty of its discount service stations. "The longer this U.S. scarcity goes on," said manager George Coates of the 1,500-member Ontario Retail Gasoline Association representing both independent and franchised dealers, "the tighter the control of the majors will be and the more independents will be driven to the wall." The industry, Coates felt, was using world prices and the supply situation to condition government and public for major price increases, plus a speed-up in pipeline projects supported by generous government grants for exploration and refining. "This association feels," said Coates, "there should be more governmental controls on energy and the irresponsible actions of the oil companies indicate they should be applied immediately." The corporations, of course, did not think their actions irresponsible at all. Their euphemism for what they were doing was "restoring normal marketing balances." What that meant was that they were at last in a position to use their control of supplies and pricing to wipe out the independents who had provided highly effective competition in the 1960s, to the obvious benefit of the motorist.

There is a scholar in Edmonton whose name, like that of the Toronto wholesaler, must not be revealed. This man has spent much of his working life in a close study of the operations of the petroleum industry. "The corporation that controls the retail market," he told me with almost oracular emphasis, "is always in a better position than you might think." It was his experience that major foreign-owned oil corporations always became "edgy" if independents threatened to control much more than ten percent of the market. This analysis, I was to find, had been substantially confirmed by the authoritative McKenzie Commission on Gasoline Marketing, which reported to the Alberta government in 1968.

That commission reported that though all eight of the world's giant oil corporations were operating in Alberta in 1965, only four of them had fully "integrated" operations. The subsidiaries of Standard Oil of New Jersey, Gulf, Shell and Texaco produced, refined and marketed oil in the province. Those four corporations owned all of Alberta's refineries, sold through brand name outlets 86.5 percent of the gasoline used by consumers in the province, tied 87.9 of all retail outlets to their brand names and sold refined petroleum to all of the remaining marketers. The four corporations sold 222,756,000 of the 257,436,000 gallons of gas traded through 3,139 retail outlets. Three of the four reported incomes higher than the Alberta government and the four together earned five times the province's income that year! In conditions of such dominance, total price control is but a hairsbreadth away, and a prolonged and deepening scarcity would remove that hair.

In any event, independent entrepreneurs whose competition threatened price structures established by the giant corporations —to the direct benefit of the consumer—get no sympathy from governments in the context of the energy crisis. "These people," says William Simon, deputy secretary of the U.S. Treasury, "lived on the margin of the industry, buying the oversupply of gasoline at lower prices and providing a useful competitive force . . . this oversupply no longer exists." "Many of the independents," echoes Canadian Energy Minister Donald Macdonald, "were set up to take advantage of surplus offshore

32

supplies, which they could pick up at bargain prices and market at highly competitive rates. That environment has changed. There is no excess gasoline around." Exit, unmourned by government, the independents.

But gasoline, of course, is but one gauge of the energy squeeze and the slaying of Henry Craigs is, as we conceded, at best a rough historical marker. For those in the business of finding and using energy resources, the problems began years before 1973. Bruce F. Willson, who describes himself accurately as a "concerned Canadian," has been living with them ever since he went into the business of selling natural gas to the industries, power utilities and householders of southwestern Ontario. As president of Union Gas Company of Canada,[1] which, with its supply lines to 250 communities and its record 1972 earnings of $14.5 million, is one of Ontario's big three distributors of natural gas, Willson is responsible for a $300 million expansion program that was drawn up in the assurance that Canada will always protect, for at least twenty-five years, the needs of its own energy consumers.

In conventional terms, Bruce Willson is a relatively young business leader with everything going for him. Yet there are times when he looks at energy developments across North America and wonders if he might not be in a dying business. Often, he glances at a simple graph entitled "Union Gas Limited: Forecast of Requirements and Presently Contracted Supplies." Vertically, it is marked off in billions of cubic feet of natural gas, horizontally in years from 1973 to 1995. A red line, ascending steadily at an angle of about forty-five degrees, represents estimated market demands and a green line, stepping jerkily down towards the base of the graph, stands for total contracted supply. It is not, for Willson, a reassuring picture. Beginning in 1973 with something over 200 billion cubic feet, the red line rises to an anticipated demand of 800 billion in 1995—a quadrupling in twenty-two years. Starting out from the same point, the contracted supply line stumbles down to 150 billion cubic feet in 1981, to 100 in 1988, to 50 in 1991 and to zero in 1993. There is, it is true, a seemingly ample margin of time for Union Gas to negotiate contracts for new supplies, but

---

1. Union Gas is ninety-five percent Canadian owned.

its ability to do that will depend on the willingness of foreign-owned producers and the men who supposedly regulate them to expand their service to the eastern Canadian market. If, say, the big Alberta producers and their price-conscious provincial government were to decide that real profitability lay in the United States market and that natural gas should gradually be priced out of the reach of eastern Canadian consumers, then the gap on the graph might never be closed.

Willson points to a second graph. This one shows the "life index," the measurement that relates rate of discovery, rate of production and remaining proven reserves of natural gas in the United States and Canada. It covers the period 1955 to 1972. The United States index starts out with the life index at just over twenty years and ends at just over ten years. The Canadian index, suggesting in 1955 a further one hundred years of possible exploitation, was down in 1972 to twenty-three years. If, as seems probable, it will be a decade before significant supplies of gas flow from the Arctic fields, a serious supply gap looms for eastern Canada simply because more than one third of Alberta's future production is committed to markets in the United States. A third graph in Willson's office plots the well-head prices of gas in Alberta if they follow the course projected for them by Premier Peter Lougheed. This line creeps upward very slowly at first, from about six cents per 1,000 cubic feet in 1950 to sixteen cents in 1972. Then, in 1973, it rises vertically to thirty-six cents and veers like a rocket into a steep-angled climb that takes it to one dollar per 1,000 cubic feet in 1990.

In Willson's mind, the conclusions of these graphs merge into a crisis of both price and supply. After years of cheap exports to the United States, Alberta and the foreign-owned producers have decided that the price achievable in the energy-starved United States market is what will determine the price of gas everywhere, save Alberta. The effect of more than doubling the price of natural gas, says Willson, will hit Ontario like a sledgehammer, adding $32 billion to Ontario's industrial production costs over thirty years and $52 billion to Canada's. Ontario, with more than ninety percent of its gas supplies drawn from Alberta, is now almost totally dependent on that source. It is a different story in the sprawling United States market, where Alberta gas is but three percent of the total supply and huge quantities have been cheaply secured on contracts lasting decades. There, higher-priced supplies from new Alberta contracts will be "rolled in" with larger supplies of cheaper gas. The consumer will pay more, but nothing like so much more as industry in captive Ontario. The result will be to penalize the manufacturer using the best fuel in Canada, to increase his costs and his prices, to weaken his competitive effort in the U.S. market and to make more precarious the jobs of his workers.

By 1973 Ontario provided a huge and concentrated market for Alberta gas with 810,000 residential and 80,000 commercial users, and 10,000 strategic industrial customers accounting for fifty-eight percent of the consumption.

What did the first, ten-cent instalment of Lougheed's price increases mean for them? For the Polysar chemicals complex in Sarnia it meant $1.7 million a year in additional costs, and a serious weakening in its competitive position. Polysar's big rivals in the southern United States were assured of gas at low cost on long-term contracts from local sources. For the Ontario Paper Company, producing newsprint in a sixty-year-old mill at Thorold, it meant a twenty percent increase in power costs, the prospect of having to use wood wastes to produce steam, and a threat to the jobs of 1,400 workers with an annual payroll of $15 million. For Algoma Steel at Sault Ste. Marie, an increase of $877,000 on the annual fuel bill might add an estimated fifty-five cents a ton to manufacturing costs. For Toronto's Abitibi Paper, it was estimated, an extra ten cents per 1,000 cubic feet of natural gas might translate into one dollar on a ton of paper. And for the Cyanamid chemical plant at Welland, officials claimed, it would mean three dollars a ton on the cost of producing ammonia. Alberta's increases would require Cyanamid to pay about sixty cents per 1,000 cubic feet, which was three times the average price paid by the chemical firm's opposition on the American Gulf Coast.

Willson, a veteran of the Alberta gas business himself, had seen trouble coming a long time ago. In 1964 he appeared before the Energy Resources Conservation Board in Calgary to oppose an application from TransCanada Pipelines to serve huge new markets in Chicago and Detroit with Alberta gas. Given the state of the province's discovery rate and reserves, and given also the growth of the Canadian markets, Willson had argued, there was no justification for such commitments to mammoth new markets. Years later, before that same board, the Union Gas counsel Arnold F. Moir was to make an eloquent stand against the pattern of price escalations soon to be adopted by Premier Lougheed.

Moir's appeal went to the heart of the developing Canadian crisis, exposing how the near-monopoly of the dominant foreign corporations applied the squeeze to consumers and how they would use their price control of different petroleum commodities to exploit government regulations. Imperial Oil, Shell, Gulf and Texaco, he pointed out, were fully integrated petroleum corporations, refining and selling both No. 2 oil and Bunker C oil in Canadian markets. "These companies," said Moir, "are not regulated as to the price they can charge for No. 2 or Bunker C oil. If the price of gas is to track the price of No. 2 oil and Bunker C, the producers have the best of both worlds. They can raise the price of the No. 2 oil and Bunker C, and then argue that the price of gas must come up to meet the price of oil. When this has been accomplished, they can again raise the price of oil and again argue that the price of gas must come up to meet it . . . . These companies are in a position to thereby control both the price of oil and the price of gas to the detriment of residential and industrial consumers."

The corporations, which operate all over the world, had argued that the Canadian price of oil and gas must follow the world price. Their star economic witness from the United States —Sherman Clark of Stanford Research Institute—had explained that "the strategy . . . is to restrain supply so that the highest possible price can be obtained. Supply and demand are still in balance but the price is higher than under competitive conditions." Commented Moir, "The truth of the matter is that, in a monopoly, by withholding supply the seller can extract an exorbitant price and this appears to be the entire strategy of the industry."

"The strategy of the producers and American users," charged Moir, "appears to be to price natural gas out of the Canadian market. If the price of gas is substantially increased, the demand for gas will most certainly be dampened . . . . The thrust is that the cost of energy for Canadian consumers should be tied to the

U.S. energy crisis, the growing world energy shortage and the Middle East problems of the international oil companies . . . . Extracting the highest possible price from Canadian consumers can benefit only the producing companies and the U.S. fourteen-state market which is in critical short supply and where higher-cost Canadian gas would have a much lesser impact when rolled into existing supplies . . . . It is submitted that the consumer is potentially at the mercy of the pricing policies of the international oil companies. The attempt to relate gas prices in Alberta to the uncontrolled price of competitive fuels in the Ontario or California market allows the international oil companies to raise the price of oil and then raise the price of gas to meet it and the ladder effect will be intolerable for the Canadian consumer." The plea was disregarded.

With Willson, then, the awareness of the energy squeeze had been growing for almost a decade. In 1971 he carried his concern to the public, through speeches, statements and letters, but had the feeling few were listening. He was, he says quietly, "roundly criticized by many colleagues in the producing industry" and often felt like a voice crying in the wilderness. There was small response when, in a 1971 Windsor speech, he warned that "unless the discovery rate of Canadian natural gas rises substantially, I might even say dramatically, Canada is heading for the type of energy crisis that exists in the United States." But when he spoke there again two years later, Willson was able to say that "we can hardly pick up a newspaper without reading the latest contribution to the energy supply debate . . . . The media and general public are becoming deeply interested and concerned." By then Union Gas was unable to contract new industrial customers, plans to convert Windsor's J. Clarke Keith generating station to natural gas had been "virtually ruled out," Alberta had announced increases in natural gas revenues anticipated to bring an additional $27 million to the provincial treasury and $167 million to the gas producers each year, the National Energy Board had been obliged to bring crude oil exports under control to protect Canadian supplies, and an Advisory Committee on Energy had warned the government of Ontario that "the period of seemingly unlimited abundance and cheap energy has come to a close . . . . Effects of the energy crisis in the United States will spill over into Canada."

In the winter of 1972–73 there were fuel supply failures and cutbacks in the United States, school closures, layoffs and rationed heating oil. In the ninety-five-degree heat of June, power companies from Maine to Washington, D.C., cut voltage by a minimum five percent. Willson had an audience now. The family in Windsor faced another $20 on the annual fuel bill and felt less certain about supply, while the worker in the auto plant felt a little less confident about the job-protecting Auto Pact that might become a trading counter in the coming American push for Canada's energy resources. Unease was seeping into the public mind, and after Henry Craigs had been shot in the stomach everyone knew there was talk of a crisis in fuels.

The two-year lag in public awareness between Willson's speeches in 1971 and 1973 parallelled almost mechanically the American experience. United States gas reserves peaked in 1967, shortages first appeared in 1970 and the situation reached "crisis proportions" in the winter of 1972–73. In Canada, the absolute decline in gas and conventional oil reserves reported in 1972, the first since Alberta's energy boom took off in the late forties, could signal scarcity for 1976—unless the rate of exports was curbed.

"We have been following the same pattern as the United States in the late 1950s and early 1960s," Willson reported to his shareholders in 1973. "It would probably be fair to say that we are about halfway towards the disastrous position the Americans now find themselves in with regard to gas supply, but we are declining at a faster rate."

The Americans had received plenty of warning from their academics and researchers, "but somehow," Willson reflects, "maybe just because of their natural optimism, the U.S. corporations chose not to heed the warning signs." Whether from optimism, self-interest or folly, there was at the start of the seventies a trendy pose of not taking energy too seriously, an indulgence widespread among readers of such works as John Maddox's *The Doomsday Syndrome*, which mocked the scholarly studies undertaken by such groups as the Club of Rome.

Nobody, naturally enough, wanted to believe we faced a crisis in non-renewable resources, and some who claimed it was phony pointed to the unconscionable manipulation of scarcities by the giant corporations as an argument in support of this scepticism. Those people had missed the point. Serious study will show that price and supply manipulation and the energy crisis are essentially the same problem; you cannot have one without the other. The giant corporations, and the mechanisms they have created, are the energy crisis.

The gas wholesaler and the Edmonton scholar provided one clue. Bruce Willson provided another. What they all had in common was their bruising exposure to the price squeeze applied by giant international oil companies, to the priorities that place serving the U.S. market before Canadian need, to the long odds facing those who must exist in the face of monopoly.

Later chapters will trace connections between the exploitation of oil and gas in Alberta and Canadian frontier regions, the operations of the world cartel of eight mammoth corporations, the emergence of a "counter-cartel" of producers in the underdeveloped world, and the transformation of oil into a sprawling energy industry equipped to profit from the depletion of all the world's fossil fuels. It will become apparent that whoever has suffered to date from the depletion of resources it has not been the energy business. Its rosy mood was cheerfully evoked by Jack Armstrong, president of Imperial Oil, Canada's largest corporation and seventy percent subsidiary of the celebrated Standard Oil of New Jersey, who opened the annual meeting by saying: "In speaking to the Annual Report, I can think of no better way to begin my comments than by repeating the first sentence of the Report... '1972 was a good year for Imperial Oil'."

The American optimism Willson had noted endured well into the supply crisis. It was only in 1973 that advertising agencies with petroleum accounts began to replace their strident promotional gimmickry with pious messages stressing the careful use of gasoline. Yet the executives of the international oil companies had not lacked documentation about the world or domestic supply situation. It was a global study undertaken by the Shell group that showed that, whereas it had taken fifty-one years for the energy demand of the non-Communist world to rise to its 1971 level, which was the equivalent of 72½ million barrels of oil a day, the demand would double to the equivalent of 145 million barrels a day in only fourteen years, and that the United States, Japan and Western Europe would be clamouring for larger shares of the diminishing reserves in the future.

In the U.S. itself, the gap between rising demand and the possibilities of supply was so enormous and widening so swiftly that the nation appeared headed for industrial breakdown and social dislocation on an unprecedented scale. The gap was apparent, in varying degree, in all forms of energy—oil, natural gas, coal, nuclear and hydraulic generation. Nuclear generation, which had been prematurely oversold by an aggressive Atomic Energy Commission in the immediate postwar period, was bedevilled by technical blunders and production problems, stalling the anticipated transition from hydro dams to nuclear plants. By 1973 the U.S. was operating only ten plants of more than 1,000-megawatt capacity and the forty-six under construction faced a legal assault from Ralph Nader and an adventurous coalition of conservation groups arguing that the U.S. industry had not overcome the safety hazards in its reactors. Against the forty-six plants being built, industry's demand projections showed 280 would be "needed" by 1985. Since the United States was also running out of rivers to dam, there were strong pressures to buy hydro from James Bay, New Brunswick and Canada's western rivers.

In oil, the classical U.S. strategy had been to develop petroleum resources by supplying most of the domestic market with U.S. oil. Developers were given a holiday from taxes and received prices far above those of imported crude, which was restricted to twelve and one-half percent of the market. U.S. prices largely determined prices on the world market, controlled by the eight corporations of the oil cartel. By developing its own supply, the theory went, the U.S. would not be dependent on foreign sources in times of war. Under such a policy, highly profitable for the large corporations which also controlled Middle East, Latin American and Canadian reserves, the number of producing wells and proven reserves both peaked in 1961. The long decline that followed speeded up in 1968 and by the start of 1973 the U.S. was importing one quarter of its crude. By 1980, the demand projections indicate 10 million barrels of crude oil will have to be imported every day—the equivalent of the daily production of eight Albertas. As a result, the U.S. is increasingly dependent on the vast reserves in the Middle East and will require 200 supertankers each carrying 2.2 million barrels by 1980. The giant corporations, meanwhile, have undertaken a global program of exploration on land and under the seas—in all the oceans, all the nations of the southern Pacific, the North Sea and Mediterranean, Africa and the Middle East, Latin America, the Caribbean and the Arctic. Their exploration of the Canadian Arctic Islands and Atlantic offshore is a sector of this program, but Canadian pipeline promoters sometimes suggest Canadian oil will somehow play a vital part in "solving" the American crisis. Given the dimensions of the supply deficit, this is total fantasy, since even the proven oilfield at Prudhoe Bay in Alaska is not expected to contribute more than five percent to total consumption.

Given the depletion of Alberta's conventional reserves, the current decline in the life index and the meagre oil strikes to date in frontier regions, a more realistic prospect, says Jim Ryan, professor of petrochemical engineering at the University of Alberta, is that Canada will be a net importer of oil after 1975 and will have to cut off exports to the United States by 1981 or soon afterwards. The petroleum industry's fantasizing over Canadian potential in conventional oil will be examined in later chapters.

In natural gas, American output is expected to decline by about one third while requirements will more than double in fifteen years. Here, Canadian frontier exploration has produced better results than with oil, but the new reserves are in regions far from markets, the gas will be very costly, and Canada's own needs are growing fast. The best and most accessible gas in the country has already been sold off to the United States at bargain basement prices.

Only coal is making a comeback after a half-century in decline, passing increasingly into the ownership of the great oil corporations, which now control the largest reserves in the United States. This industry claims it will double output in fifteen years, mostly by strip-mining hundreds of square miles of western countryside, to the dismay of conservationists striving to preserve the landscape and health authorities working to preserve clean air. It is ironic that the oil-based energy corporations now plan to use coal increasingly for the production of substitute gas that will command high prices. Before such prices were attainable for gas produced from coal, and while there were still substantial reserves of natural gas in the ground, the oil corporations resisted coal gasification. But in the 1980s both gasification and the extraction of synthetic crude from the Athabasca tar sands in Alberta are certain to be important. Work on exotic new chemical fuels, harnessing energy from the sun, the sea, the winds and animal wastes is unlikely to be sufficiently far advanced.

Canada's energy resources, then, will never be more than marginal in terms of the American supply deficit, but they will be of vital significance for this country's future prosperity. Their marginality does not mean that they will not be attractive enough to be the object of intense and even menacing U.S. pressures, as recent Ottawa disclosures have made clear.

In the short run, though, the most immediate pressure the energy crisis will exert upon Canada is that of price. Because of the domination of the Canadian oil and mineral industries by American corporations and the worldwide control of oil prices exercised by the large corporations, United States prices will spill over into Canada, with disproportionate effects. The pressures for further massive investment in such giant energy projects as the $6 billion Mackenzie Valley pipeline and the $6 billion James Bay scheme, officially expected to total as much as $70 billion in the present decade, will of course serve to accentuate the distortion of the Canadian economy created by the inflation of prices caused by American scarcities.

The American crisis was not produced by the energy corporations alone, but by the entire productive and distributive system those corporations epitomize. The dynamics of the most acquisitive society in human history have been spinning out of control. The U.S. is caught up in a mindless merry-go-round of growth and development to produce more growth and development.

It has become like a hydro utility with a promotion-minded management, which produces more and more "feedback" that will push it farther and faster in the direction in which it is already leaning. The utility structures its rates and promotes the use of electricity in a widening range of appliances so aggressively that it creates an accelerating cycle of demand constantly running ahead of productive capacity. The United States has become a nation racing to catch up with its self-created demand curves. It employs what the American economist Paul A. Samuelson terms "manipulated fads engineered by profit-seeking advertisers" to create what his colleague Kenneth Galbraith called a society of "private affluence and public poverty."

The Canadian advertising man Jerry Goodis has seen the connection. He said recently that marketers would have to give some things up—the line extension, the fourteenth flavour, the twenty-cent packaging around ten-cent goods.

He continued: "If we don't... some time around 1995, we're going to be sitting around with our cavity-free grandchildren surrounded by all our wonderful products... our quiet-ride Fords, our better-seven-ways snowmobiles, our dependable Maytags. Our hair won't have the frizzies... we'll only need deodorant every other day... we'll have tried it and liked it... we'll have found out what we've been missing... we'll have taken five for fifty... and margarine will taste just like butter. But Mother Nature won't have been fooled. We'll have wonderful products. But there's going to be no gas to run them. No hydro to heat them. No fuel to start them. No juice for the microwave ovens. No energy to turn the generators to make any more power."

In 1970 the United States, with six percent of the world's people, was consuming thirty-three percent of the energy used in the world and the individual American was estimated to be using energy equivalent to the muscle-power of a retinue of 500 strong slaves. Energy demands in California were doubling at such a pace, reported Rand Corporation researchers in early 1973, that 130 giant nuclear reactors would have to be spaced at eight-mile intervals along the entire Pacific coast in order to meet the demand curve in twenty years' time. That demand curve, the Rand people told the state, should be reduced by sixty percent, with subsidies and tax incentives to users of alternative power and through even drastic changes in lifestyles.

Artificially-fostered demands far outstrip the increases attributable to larger populations and increased family formation. They become victims of "exponential growth," doubling themselves at ever-diminishing intervals. The University of Manitoba's Dr. Robert W. Newbury explains the process with the vivid analogy of the lily pond. If you know that only two lily pads float on the surface on the first day, and four on the second day, and eight on the third, and also that the pond will be covered with lily pads on the thirtieth day, you can figure out that enough lilies to cover half of the surface must appear on the twenty-ninth day. America, Newbury says, is in the twenty-ninth day of using up its energy resources.

The American people, always ingenious, conscious of the dilemma in energy resources, are attempting to work out technical, social and lifestyle changes that could enable them to use resources less wastefully. But their chances of achieving these innovations must be accounted small, because most of the changes would affect the profit mechanism of the corporations in effective control of U.S. society. For example, America has always had huge reserves of coal. If years ago, like Britain, it had begun to produce substitute gas from coal reserves, the country might have been better equipped to produce domestic cheap energy, but the primarily coal-mining corporations might also have supplanted Standard Oil of New Jersey as the commanding industry in the energy field. Jersey Standard found it preferable to keep the gasification process out of the U.S., rather than risk losing its leadership. Many of the energy-conserving schemes being currently advanced would reduce the profitability of many corporate operations and, for that reason, they must be accounted long shots. The corporations, themselves the creations of nineteenth century enterprise, now react defensively and ruthlessly against any entrepreneurship, any technology and any innovation that intrudes upon their market control. Thus, the U.S. National Petroleum Council, a lobby of the corporations, declared recently that "the nation's lifestyle is perhaps the most fundamental determinant of energy demand." Having said that, it then opposed any "restrictions that would alter consumer habits." Those habits, after all, were fostered by corporations.

Thus every rational measure to conserve energy—stiff taxation on wasteful large automobiles, strict standards of insulation on buildings to reduce energy use for heating and air-conditioning, a ban on glass office towers, penalization of heavy industrial users of electricity, a massive swing to buses and rapid transit with a ban on cars in downtown districts, prohibition of inefficient home-heating by electricity, increased taxation on products with a high energy component—is likely to be snuffed out by the dead hand of corporate self-interest, even if promoted by political authority. But alternative values are emerging that will inevitably challenge the corporate lobbies as the situation deteriorates. The concept of high "standard of living," for instance, as perceived by developers and growth-at-any-price propagandists, has become a dangerously crude and entirely quantitative notion. The influential environmentalist Russell E. Train advances a superior concept. A slowdown in the use of energy, he points out, could actually improve qualitative living standards, by shifting emphasis from industrial production to better services, education and arts, recreation and more durable products. "The real issue," as Train sees it, "is not whether resources will last one hundred years, two hundred years or even longer. The real issue is how much are we willing to pay, in real costs and in environmental degradation, to supply our spiralling energy demand?"

Before the energy crisis reaches its climax, the issues will have polarized Americans as well as Canadians in a new and profound debate about the future of our societies. Within each nation-state there will be a conservation party and a technocrat party. The ideology of the conservationists will be in the tradition developed by Malthus, Ricardo and John Stuart Mill, all of whom anticipated an inexorably tightening scarcity in non-renewable resources. This group may be expected to emphasize the social costs of large-scale resource development, almost invariably damaging to the environment and invariably treating the environmental "property" of society as a "free good" in the corporations' search for profit.

The seventy world scholars of the Club of Rome endorsed this view in their 1972 prophesy: "If the present growth trends in world population, industrialization, pollution, food production and resource depletion continue unchanged, the limits to growth on this planet will be reached some time within the next one hundred years. The most probable result will be a rather sudden and uncontrollable decline in both population and industrial capacity . . . ."

The other view, dominant still in the corporations and in Canada's Liberal establishment, is that technology will find an answer to every problem. Though often expressed in the pseudo-scientific terminology of the engineer and the organization man, this belief is ultimately mystical. In practice, it is a self-deceiving rationale for continuing on familiar paths, accepting that however irrationally corporations or individuals consume energy, there will always be another breakthrough, a new technological lease granting the corporations another decade or so in which to fulfil their manifest destiny of exploiting and consuming boundless wealth. Such a breakthrough in the next fifteen years of the crisis appears improbable. Such thinking is more likely to produce a breakdown.

In Canada the debate over standards and values will be invested with special urgency by the threat to national survival represented by the continentalist approach to North American resources in the period of energy depletion. The continental resource pool is no longer an idea but a physical emplacement in Alberta, on the Columbia River and James Bay, in the Mackenzie Delta, the Arctic Islands and the Atlantic offshore. The conservation of Canada is an even more pressing matter than it was when General Andrew McNaughton first perceived the issue in the fifties. His concern to use Canadian resources to enhance per capita incomes here instead of servicing American industry is as valid as it ever was. But there is a new aspect. Since McNaughton lost the fight to save the Columbia and the Arrow Lakes valley was drowned, the destructiveness of the continental approach to resources has been vividly displayed to Canadians. The casual sacrifice proposed for the native peoples and societies of James Bay, South Indian Lake and the Mackenzie Delta have dramatized the exploitive callousness of "development" as it is practised by the energy corporations and their continentalist friends. Such critics of destructive resource development as the Dalhousie Four are not talking of Canadian survival in terms of a fight over financial control in remote boardrooms, but about the preservation of living societies and physical landscapes. Every time an earthmover crashes through a trapline, a dam drowns a spawning ground, tundra, bush or delta is laid waste or shoreline fouled, something of Canada is lost. In northern communities, the arrival of developers brings a psychic shock, a sudden obliteration of tangible heritage that southern Canadians are only now beginning to understand.

The irony comes when Canadians are told that, in the context of the energy crisis, there is a "moral imperative" to share their resources with the United States. The record in this book will show that energy shortages are already on the horizon for Canada because the best and most accessible resources we had have gone to service U.S. corporations. The usage of one third of all the energy ever consumed in the world has not saved the United States from crisis. What remains in Canada is inconsequential in the dimensions of American demand, vital in the context of Canadian sovereignty. If the resources that remain were programmed to service and develop Canadian industry under a long-term national plan, then prosperity and independence might still be achieved.

If the best remaining resources are swiftly depleted and Canada is unable to buy fuel on inflated world markets, we shall some day be unable to heat our homes. The geophysicist J. Tuzo Wilson has pointed out that in such a situation some Canadians, particularly northern Canadians, would ultimately die. What the Dalhousie Four are saying is that we should preserve the remaining environment and economy through what is left of the Petroleum Age, managing our resources with care, refining our nuclear programs and controlling our uranium supplies, while developing the sophisticated research that will lead to new sources of energy.

Tuzo Wilson, who was born before there were cars, does not expect petroleum to last out his grandchildrens' time. "All fossil fuels," he has said, "will only last for a brief episode in the history of man." A nation might prove less finite, given a moral imperative equal to its times. If that imperative were to husband the resources still retained and to shun the trap of artificially-fostered demands, it might be possible to ensure that there will still be a Canada one hundred years from now.

Chapter Three

Paradise Lost

"Increasing public attention is being focussed upon
possible sovereignty difficulties arising from large
concentrations of foreign ownership in certain Canadian
industrial sectors. It is something of a paradox that a
protective policy should develop concerning foreign
ownership of developed enterprise and at the same time
nothing be done with respect to the protection of one of
the basic assets upon which so much industry and
virtually all settlement so crucially depends."

—Ian A. McDougall, Faculty of Law, Dalhousie University.

The great Canadian sellout this book chronicles begins on the
Columbia River. Here squabbling federal and provincial politicians threw away the greatest single energy resource of the
nation and the continent. It took two decades of study and
negotiation, of scheming, betrayal and intrigue to realize the
Columbia River treaty; it is taking another two decades for
Canadians to realize the damage that has been done.

This tragic deal, the first of Canada's postwar blunders in
large-scale resource development, epitomizes the folly and haz-
ard represented by the economic theory of a continental policy
in resources and the political doctrine of North American continentalism. Here in the soft, mild fruit garden of the nation,
where nature and climate offered unrivalled opportunities for
the good life, Canadians pursuing factional advantage and narrow ambition could agree on nothing save that they would
surrender their Paradise. Through a combination of opportun-
ism, greed and parochial interest, these men contrived to lose

control of the flows and uses of the 480 miles of North America's third largest river that flows through Canadian territory.

The Dalhousie scholars defined a bungled Canadian resource project with some care. It was, first of all, an undertaking in which the long-term interests of province and nation were sold spectacularly short. That happened in the Columbia River treaty because the industrialization that might have been fostered in British Columbia was transferred to the Pacific Northwest of the United States and thousands of jobs were exported with it. The treaty was a deal, said the Dalhousie Four, that caused needless environmental havoc. This chapter will show how it triggered a chain of natural disaster that ricocheted from the Arrow Lakes Valley to the Athabasca Delta. A third common characteristic of bungled developments in an "unimposing" involvement by the federal government, a word that appears positively charitable when applied to the inertia, incomprehension and ineptitude of the Conservative and Liberal governments that negotiated away the Columbia River.

These politicians in Ottawa and their provincial counterparts are prime targets of the Dalhousie resources critique. "Sellout" and "giveaway," we know, are strong words—strong and judgmental. But in postwar resource transactions the sellers were almost invariably Canadians and the stigma of sellout must bear, not upon the American buyers who seized their opportunities, but upon those Canadians who permitted the nation's integrity to be compromised and its potential diminished. It is, surely, an essential function of Canadian leadership in our time to recognize the United States as a foreign nation-state pursuing, properly or otherwise, its national interests and seeking to ameliorate, sometimes with ruthlessness, its convulsive economic and social tensions. To export the environmental costs of energy production beyond national boundaries, to use pressure to acquire needed resources at bargain prices from weaker countries may be, in American eyes, no less than a patriotic act, which, if it carries moral burdens, is a question for the American conscience.

General Andrew George Latta McNaughton, war hero, engineer and diplomat of beguiling candour, understood all this. As Canadian joint chairman of the International Joint Commission, which regulates disputes between the two nations over boundary waters, he saw Americans he respected—politicians, civil servants, diplomats and fellow engineers—pursuing their country's interests in ways damaging to Canada. When he set out to warn his countrymen of the dangers implied in these actions, the better Americans understood and respected his stance.

Within the American nation-state, Canadian political leaders have frequently been slow to recognize, corporations have concentrated more economic power than many of the world's nations possess and have imposed seemingly irreversible dynamics of growth upon the entire society, changing both consumption patterns and lifestyles. Since the Second World War these corporations have promoted geometrically increasing demand on a shrinking resource base, leading to an energy crisis many thoughtful Americans know must end in industrial and social breakdown.

McNaughton's fight in the fifties and early sixties against the sale of the Columbia River was a mature nationalist response to postwar American expansionism into Canada. When the U.S. decided it must control the water systems in all quarter million square miles of the Columbia basin, including 40,000 square miles of British Columbia, it was creating, McNaughton saw, an almost classical conflict of national interests.

Columbia; it is not that river's immensity alone that makes it the greatest single source of potential power in North America, but rather its singular geography. The river is a hydro engineer's dream. Its magnificent 2,652-foot drop between source and sea makes it one of those rare waters where, even today, the benefits of power dams can be shown to outweigh the costs. Often, in less desirable hydro projects such as Hydro-Quebec's James Bay scheme, the slow-falling rivers are only marginally suitable for power generation. But the Columbia, rising high in the mountains near the provincial border with Alberta and looping like a great coiled rope 480 miles through British Columbia before it crosses the international border and sweeps through 700 miles of the American northwest to empty into the Pacific Ocean, represents an estimated fifteen percent of all the hydro-electric potential in the world! Had there been no Columbia River treaty, more than 2,000 megawatts of that power might have been harnessed in Canada and some 14,000 megawatts in the United States. Two thousand megawatts is a considerable power installation.

If the Columbia River were to be developed in Canada's interest, as McNaughton had long advocated it should be, dams would be built high in the mountains and the river's racing flow would be harnessed to power the populous lower mainland and the sprouting company towns farther north. Instead, under the treaty signed in 1961 and ratified three years later, dams were to be clustered near the American border. Canada undertook to build storage dams on the Columbia that would be controlled, as if by a tap, in the state of Washington. Their purpose would be to provide peak flows when they were needed by the Bonneville Power Administration for its giant Grand Coulee dam and the series of cascade dams downstream.

After the river had been lost to Canada, in a letter to External Affairs Minister Paul Martin, McNaughton quoted an eulogy of the Columbia treaty by the chairman of the Bonneville Power Administration. "An opportunity for a strong industrial development program," the American called it, "a spur to new industries, new jobs, new profits and new payrolls." McNaughton went on to ask: "What does this mean? It means that our industries, in place of being stimulated and expanded, are to be brought under the close-range competition of new American production with power in very large amounts supplied for half a century at a small fraction of the unit costs in Canada."

The Americans, not unnaturally, wanted to acquire cheap power from the Canadian part of the river. One effect would be to undercut the manufacturing industry so tenuously established in British Columbia. The U.S. Departments of State and the Interior had long been subjected to pressures from industry and the military seeking Canadian storage. In 1954 the American Kaiser Aluminum Company, engaged in competition with the Aluminum Company of Canada's plant at Kitimat, had won permission from Social Credit Premier W. A. C. Bennett to build a small dam at the outlet of the Arrow Lakes on the main stem of the Columbia that would yield Kaiser some $14 million a year, with British Columbia collecting an annual $2 million. Described by then federal minister Jean Lesage as a childish "fire sale," the scheme was vetoed in Ottawa. But it was American industry's first formal recognition of the potential benefits of Canadian storage and it is curious that, having accepted the principle of servicing U.S. corporations in the Kaiser deal, Bennett was to reject later an application from a private American power consortium that wanted to build a $425 million dam at Mica Creek. The terms offered by that consortium, ironically, would have proved more advantageous to British Columbia than those Bennett was eventually to receive from the Columbia River treaty. The other pressure on Washington came from the U.S. Army Corps of Engineers, which had been eager since 1948 to build a large dam on the Kootenai River (known as Kootenay in its Canadian reaches) at Libby in Montana, flooding more than 17,000 acres of southeastern British Columbia.

The real national priorities of the period were stated with luminous clarity by Larratt Higgins, the Ontario Hydro economist who was to become McNaughton's closest colleague in the fight against the Columbia sellout. "The whole point about the development of Canadian resources is not to develop them for the sake of developing them, but for the sake of maximizing Canadian per capita real income over the long run," he said. "It does not follow that integrating them into United States operations will achieve this. Our American friends are in no doubt about their objectives ... to maximize their per capita incomes and not Canada's, and integrating our resources into their operations will certainly help them achieve this purpose."

There was, then, more than a decade ago, a fully-developed economic case against energy sellout. It did not stop the Columbia River treaty, nor could it hope to convey the tragic scope of the treaty's consequences, which would emerge only with the sophisticated environmental criticism of the late 1960s.

More than any other single force, it was sustained pressure from the U.S. Corps of Engineers that brought the Columbia to the international bargaining table. Though, throughout the long years of negotiation, the Americans were to appear as consistently the better bargainers, they were not free from conflict behind the scenes. The Departments of State and the Interior wanted the treaty signed so flows from the Canadian Columbia could be controlled for flood protection, for municipal and industrial uses and for power generation; the engineers were primarily concerned with building the Libby dam in Montana. The Americans were seeking 15½ million acre feet of water a year (an acre foot is the quantity of water that covers an acre to the depth of one foot), 8½ million acre feet to provide fully effective flood control storage, the rest for power generation and "consumptive uses"—irrigation, industrial processing, municipal water and sewerage systems.

In 1948 the American segment of the Columbia River basin had sustained $100 million in flood damages and it seemed important to their engineers to gain control of the upstream flow for that reason alone. Since 1945 the International Joint Commission had been surveying the Columbia and Kootenay rivers. Preliminary international exchanges had taken many turns, but both McNaughton and his U.S. counterparts had come to see the matter of control of the Canadian part of the Columbia as the crucial question at issue between the nations.

Power generation was also important to the U.S. In Washington, the Bonneville Power Administration had built the huge Grand Coulee and Bonneville dams, which were imposing but not notably efficient. The Columbia south of the border was swollen in summer after Canadian mountain snows had thawed, a meagre trickle in winter time when Washington industry demanded most power. Seventy percent of the annual flow from upstream crossed the border between the beginning of June and the end of September. Huge storage dams in British Columbia, which could be opened or closed in accordance with Bonneville's supply needs, would guarantee a plentiful year-round flow for Grand Coulee and the smaller dams downstream.

"In retrospect," says Larratt Higgins, "it's hard to gauge where the American priority lay because ideas were changing rapidly between 1958 and 1964. Certainly, before 1958, the electricity potential was what they had most in mind, though the engineers had long pressed the flood control aspects and their scheme for Libby. But the testimony in the later Senate hearings showed the Americans putting more and more stress on the consumptive values involved in the transfer of such large volumes of water, of the enormous benefit and swiftly rising values of water for municipal, irrigation and industrial purposes in the American southwest."

But when negotiations opened, Higgins says, "the Canadians were talking primarily about a power treaty, while the Americans were negotiating a water supply and flood control treaty."

Treaty negotiations must be conducted by governments, and McNaughton, probably the best informed individual Canadian on the resources at stake, had no official part in them. He was impelled to carry his warnings of an impending Canadian give-away to the public. His reward would be arbitrary "retirement" from his post as Canadian chairman of the International Joint Commission. His eventual replacement would be Arnold Heeney, one of the originators of the theory of a continental pool in energy resources.

In practical terms, the Americans began by pressing for Columbia River storage dams in the extreme south of B.C., and for their own dam at Libby. This plan would ensure that only the United States could derive significant hydro power and flood protection from the two rivers. They would both be harnessed to serve U.S. needs.

McNaughton had nurtured other ideas about the Kootenay, which flowed through the country of his boyhood. Before the First World War, he remembered, the Canadian Pacific Railway had proposed the diversion of the Kootenay into the mainstem Columbia, but had lacked the technology to do the job. After World War II the scheme posed no technological difficulty and the general actively supported British Columbia interests anxious to revive the diversion scheme, which derived its potential from a freak of Canadian geography.

The Kootenay River, like the Columbia, rises in the mountains near the Alberta border. Unlike the Columbia, which arches north to Mica Creek, the Kootenay flows almost due south, plunging across the international border into Montana before it curves northwards back into Canada and pours into Kootenay Lake.

The geographic freak is at Canal Flats. Here, the upper reaches of the south-flowing Kootenay pass within one mile of the north-flowing Columbia, and at the same elevation. A shallow canal has long joined the two rivers, transferring small volumes of water between the two river systems.

To enlarge that canal, to re-channel the rising Kootenay, to lock its mountain rush into the Columbia, thereby swelling the mainstem's flow and enhancing its power capacity within British Columbia, appeared to McNaughton as no more than engineering common sense. A Columbia Lake reservoir high in the mountains, the general argued, would have enabled hydro engineers to control the flows into both the Columbia and the Kootenay, providing new options for power generation. Though massive river diversion schemes have proven in recent years to be almost universally disastrous, the Kootenay-Columbia plan appeared much less damaging than, say, Manitoba's crude Nelson-Churchill diversion or the widely destructive James Bay scheme. This was a rare diversion proposal that appeared to possess a built-in natural logic, a merging of smaller river into larger that might be accomplished without mounting an assault upon the region's natural system. Had McNaughton's scheme been adopted, there would certainly have been controversy over the loss of winter grazing for game in the east Kootenay mud-flats and the inundation of resort areas around Lake Windermere. Against this, the general claimed 300,000 acres of the dry benchlands could have been made arable. It seemed to some that the Kootenay must have been born to serve as a tributary to the Columbia.

Whatever the effects of diversion might have been upon the ecosystem, there was no question of the project's engineering feasibility, no doubt that it could have produced twenty percent more energy at ninety-seven percent of the unit cost to service development in British Columbia than was possible under the treaty arrangements. It would also have made it impossible for the United States to build a dam at Libby.

In 1959 it looked as though McNaughton had won a victory when the Americans let it be known they were ready to drop the Libby plan. That triumph was a momentary thing, abruptly overturned by the zigzag policies of Premier Bennett. The ebullient former hardware merchant was operating the province on aggressive chainstore lines and his policy switches were rarely predictable. As External Affairs Minister Howard Green was to tell the Commons, Bennett's government "turned right around and changed their minds completely and said 'We will not stand for a dam in the East Kootenay'." Since both Canada and the U.S. agreed that the Kootenay had to be dammed somewhere, to prevent floods, Bennett's switch ensured that Libby would be built after all. With Libby, the Americans would win the right to divert Kootenay waters for consumptive use in Washington, Oregon or California, and Canada would lose for twenty years what McNaughton had seen as the vital option of plugging the Kootenay into the Columbia.

Looking back at that reversal, Larratt Higgins says, "It was at the moment that Bennett cast his veto that Canadian water policy died. It has been in limbo ever since." The Columbia treaty as it was emerging would deprive Canada of control of both the British Columbia rivers and salvage only U.S. agreement to the principle of a Canadian half share in "downstream benefits"—extra power generated in the United States because of the water released from Canadian storage dams.

The bitterness revealed in Howard Green's account was symptomatic of a widening rift within the Canadian negotiating camp, a weakness the Americans would not be slow to exploit. Green himself was but a bit player in the developing tragicomedy, in which E. Davie Fulton, Canada's chief negotiator, and the impulsive Bennett would have the starring roles. Public attention was soon riveted on the feud between the federal and provincial teams, a hostility that extended down to the level of advisory economists and engineers, and incidents in the personality feud were soon receiving more attention from the media than the issues at stake in the treaty itself. Concessions to the United States attracted little remark. But when Davie Fulton made a pilgrimage to Victoria on treaty business and Bennett ostentatiously contrived to be "out of his office," it was an instant national story.

As Fulton himself later told it to Parliament, he was "astonished" when Bennett suddenly announced that construction was to begin on Columbia dams at Mica Creek and at Duncan and High Arrow near the American border. Of these, only the Mica dam would contribute any power to British Columbia. High Arrow, designed to provide storage for Grand Coulee, would back up Columbia waters 150 miles from Castlegar to Revelstoke, drowning ninety percent of the habitable farmland within sight of the river. On the American side, Libby was to go ahead, backing water forty miles into B.C. from Montana and turning farms into mudflats.

The Fulton account related more shocks. When Prime Minister John Diefenbaker and President Eisenhower signed the treaty in Washington on January 17, 1961, Fulton would tell the Commons, it was their understanding that Canada's half share of the downstream benefits of Columbia River power was to become "the next major source of hydro power to supply British Columbia's requirements." But then, Fulton claimed, Bennett's government performed "a surprising contortion. Its position moved from an insistence on marketing some of the downstream benefit power in the U.S. while it might be surplus to our requirements—a position which was accepted throughout—to a refusal, after the treaty was signed, to proceed with any development at all unless the whole entitlement was sold in the United States and paid for in advance on a basis which would pay for the three treaty dams at no cost to British Columbia."

Fulton's account, explaining away the whole bungled affair as a Bennett double cross, was itself an over-simplification. Foxy, even Machiavellian, as the old hardware merchant might be, his "contortion" had been neither so sudden nor so surprising as Fulton was suggesting. Pathetically, the debate over a significant national resource was descending into an acrimonious squabble about the receipt of a letter. Bennett was able to show that he had never stated his accord with the treaty proposal advanced by the federal negotiators. On January 13, four days before Diefenbaker's trip to meet the retiring American soldier-president he revered, an ambiguously-phrased letter had gone out from Bennett's office, specifying that Ottawa's version of the financial arrangements for the treaty was not acceptable to British Columbia. Diefenbaker left for Washington before that letter was received and Fulton was to claim that Bennett's letter did not arrive in time. Even at the time, that seemed a lame excuse, since Bennett's actions and statements through December 1960, and early January 1961, had made it crystal clear that Ottawa's financial proposals had not received the province's assent.

Dealing with Bennett, of course, could never have been easy. He often strained credulity with his semantic ploys. He justified his opposition to a dam in the East Kootenay, for instance, by saying it would create a "transportation barrier"—even though the site lay in a swamp and a road was proposed for the crest of the dam. Later, when he wanted to dam the Peace River, he would describe the project as creating "a water highway"—even though its effect would be to choke once-navigable waters with timber. But he was concerned with larger ploys than merely semantic ones. While Ottawa's negotiators were floundering through their sessions with the Americans, Bennett, acting independently, was orchestrating an entirely different stratagem for the province's development—the famous Two Rivers program.

Despite his flamboyant feuding with the central government, Bennett was essentially reconciled to the sale of the Columbia because, since the late 1950s, he had been captivated by the enormous potential of development on the northern Peace River, where Swedish industrialist Axel Wenner-Gren, proposing to exploit mineral and timber resources, was demanding cheap power. Power from the Peace would call for a gigantic installation, six times bigger than Grand Coulee, because the river was 600 miles from the Vancouver market. But with new technology huge volumes of electricity could be transmitted long distances at very high voltage and with small load loss. In August 1961, Bennett expropriated the Peace River Power Company and the privately-owned B.C. Electric Utility—"dishing," in the process, the ostensibly socialist New Democrats and prolonging his own reign in Victoria—and issued construction licenses for the Peace, High Arrow, Duncan and Mica dams.

Though denounced as a madman by Fulton, as a second Castro by U.S. newspapers and as "King Cecil" by the NDP opposition, Bennett had covered his bets. In 1960 he'd ordered discreet studies on alternative energy sources for the lower mainland market, which was growing at a projected eight percent per year. The alternatives studied were Hat Creek coalfield near Ashcroft and the Clearwater River, a tributary of the North Thompson. The studies showed that either source would be cheaper than energy from the Columbia developed by the province alone, but neither of them would be as economic as the Columbia if the United States bought or returned half the benefits of downstream power.

Now, the merchant's masterstroke. Bennett refused to permit ratification of the treaty until the U.S. agreed to finance all the treaty dams on the Columbia in exchange for all the downstream benefits for thirty years. The U.S. was to pay $274.8 million for downstream benefits and use the power, thereby helping finance the Peace, the river Bennett had destined to light up the lower mainland. Now the premier had good financial cards to promote his Two Rivers program of provincial development through the export of power to the United States. He had conducted an adroit political manoeuvre at the expense of Canada's future. Even if a major resource was to be lost to Canada, immediate provincial needs would be served.

If Bennett's performance fell short of far-sighted leadership, he could, retrospectively, claim that he had at least promoted good financial deals for his immediate constituency. The federal leaders, charged with the husbandry of all the nation's resources, could not say even that. Bennett's wheeling and dealing, parochial, short-term and politically-inspired at it was, had more purpose to it than the muddled federal involvement, and achieved in its own narrow terms a measure of short-run success.

Ottawa was not successful at all. The performance of Conservatives and Liberals was uniformly dismal. Fulton, before he abandoned Ottawa to be rejected by his own constituents in the provincial general election of 1963, was obliged to eat the brave words he had spoken in a celebrated speech denouncing the Bennett "sellout" of the Columbia. Fulton had a principled objection to the export of power. But Larratt Higgins, who had harried the federal advisers for years, recalls that Fulton "ultimately decided that the treaty which was signed was better than no treaty at all. When the crunch came, his options were to break off negotiations or to take what he knew was second best. He took second best. Perhaps the only justification for him is that he never really knew how far away from first best that was!"

If the Tories had blundered, the Liberals, with the late Lester Pearson, Paul Martin and Jack Davis conspicuous among them, would manage to compound every error. When they took office, the Columbia treaty had been signed but not ratified and McNaughton and Higgins entertained hopes, if not for long, that something might be salvaged in the Canadian interest.

By the time the Liberals took power, these nationalists had mounted a vigorous lobby and the lines of communication with Parliament seemed open to them, despite the Liberals' bewildering propensity for sudden and unexplained switches in policy. Higgins had spoken to the "power study group" of the Liberal caucus, presenting a pragmatic substitute for the Columbia treaty—a plan to build only the Mica Creek dam and provide the Americans with some storage without formal treaty commitments. Higgins had been well received; "I think you're on the right track," Pearson wrote him later. After the Higgins presentation to caucus, the chameleon-like Jack Davis, a treaty supporter in 1962, became a treaty opponent in 1963. Paul Martin, moving into External Affairs, became the target of a stream of impassioned correspondence from the ailing McNaughton. "My counsel to you, as an old friend," said one of the letters, "is to withdraw from this dangerous imbroglio, while you yet may, for the sake of Canada...." But the old pro politician from Essex County was not perceptibly moved. "Talk to me about the Auto Pact," was his advice to one visiting journalist, "don't talk about the Columbia, it bores me." And Martin would pick the brains of the critics, send them soothing letters and hope they would then go away.

Before long the nationalists were concluding reluctantly that the Liberals did not mean business and could not be trusted. The key to their actions, all along, was held by Lester Pearson, always so disarmingly genial in his social contacts with the nationalists, so enigmatic in his political aims and so opportunistic in his political timing. A year before his assumption of office, after he had met President John Kennedy at a glittering Washington dinner for Nobel Prize winners, Canadian journalists had picked up that Kennedy had emphasized the need for Bomarc missiles to be based on Canadian soil, while Pearson had mentioned a protocol that would enable Canada to ratify the Columbia River treaty. Within one month of taking office, Pearson had announced the acceptance of the Bomarcs in Canada and Ottawa's intention to negotiate a protocol to the Columbia treaty, decisions that press gallery cynics were not slow to relate to the switch in campaign donations by multinational corporations from the Conservatives to the Liberal party.

Throughout these years of intrigue, opportunities for the public to express dissenting views were severely circumscribed. Even the articulate nationalists were not permitted to relate one aspect of the sellout to another. Thus, witnesses at the public hearings on the flooding of British Columbia valleys for treaty dams were ordered not to discuss the Columbia treaty itself, while those appearing before the Commons' External Affairs Committee were told it would be out of order to discuss the dam-building licenses! Both Ottawa and Victoria had come around to acceptance, but neither would provide its citizens with the opportunity for informed debate. Between the federal and provincial governments there was by now not so much agreement as the temporary concordance of differing political self-interests; for the long run, both nation and province were to prove losers.

As a result of the Columbia River treaty Canada gained: an American market for British Columbia for $274.8 million in downstream power benefits; financing for three storage dams on the Columbia River; $68.3 million for flood control benefits; $112 million in interest and other payments; some power benefit from the flooding of Mica Creek. It comes to a rough total of $455 million.

Canada lost: control of the flows of the Columbia and Kootenay rivers; millions in power potential; billions in consumptive values; land flooded by High Arrow and Libby dams, which provided no power, flood control or consumptive benefits to Canada; cost of compensation to landowners; cost of providing permanent flood control for the state of Washington; cost of clearing Canadian land to be flooded for a dam located in Montana and serving only the United States. These items add up to a total that has never been and perhaps never can be computed.

Cash payments for the downstream benefits were made in annual instalments of $30 million, the final payment reaching Victoria in 1971. In order to accommodate the United States in its balance of payments difficulties, interest payments were received at four and one-quarter percent; the difference between four and one-quarter percent and the varying interest rates prevailing on the market during the period of payment represents a loss of at least $20 million to the provincial treasury.

The treaty provided nothing for the enormous consumptive values of the Canadian Columbia's water resources. At $39 per acre foot, they would amount to $4.5 billion. It was this omission that prompted environmental lawyer Ian McDougall to assess the treaty as "an unparallelled squandering of Canadian resources and sovereignty."

Larratt Higgins said at the time that "it will cost Canada

about $100 million to give the Columbia away," but he now concedes that this estimate was ludicrously low and does not reflect consumptive values. When New Democrat Dave Barrett succeeded Bennett as premier after an election upset late in 1972, he said simply, "We were skinned."

In long-range economic terms, there is something worse than the tangible losses. Canada's self-denial of future options, of the capacity to use its own waters for irrigation, municipal or industrial use, is now seen as an irrecoverable folly. The developmental options of the future have been circumscribed. Once the storage commitment had been made to the United States, surrendering Canadian use of the flows, it meant that several avenues of development would prove uneconomic for future provincial governments. If those governments wished to draw water from the system for consumptive use, they could do it only by pumping the water over a divide—a costly, even prohibitive engineering process. For the Americans, diversion of controlled Columbia flows for any consumptive use they choose can be achieved at a low cost—through the force of gravity.

Economists later found another grotesquely unfair aspect to be the evaluation of the controlled waters delivered annually to the Bonneville Power Authority. These values, the treaty ruled, would diminish from one year to the next. The rationale for that was that, in Bonneville's "mixed" system of electricity generation, the proportion of "base load" derived from American thermal generation, would steadily increase, with power from the Columbia storages being reserved increasingly for "peak" periods of production. In fact it is now clear that thermal and hydro generation are permanent and complementary aspects of the Bonneville system, with the growing use of reversible pump turbines at the American dams permitting a steadily growing proportion of the Canadian storage water to be drawn out of the system for consumptive use. The consumptive values of water, in fact, escalate about as rapidly as the costs of the construction industry and have risen more than fifty percent since the treaty went into effect. But the treaty determined that the more the American Pacific northwest enjoyed this increasingly valuable Canadian resource, the less it would be required to pay!

Short-term gain for a narrow provincial interest, exploitation to service the U.S., "unimposing" federal involvement—all the hallmarks of ill-considered resource development are glaringly apparent in the Columbia River treaty.

But there is one further criterion of the ill-considered resource project that fits the Columbia case—it was undertaken without regard to the social and environmental consequences. "Our grandchildren," wrote Donald Waterfield in *Continental Waterboy*, "will not be operating the sluice gates of Columbia's dams without any compensation with any enthusiasm, particularly when they recall that their grandparents improvidently spent $64 million of flood control payments largely in destroying the Arrow Valley."

Waterfield, a humane, contemplative farmer rooted in the Arrow Lakes country, became in the years of treaty negotiation the rueful prophet of Canada's paradise lost. He fought the proposal to flood his beautiful valley with all the tenacity of a pastoral man driven to rebel against the ruthless exercise of power. For him, as for the Anglican cleric V. B. H. Pellegrin, it was a countryman's protest against destructive development that will not pause to consider its human and natural victims. "In times of stress," argued Pellegrin, "we are urged to show in visible ways what our fatherland means to us, to pay the price of self-determination and, if necessary, to die for it. You can't expect us now to give away what many have died for just because the government feels that it is a convenient way of making $65 million or thereabouts." But, in the end, they did give it away.

The Columbia treaty, Bennett's pre-condition for the Peace development, was to become the first link in a long chain of social and environmental disaster. The first victims were Waterfield's people, the farmers and retired folk of the Arrow Valley. Next came the Peace River natives whose hunting grounds were inundated by the Bennett Dam. Later, 700 miles away in neighbouring Alberta, the Peace-Athabasca Delta was to be recognized and studied as an "ecological disaster area."

To create the 600-foot Bennett Dam, 680 square miles of wilderness, habitat of an estimated 6,000 moose and the Tall Grass Indians who hunted them, were turned into choked wastewaters of floating timber. And when the dam gates closed, the delicate seasonal mechanism sustaining the faraway Peace-

Athabasca Delta was shattered. For centuries before 1968 the spring flood from the Peace had poured into the Slave River, forcing waters from Lake Athabasca back into meandering channels and small, shallow lakes, renewing the cycle of life in 1,000 square miles of delta swamplands. When the Bennett Dam closed, Lake Athabasca and the delta waters dropped several feet and, starved of the replenishing spring flood, small lakes dried out and larger ones shrank, leaving stranded muskrat dying on the banks, fishkills and empty traps that would cripple the subsistence economy of 1,300 Athabasca native people.

The connecting link in this macabre chain was the sellout policies of W. A. C. Bennett and his ineffectual counterparts in Ottawa. Oddly, Alberta's Social Credit government did not protest what the scientists called the death of a delta. Perhaps it was because Alberta had its own scheme for wringing fast bucks from the ruin of rivers. Alberta proposed to compound the deterioration of the delta with a dam on the Pembina River, a tributary of the Athabasca, that would, as the next chapter shows, help promote water exports to the United States. Only the election victory of Peter Lougheed's Conservatives saved the wounded delta from this further refinement in the re-engineering of natural systems.

It was this very prospect of massive water export—"consumptive uses," in Columbia treaty language—that McNaughton most resented. The treaty was negotiated at a time when western U.S. politicians were preoccupied, sometimes to the point of obsession, with the idea of diverting Canadian rivers they considered "wasted" in the Arctic. Canadian continentalists such as Lester Pearson and Jack Davis (later, ironically, minister of the Environment in the Trudeau government) had talked excitedly about potential water exports "as important as wheat or oil."

NAWAPA, the North American Water and Power Alliance, was a $100 billion scheme to turn the Rocky Mountain Trench into an inland sea providing the United States with new irrigation, navigation and power. It was not published by the Ralph M. Parsons engineering company of Los Angeles or endorsed by a U.S. Senate subcommittee until the Columbia deal had been clinched.

The timing could scarcely have been coincidental. In the Columbia treaty, Canada, wittingly or unwittingly, abandoned the traditional shelter afforded by the Boundary Waters Treaty of 1909, which protected the integrity of national waters and established the International Joint Commission as a machinery for settling disputes over boundary waters. The Columbia treaty, therefore, removed a constitutional barrier to the promotion of such schemes as NAWAPA. If NAWAPA ever goes into effect, Canadian rivers flowing to the Arctic will be reversed. Five hundred miles of Rocky Mountain Trench, from around Prince George south to the Montana border, will be drowned. The Columbia will be diverted into the Kootenay—the reverse of McNaughton's scheme for British Columbia power development. NAWAPA, the Parsons company claimed, would draw water from river systems with total flows of 663 million acre feet. It would deliver 20 million acre feet to Mexico, 78 million to the United States and 22 million to central Canada.

One strategic tap for NAWAPA's Rube Goldberg labyrinth of dams and diversions is already in place close to the Montana border—the Libby dam. There, each year, five million acre feet of Kootenay waters pass to the U.S. for power, flood control or consumptive use, as the Americans choose. It is at least arguable that in the Columbia treaty Canada gave an implied sanction to NAWAPA and to Libby as a locking piece in the jigsaw, and that the Americans' interest in big diversions may explain their persistent pressure to build Libby, despite its dubious economics.

Water exports were never part of W. A. C. Bennett's design for his province. "We will not sell our water," he said more than once, and it can be assumed that he meant it. What cannot be assumed is that the American negotiators, who had witnessed McNaughton's official banishment, Bennett's "contortions," the embarrassment of Fulton and the impassive nonchalance of Martin, would take Canadian refusal to sell water too seriously. Why should they, once Libby was won?

The treaty certainly jeopardized the formulation of sound national water policies for Canada. McNaughton, who had laboured more than a decade in the effort to put consistency and order into Canada's approach to the regulation of the waters it shared with the United States, saw the precedent-shattering treaty as both dangerous and revolutionary, bearing the potential to disrupt the entire body of custom and law that had grown out of a century of disputes over boundary waters.

As Larratt Higgins wrote in *Close the 49th Parallel:* "In place of cooperation by national entities, the Canadian portion of the Columbia basin has been placed under international control, which is to be based upon the greatest good for the basin as a whole. The American portion of the basin remains under American control. This means that, in cases of conflict, Canadian operation must give way to the majority interest with no compensation for lost opportunity. In other words, the costs of cooperation are to be borne by Canada while the benefits will be reaped by the United States wherever a divergence arises. The Columbia River treaty is not for cooperative development and operation; it integrates the smaller but vital Canadian part of the basin into the whole."

Creation of this constitutional double standard in boundary waters matters called into question the validity of the International Joint Commission and all the jurisprudence of the past. Other shared watersheds remained under the protection of the Boundary Waters Treaty of 1909, which had been premised upon the development of North America by two separate nations and formulated procedures for resolving conflicts between those nations. The Columbia basin alone was to be governed according to the precepts of an integrated continental economy under a treaty that made no provision for the possibility of conflict. The arrangement relegated Canada to a status below that of a nation-state.

In the light of changing energy priorities since 1961, the Columbia River treaty is more demonstrably a great Canadian loss than it is a great American gain. One gain is clear, even from United States studies. Power and flood control comparable to that purchased from Canada for $344 million, before interest, would have cost $711 million to develop within the states of Washington and Oregon. Yet John V. Krutilla, an American resource economist respected on both sides of the border, has published an exhaustive analysis suggesting that, in strictly economic terms, the treaty was no bargain even for the U.S. Nor, he argues, was it an effective international agreement, since resources were wastefully developed. In effect, Krutilla agreed with McNaughton that the wrong projects had been chosen for development. As for Libby, Krutilla says its benefits don't match its costs.

If Krutilla is right about this, two interpretations are possible. One is that the American Columbia negotiators were as confused about what they were doing as their Canadian counterparts. That seems unlikely. The second interpretation is that hydro generation and flood control were never the central issues they appeared to be and that, even at the official diplomatic level, the Americans were preoccupied with consumptive use. There is abundant evidence that what they most wanted in the early 1960s was Canada's water. By surrendering the consumptive uses of the upstream Columbia, the treaty tacitly endorsed the notion of a continental resource pool, which McNaughton had termed "that diabolical thesis." The treaty makes sense if considered a logical prelude to NAWAPA or some more sophisticated scheme for the export of Canada's waters.

In summary, McNaughton's 1959 critique was a valid one. The resources of the Columbia and Kootenay rivers were not developed to maximize per capita incomes in Canada. The cross purposes of provincial and federal leaderships were exploited by the Americans, and the central government missed a number of opportunities to make its presence felt. Fulton, for instance, declined to insist that Bennett apply for the licensing of his Peace River dam project under the Navigable Waters Act, an omission that, years later, would embolden Quebec to flout federal authority in its even more disastrous James Bay project.

Criticisms mounted by the environmentalists in the years after McNaughton's death were also valid. The treaty began a chain reaction of destruction in the natural systems of western Canada.

And Donald Waterfield's outrage proved prophetic. Bountifully endowed stretches of Canada, where there had once been timberlands, cherry trees and settlers living in a pleasant climate, drowned behind the dams without any promise, prospect or possibility of adequate compensation.

The Columbia sellout became a precedent for a wide variety of resource giveaways across the country, in all of which Canada's interests were placed second to the prospects of short-term gain. In the nine years since the treaty's ratification there has been little practical evidence of any real break with the Columbia tradition.

But it is heartening that one small attempt has been made in British Columbia itself. There was, surely, a hint of stiffening resistance in the 1973 decision of the new provincial government to forbid the flooding of the Skagit River Valley which was proposed to keep the neon signs flashing in the nearby city of Seattle. Compared to the Columbia, of course, the flooding of ten square miles of Canadian land around the trout-filled Skagit is no more than a piddling affair. But it became symbolic because the Skagit is one of the last dam-free Canadian streams within a day's drive of Vancouver, because anglers and conservationists cherished the valley that would be drowned by increasing the height of the Ross Dam in the state of Washington, and because Canada's ambassador in the American capital had engaged in genteel lobbying against the flooding plan. Now a political decision in Victoria appears to have saved the Skagit Valley, reinforced by predictable after-the-event support from Environment Minister Jack Davis.

In Bennett's heyday, that small assertion of integrity would have been less likely. Development came first and fast when he sniffed sulphur in his nostrils and pronounced it "the smell of money." The British Columbia of the 1960s would have pocketed the $3 million offered by Seattle for one hundred years of power, and applied it quickly to some other dam on some other river.

Skagit is a paradise regained. And, even now a stubborn rearguard action is under way against the Columbia defeat. In the spring and summer of 1973 a series of information meetings brought British Columbia leaders together with a number of authorities on water and constitutional questions, including men who had been close to McNaughton in his last years. Premier Barrett, one of them found, remained "very serious about the Columbia—serious and even determined."

Any effort to regain that squandered asset, he must know, will prove a difficult and complex undertaking, against tremendous odds. The only time Canadians can insure the future of any resource is when that resource is under Canadian control.

Chapter Four

Dam Them All!

"Undiluted engineering talent, when applied to water problems, generally leads to disaster."

— Larratt Higgins.

There is a fast-acting antidote to any assumption that Canadian water export to the United States has become a dead letter: a phone call to Frank Moss in his office in Utah.

Frank Moss has one of those shudderingly confident telephone voices. The United States senator for the "dry" state of Utah is known to Canadians as the man who would buy our water, the tireless propagandist of that California-hatched scheme, the North American Water and Power Alliance (NAWAPA).

At a price of something like $100 billion, NAWAPA would turn around the great Arctic-flowing rivers of Canada and drain them into the American West and Mexico. Most Canadians who ever considered the notion shared General McNaughton's revulsion, a reaction politicians and bureaucrats have discreetly noted. For that reason NAWAPA has become a matter of declining fashionability in our politics. It is no longer talked about. Sometimes it is presumed dead.

Even Senator Moss admits "it's delicate. We must be sensitive about this," he says with careful tolerance. "The Canadians have to come to the conclusion that it is of some benefit to them. I have tried to indicate to our negotiators that they must present the matter of water exports from Canada as one that will be mutually beneficial to our countries.

"NAWAPA," he persists, "was a very centralized system.

It seems to me now we shall not be able to do it quite that way. We might have to do a piece at a time, as each piece becomes feasible."

Eight years earlier, Moss had been more direct. As chairman of the U.S. Senate's Western Water Development Committee, he had rammed through a resolution demanding "diversion of surplus Arctic waters." Now he was taking a detour. But it would be optimistic to think that Canada is out of the NAWAPA shadow. A wiser reaction would be that the threat to the whole has receded—but we had better keep a careful eye on the individual parts. Nowhere in Moss's conversation is there any weakening in the conviction of absolute rightness and inevitability of using Canada's "wasted" rivers to service American industry and agriculture and to flush away the sewage of American cities.

NAWAPA, designed by the Ralph M. Parsons engineering company of Los Angeles, was touted as the biggest public works project in man's history. It involved building the biggest dams in the world, creating an inland sea in the Rocky Mountain Trench of British Columbia, a ship canal across the prairies to the Great Lakes, tunnels, spillways and reservoirs to shift an ocean of water from the Canadian northwest to seven provinces, thirty-three American and three Mexican states.

NAWAPA engineers would seal off the Arctic-flowing rivers in Canada and Alaska. They would pump the flow through pipelines 1,000 feet up to the Rocky Mountain Trench. Then they would flood the interior valleys for 500 miles from Prince George to the Libby dam. And then they would spill it southeast to the American drylands.

It was too monstrous to be palatable in Canada. So, through the late sixties, water and construction engineers worked on variants. One scheme would gather up the waters of the north-central prairies for delivery to the American midwest. Another would plug James Bay into the Great Lakes. Why did such schemes sprout at that time? It was only partly because of the crude state of the environmental science of the day. It was also because the Columbia River treaty had signalled to Washington that Canada's rivers could be sold for consumptive use by Americans, and the price was right.

There were plenty of salesmen. Jack Davis trumpeted continental water sale as an "inspiring" idea. Tory Alvin Hamilton, pepped up with the adrenalin of John Diefenbaker's "northern vision," was just as keen. Even in 1970, Pierre Elliott Trudeau was saying on television, "If people are not going to use it, can't we sell it for good, hard cash?" Though respected geographers such as McGill's Dr. Trevor Lloyd could dismiss NAWAPA as "an exercise in sophomore civil engineering which has received far greater attention than it deserved," Canada's leaders appeared to suggest that, if water export could be worked out on a basis less nightmarish than NAWAPA, there might be a deal.

This was when the "studies" began. Pressed about water, the only intermittently nationalist Energy minister, Joe Greene, explained that Canadians didn't know enough about their water supplies. There could, therefore, be no quick decisions. There would have to be "inventories." It was true that little was known. Canada had more than one quarter of the world's fresh water, more water per capita than any other people. But the flows of few northern rivers had been measured.

The Canadians of the sixties were susceptible to the environmental misconceptions of the time. It was assumed, for instance, that waters flowing to the Arctic really were "wasted"; the delicate natural and economic harmonies of northern systems were not understood. It was thought irrigation was always a boon to agriculture; only after the costly lesson of the South Saskatchewan dam was it realized that a dryland farmer could have sound marketing reasons for rejecting irrigation. Moss's belief that vast regions of the United States are "starved of water" was then unchallenged. U.S. scientists have since shown that the problem is not a general shortage, but a maze of local difficulties arising from pollution, waste and corporate greed. The disasters of the engineering approach to river systems, soon to be seen from Aswan to the Athabasca, had not emerged.

So the need for inventory was real. But the studies of the sixties were not launched in a spirit of scholarly inquiry. They began in the aftermath of the Columbia sellout, while American lobbyists clamoured for Canadian water and academics won reputations by demonstrating how water could be marketed at a profit. A decade of study was starting in dangerous ambiguity, with a predisposition toward giant river engineering, in official secrecy and against a background of academic huckstering.

Alberta provided a classic example. The rise and fall of its Prairie Rivers Improvement, Management and Evaluation (PRIME) scheme mirrors precisely the changing priorities of the decade. Developed by seasoned practical water management people using the utilitarian approach of the early sixties, promoted vigorously by a scientist-salesman, adopted by a provincial government that saw non-renewable resources simply as "commodities," PRIME was shelved in 1971 by a new government with a more sophisticated view of the dynamics of development.

The conventional wisdom of the post-Columbia period was that rivers are a moveable convenience. If rivers flowed in the north and the people lived in the south, you re-channelled the rivers to where the people were. That had been the stated purpose of California's State Water Project and PRIME's was almost a carbon copy. The Alberta Department of Agriculture's Water Resources Division pointed out that eighty-nine percent of the water passing through the province was carried north by three river systems. The eleven percent of the water that flowed south had to service eighty-five percent of Albertans. "The logical solution," it was argued, "is to divert northern waters southward where they are more urgently needed."

Two men are synonymous with PRIME. Reginald Bailey, a twenty-four-year veteran of water management and head of the Water Resources Division, is a civil servant of super-professional reticence. Never, in years of promoting PRIME, did he relate the scheme to the prospect of water export. Yet the public always associated the redeployment of the rivers with the export of water. One reason was that both Ernest Manning's and Harry Strom's Social Credit governments were always very receptive to U.S. investment. Another reason was the continuing prominence of the second man associated with the scheme—Dr. Arleigh Laycock.

From the geography department of the University of Alberta, Dr. Laycock constantly encouraged the discussion of water exports, before and after his 1971 election as president of the American Water Resources Association. He says now that his advocacy has always been to persuade Canadians not to reject out of hand exports that would be in the national interest. But he has also suggested the sale of "options" on future use of Canadian rivers and argued that one or two percent of all the nation's water could be sold. By increasing PRIME transfers beyond what was needed for southern Alberta irrigation, he suggested, water could be made available for export, "economies of scale" achieved and American money attracted for building dams and reservoirs. The potential export routes were easy to see. PRIME would shift Athabasca waters down to the Bow and Oldman river irrigation districts south of Calgary. It would not, then, be a great step to divert water into the Missouri system by way of Alberta's Milk River or the border-hugging Souris.

But it did not happen. Alberta environmentalists pointed out that more diversions from the Athabasca would compound the havoc wrought by construction of the Bennett Dam on the Peace. Anti-PRIME stickers festooned car bumpers in Alberta's 1971 election campaign. Campaigning Conservative William Dickie warned of a "domino" effect from PRIME diversions, the damages of each project demanding a further project to patch up the environmental damage. Dickie is now resources minister in the Lougheed government.

"Bringing northern rivers south doesn't fit the pattern now," says a senior civil servant. "The general approach is to bring development to the resource. This government rejects water exports and doesn't see spending millions diverting rivers. It would rather build a transportation network and promote "spin-off" industry where the resources are—in the north."

Reginald Bailey went back to the drawing boards. Under water management policies being worked out now, he says, "the development of the water resources within each river basin will be given high priority. Inter-basin diversions are given a very low priority." Interestingly, he says "the most significant thing influencing this change in policy has been the public's recognition of and concern for environmental factors. PRIME was a concept geared to meeting water shortage. Today, environmental effects have become a factor in assessing the costs and benefits of any project. We know we can't measure all the costs in dollars."

Dr. Arleigh Laycock "feels badly" that transfers are being de-emphasized, but does not believe it will last. Environmental-ism has scarcely modified his views. He never felt, he says, that NAWAPA had much potential. But Canadians should consider other schemes. They might transfer northern Ontario waters to the U.S. by way of the Great Lakes. Water could be used as the medium to pipe western potash to Chicago, then be separated and distilled at an agreed price. Canadian water could be sold for "supplemental" use in a trans-border irrigation network, operating like the power grid that already links western provinces with some American states. "Such a scheme," Laycock says, "would have a major impact on, say, the Nebraska Sandhills, but not involve more than ten percent of the exported waters in transfers over a major distance."

The real emphasis of his advocacy, he maintains, has been to "get proper studies." But what are proper studies? His favourite is the four-year, $4,700,000 study undertaken by the Saskatchewan-Nelson Basin Board, jointly financed by Ottawa and the three prairie provinces. The eleven-volume report is now stacked on Reginald Bailey's desk in Edmonton and those of his counterparts in Regina, Winnipeg and Ottawa.

"It will, almost inevitably, mean water exports," Dr. Laycock says. "They're talking in terms of transfers of such volumes that it's nonsense to think on that scale unless it's for export. The board doesn't say that, I know—it's politically tough. But that's the way it makes sense."

Nowhere in its media brochures prepared by Foster Advertising of Toronto does the board mention exports. But if Ottawa and the prairie governments had decided in advance that water exports must come one day, they would have ordered an identical study. Study Director E. F. Durrant proclaimed the 1972 report as "precedent-shattering in its scope and magnitude—a truly important chapter in western Canadian history." He could be right.

The report, Durrant said, "presents an inventory of river flows at 145 points in the basin. It gives the results of preliminary investigations of possibilities for storing and diverting the flow of rivers to increase the usable supply of water." The stated premise, in fact, was an amplification of the rationale justifying PRIME: "There is not enough water in the Nelson-Saskatchewan basin to cope with the present and the projected needs of the future based on existing use patterns."

The board made detailed appraisals of the sites of fifty-five dams and twenty-three river diversions across the basin and classified every one of them "practical engineering projects." They worked out how existing dams and diversions could be used to augment flows, then packed new dams, storage reservoirs and diversions into the equation. Their final computation showed flows that could be achieved if eight added reservoirs were coupled with external diversions from the Peace-Athabasca and Churchill rivers.

Their conclusion: "To effect a major increase in river flows, of the magnitude expected to be needed in future, it would be necessary to divert water into the basin from sources outside its area."

Predictably, the board does not answer the next questions—the vital questions behind PRIME magnified now to a scale as wide as the prairies. Where will you find the billions for all this monumental engineering? Can you redirect the great northwestern rivers to the central prairie and stop them there? Why not finance it by siphoning off a "surplus" to flow to the American midwest?

At this point Dr. Laycock begins to make sense. How can you bring that geographic upheaval shuddering to a halt at a line on a map? If you turn around the Peace-Athabasca, surely, you set in motion a process that will not stop at the southern political limit of the Saskatchewan-Nelson basin.

The entire elaborate study, in fact, provides the outline structure for an updated NAWAPA.

Remember all this began in 1967. Remember that when the Energy minister of the day, Joe Greene, was asked about Canada's policy on water exports, he replied, "It's the same as it is in regard to any of our other energy resources, namely that if there is an amount that is clearly surplus to Canadian need, present or future, then this energy source is for sale to the extent of the surplus. With regard to water, we do not know whether there is a surplus because we do not have sufficient inventory of our total waters. We do not know what is the Canadian need for the future.... We don't know that there is a surplus and therefore there is none for sale. That is the Canadian position."

Nothing more definitive has been said since. The Nelson-Saskatchewan study is consistent with this position. A future declaration that studies had shown Canada possessed a water surplus would not be inconsistent, either.

Larratt Higgins believes that massive diversions for consumptive purposes almost invariably prove to be natural disasters. Richard Bocking orchestrated this theme in his 1972 book *Canada's Water: For Sale?* He showed that even in the U.S. contemporary water scientists now reject the rippling violence of river diversions upon the ecosystem. Engineers such as the University of Manitoba's Dr. R. W. Newbury are moving toward a higher understanding of water projects. The Saskatchewan-Nelson study, like the Churchill diversion and James Bay, is already close to obsolescence in scientific terms. The danger is that the politicians may also be obsolete. Has there been an evolution in their horse-trading psyche to match developing science? It is not inconceivable that Ottawa could approve water sales without knowing what it was doing. Bourassa has done something like this in Quebec. More improbably, Schreyer has done it in Manitoba. In the absence of massive public pressure, what guarantee do we have that Trudeau and Jack Davis will not do it in Ottawa?

The master map of the Nelson study reveals a clear pattern. Huge volumes of water are moved southeast from the remote northwest. Existing dams and reservoirs frame a skeletal export route. One prong carries water from the Peace River country through a Smoky River diversion to a dam at Hairy Hill, thence down to the South Saskatchewan dam, the Qu'Appelle and the Souris. Another prong, akin to PRIME, starts at the Old Man dam on the Athabasca and moves through the Macleod, Chip Lake and the Pembina to the North Saskatchewan, Battle and Red Deer rivers, plunging south to the Oldman and Bow. An eastern diversionary route flows from Lake Athabasca down to the Churchill system and out through Frog Portage. The Dauphin is thrust south into Lake Manitoba, south again to the Souris, close to the sprawling Missouri system.

When the U.S. launched its current push for a continental energy deal in 1969, water was said to be off the agenda (though hydro-electricity was on) because the Canadians didn't have the facts. Since then Ottawa has been busily ensuring that we do have the facts for some future round of continental energy talks.

76

The Nelson basin study is not unique. A similar $4 million federal-provincial study was launched in northern Ontario in the mid-sixties. The pretext—that diverting the rivers that flow to James Bay could end the problem of low water levels in the Great Lakes—was never plausible. Old-timers in the Ontario cabinet recall the prophetic grumbles of Premier John Robarts that they'd be likely to cause floods in high-water years if they messed around with inflow to the lakes. Ontario Hydro is no longer interested in remote generation sites. Ontario's Environment Minister James Auld and Environment Canada's policy-making Alex Davidson deny the study is related to water export. "We don't even talk about diversions any more," says a senior man at Queen's Park, "it's become a dirty word."

But the export question does not go away. Larratt Higgins, who has watched the curious undulations of water politics for decades now, says there's been no firm national policy since Jean Lesage left the federal cabinet. In 1964 the Columbia treaty led the Americans to think that Canadian water could be bought for consumptive use. Nothing decisive has happened to shake that belief.

In 1973, the demands of new technology were added to the American pressures that stemmed from folkloric fears of drought. The U.S. coal industry, increasingly dominated by the giant corporations of the petroleum cartel, proposes for the 1980s a mammoth program of coal gasification. The coal that will be used lies in the arid regions of the American West. The production of substitute natural gas from coal requires enormous volumes of water. And the U.S. Department of the Interior has let it be known that water from Canada's western rivers might be a prerequisite for successful large-scale gasification. Free-spending coal lobbyists will bring an important reinforcement to Frank Moss's crusade for Canadian rivers.

In environmental terms, the "state of the art" has been transformed since NAWAPA. The Bennett Dam and the Athabasca Delta dramatized the folly of brutal interference with river systems. Arctic studies showed northern rivers do not "waste" their waters but sustain a complex and delicate natural system, which is the basis for the subsistence economy and social patterns of Canadian natives. Modern economics showed irrigation to be no agricultural panacea. And using added waters to spread sewage over wider areas is no longer seen as an acceptable substitute for pollution control.

In national terms, selling water would represent a drastic reduction in the exporting nation's future options. A nation that contracts to sell water can't turn off the tap when its own development requires change. Once kitchen taps in Denver and Tucson turn on water that starts out from the Athabasca, certain options in northern Alberta's development will be foreclosed forever. Once Canada has lost the ability to develop along its water courses, it will be, in an irreversible sense, a colony rather than a nation.

Not that selling our water would solve the Americans' problems. The U.S. conservationist David Brower has pointed out that "good neighbour" Canadians could only give away rivers for a finite period. Then, Brower said, Canada "will have used up its wilderness and wild streams and the neighbour in the south will still be thirsty. The neighbour to the south will have grown bigger and bigger and thirstier and thirstier. And there will be nowhere else for it to go."

None of this impresses Dr. Arleigh Laycock. Water export, he feels, will soon be back in fashion. "One dry summer on the prairie," he says, "that's all we need to bring it back."

Chapter Five

The Closing Pincer

"The natural gas that could have formed the basis for a wave of industrial expansion based upon cheap energy has long since been sold off to an export market at 'bargain basement prices'."

— the Dalhousie Four.

Oil, the largest, the wealthiest and the most powerful industry in the world, is squeezing Canada in a continent-sized pincer grip.

One arm of the pincer sweeps eastward from the bleak north slope of Alaska to the Mackenzie Delta, then takes off in a soaring arc through Canada's Arctic Islands. The other arm jabs up from New England and curls around the Maritimes' shores from Sable Island to Labrador. Hundreds of exploration crews blast and drill in their search for the natural gas and crude oil that may lie in quantity under the northern permafrost and the Atlantic waters. They are seeking Canada's "frontier resources" in energy.

Edmonton, once a destination in the ambitions of oil men, is now a staging post on the way to the new frontier, and Alberta's great gas boom is becoming an episode tinged with the nostalgia of past triumphs. The gas itself, of course, is still pumped from southern Alberta wells, still flows to market through thirty-six-inch pipe and still services factories from California to Delaware. But the discovery of Alberta natural gas passed its peak in 1971. Since 1968 the oil industry has spent more on exploration and development in Alberta than the value of new resources found. So now it is moving along, as it moved long ago from Pennsylvania to Texas and Oklahoma, to Wyoming and through Montana to Alberta. Exploiting finite reserves, the oil industry must be mobile. Professor Jim Ryan, the immensely knowledgeable petrochemical engineer at the University of Alberta, calls it "an industry that votes with its feet." And today it is voting heavily for the Canadian frontier.

Twenty years ago, when they were younger and leaner, some of those frontier-bound oil men were moving into Alberta fields from the United States, drilling, testing, installing pipe for a binge of selling that was to last two decades. Natural gas, once burned away at the wellhead as a waste product of oil extraction, had been recognized as a wonder fuel and it was abundant and accessible here. It was cheap and clean, easily extracted and easily moved. Elsewhere its cheapness and efficiency would catalyze a rich diversity of industrial development and the creation of many manufacturing jobs—elsewhere, but not in Alberta.

Those oil men have seen phenomenal change in their twenty-odd years in Alberta. Inside the province, a spirited new political regionalism has emerged. Outside, the pattern of relationships in the worldwide business of oil and gas extraction, distribution, refining and marketing has been transformed; the accelerating depletion of domestic resources in the face of geometrically-rising demand has pushed the United States into an energy crisis; and Canada's traditional readiness to sell off its considerable but not limitless resources in energy has become a point of national controversy. Yet even now, as oil prepares its great new foray for Canadian resource wealth, the consequences of the industry's historic thrust into Alberta are neither widely discussed nor widely understood.

The curving arrows of a giant industry's pincer squeeze are less visibly dramatic than the racing advance of armies deployed for *blitzkrieg*. But, in their context of the history of nations, they move with similar dynamics of speed, cohesion and penetrating strength. Industrial strategists, like generals, test and probe for defensive soft spots, exert growing pressures, skirmish and feint and then—armed with the element of surprise—enfold the target region in an encircling lunge, tightening the squeeze until control is assured. On oil's world battle map, the pincer movement that engulfed Alberta was a successful local operation; it was in many respects the model for today's monster squeeze. The men who prompted this book considered the oil industry's leap into Alberta a highly relevant component of today's debate over Canada's energy resources.

In a 1972 brief to the Canadian Council of Resource Ministers, Dalhousie's dean of Law, R. St. J. Macdonald, and his colleagues Douglas M. Johnston, Ian A. McDougall and Rowland J. H. Harrison argued that large-scale resource projects had been bungled all over Canada. When the former Liberal cabinet minister Eric Kierans skimmed the pages of their *Economic Development with Environmental Security*, he termed it "the record of a nation on the way to being a colony." Since the Dalhousie group combined the talents of international, marine, constitutional and environmental law, it was not hard for them to define just what constituted a bungled resource project. It was, in summary, a project on a large scale, undertaken within a province without regard for the long-range economic interests of its citizens or of Canadians at large, launched to service the United States, and characterized by federal-provincial dispute about how the resource should best be used. In the eyes of the four scholars, the export of Alberta's natural gas through the 1950s and 1960s had every qualification to be considered a bungled resource project.

Their critique was not "academic" in any cloistered way. They were concerned about Canadian jobs. They felt, like Kierans, that a prosperous and independent Canada could develop only if the capital-intensive process of extracting energy resources was undertaken to service the labour-intensive process of manufacturing finished goods inside Canada. The Columbia River treaty and other water export schemes had the effect of transferring a cheap Canadian resource to the United States for the purpose of enhancing American per capita incomes. Exactly those dynamics, the Dalhousie Four declared, were at work in Alberta's sales of cheap gas for the service of industry inside the U.S. For twenty years the governments of Alberta and Canada permitted Canadian opportunity to drain away. The best, most accessible gas in the country was sold cheaply to the U.S., and the possibility of an industrialized Alberta was sold with it.

The sad thing is, of course, that such a global critique was only possible in retrospect. At the time that it happened, no one considered the gas boom as a pincer movement in which the world oil business captured the petroleum resources of Alberta. The gas boom appeared an entirely natural sequel to the oil boom that began with the discovery at Leduc in 1947. The huge exports of the 1960s did not happen in an economic and political vacuum, but no one then was relating them to the racing depletion of U.S. resources or to the growing resistance in other petroleum-producing countries to control by the eight giant companies Albertans call "the majors," or to the progressive transformation of the oil business into a highly diversified energy industry. Marketing the gas, at the time, was seen simply as a happy windfall for the international corporations already making a fortune in selling Alberta's oil. Gas was a commodity; it made sense to send it to market. In the 1950s, at least, the contribution the gas might make toward the establishment of an industrial base in western Canada was scarcely considered. Alberta was in a rudimentary stage of industrial development and the branch plant mentality went unchallenged. When Premier Ernest Manning, anxious to gain first-hand knowledge of the business, visited Texas before formulating the rules governing gas exploitation in the province, it was considered simply as a mark of his shrewdness and foresight. His Alberta was in a selling mood, and appeared to be thriving on it. Only later would it be seen that the province was wide open to what Kierans calls the "come and gut us" approach. Only later would the connections appear. And by that time one third of all the gas the province had produced had been exported to the U.S. The traditional nightmare of Alberta producers was of being denied markets in the United States by regulations protecting American producers; selling, in their eyes, equalled prosperity, and how could anybody have too much of that?

But the Dalhousie Four saw that the pincers had indeed closed around the choicest resource region in Canada. The gas that was easiest to get at was sold at the lowest prices, without a thought about future industrial needs in the rest of the country. In the 1960s and early 1970s, the nation lost hundreds of millions of dollars because gas prices took no account of the swift North American transition, from a buyers' market to a very strong sellers' market. The labour-intensive industrial development that cheap energy supplies might have fostered in Canada was in fact under way in California and the American Pacific northwest. The fire sale was checked, on federal authority, only after it had become obvious that the rate of increasing demand, consistently underestimated, had outstripped the possibility of supply, always unreliably computed.

"Never again," concluded the Dalhousie Four, "will Canada have gas more accessible than what was removed from the southern part of the western sedimentary basin and sold to the United States at an average twenty-six cents per 1,000 cubic feet—some of the cheapest gas in the world."

There is, as Jim Ryan has explained, a cycle of birth, adulthood and death in the exploitation of a non-renewable resource. "In spite of erratic behaviour," he says, "it is possible to analyze the growth and decline of reserves as the industry grows, matures and finally dies. In the early stages of development, the discovery rate is usually large and the production rate small; consequently, the reserves grow quickly. As development proceeds, the production rate slowly begins to climb and the discovery rate decreases. This pattern continues until the production rate is equal to the discovery rate, at which time the proved reserves on hand are a maximum. When the production rate exceeds the discovery rate, the reserves decrease. In the final stages of development, the discovery rate falls essentially to zero; however, the market created by the previous production remains. The production attempts to satisfy the market until all reserves are depleted."

When you apply that science to the record of the Canadian fire sale, the awesome fallibility of those responsible for regulating resource exports becomes transparent.

In the decade 1960–1970, Canada's production of natural gas, eighty-five percent of it in Alberta, more than tripled (from .58 trillion cubic feet in 1960 to 1.8 in 1970). In the same period the nation's reserves were not even doubled (moving from 30 trillion cubic feet in 1960 to 53 in 1970). Alberta in 1970 was passing over that plateau at which production rate equals discovery rate. Reserves, which increased by about one half between 1965 and 1970, increased by only one trillion cubic feet in 1971. One trillion cubic feet equalled about six months' production of gas! In 1972, for the first time, the nation's reserves registered a decline.

Yet, incredibly, despite the clear warning signals, the National Energy Board, supposed watchdog of natural gas exports, imposed no curb on foreign sales before the summer of 1971. In 1970—when the life index of Canadian natural gas had already registered a significant decline—the board licensed American pipeline corporations in a series of massive exports. One year before a crisis in supply became apparent, the board was on an export binge. So much for its predictive powers!

	Canadian Natural Gas Proven Reserves		
	Production	Year-End Reserves	Years of Supply
1960	0.58 tr. cu. ft.	30 tr. cu. ft.	52
1965	1.25	40	32
1970	1.80	53	29
1971	2.00	54	27
1972 (est)	2.40	45	23

The last line of the above table does not mean that Alberta will be producing gas for another twenty-three years. Not at all. Even if the rate of demand were not rising, much of what remains would be impossible, or uneconomic, to extract. Much of what's left is gas with high sulphur content—what the industry calls "sour gas." Sour gas in the foothills of the Rockies is, says Jim Ryan, "the only untapped supply left in Alberta." He reckons "it might take a $100 million processing plant just to get the sulphur out of the gas. It's pretty hard to justify drilling when you face that kind of initial expense."

By the end of 1972, then, Canada had sold more than one third of all the gas it had ever produced (6.9 trillion cubic feet of a total 17.2 trillion) to the United States and was committed by contract to sell one third of what was left before 1995. Yet it was not until 1971, with a supply deficit of one trillion cubic feet staring it in the face, that the National Energy Board began to block the export applications submitted by giant American-based corporations. More than 16 trillion cubic feet of future production is locked into American contracts today!

But the force of the critique of Canada's gas sellout cannot be measured by statistics. Natural gas is a unique Canadian resource. It is the only energy resource we have that, within the near future, could be totally harnessed to an expansive domestic economy. In 1972, the one trillion cubic feet of Canadian natural gas exported to the United States constituted three percent of U.S. consumption, a figure that was noteworthy chiefly because American gas suppliers fell about three percent short of their contractual commitments to industry and utilities in 1972–73, the first winter of their energy crisis. Theoretically, therefore, if all the gas produced in Canada in 1972 had been exported to the United States, there would have been no shortage there that winter. It is of course a highly theoretical point, since the shortages were regional and U.S. demands are rising so rapidly that a five percent shortfall was anticipated for the winter of 1973–74, and it serves only to emphasize that Canadian natural gas is but a marginal contribution to alleviating the American energy crisis—a drop in the bucket.

If the 1 trillion cubic feet Canada exported was marginal for American consumers at large, the 1.4 trillion this country used domestically was of crucial importance. Manufacturing in Montreal and Toronto depended on it. Without it, businesses would be ruined and workers would lose their jobs. The task force on energy headed by Dr. John J. Deutsch of Queen's University, reporting to the Ontario government in the spring of 1973, noted the rising curve of exports with some concern. Export markets, accounting for twenty-six percent of Canadian gas production in 1960, were receiving forty-six percent by 1970. Though Ontario remained the largest regional market, it was getting only twenty-nine percent. Unless major frontier supplies were opened in this decade, the Deutsch report predicted, exports would have to end soon after 1980. In 1960, Canadian industry was buying thirty-seven percent of natural gas output, but by 1970 increased exports had driven the proportion down to twenty-nine—a clear impediment to the potential growth of manufacturing in eastern Canada.

Canadians, says Dalhousie Professor Ian McDougall, have been "duped" into selling too much gas too cheaply. But how? We have, after all, two seemingly sophisticated agencies specifically charged with the wise husbandry of natural gas: the Energy Resources Conservation Board in Calgary and the NEB in Ottawa. How could both be duped? It may be true, as Mc-

Dougall wryly notes, that "regulatory bodies generally become captivated by the priorities of the industry they regulate," but that alone cannot explain the involvement of such disparate agencies, subjected to such different pressures, in a series of decisions that appear, at least in retrospect, to have been basically anti-Canadian.

It is at this point that any socio-economic interpretation must falter. No analysis of the multinational corporation can explain entirely the gulf in communication between those who make decisions in Ottawa and those who make them in Calgary. At a certain point, questions of regional and economic interest cease to be matters of purely rational debate. Human quirks and fixed attitudes enter the equation. At least until the late 1960s, thirty men holding some one hundred petroleum and pipeline directorships in the boardrooms of Calgary were assumed to make most of the major decisions about oil and gas exploitation in Canada. More recently, with the development of a united front of multinational executives and federal politicians interested in promoting northern pipelines, the focus of decision-making has veered to corporate head offices in Toronto and their lobbyists in Ottawa. But even today Calgary's top thirty (in comparison with whom, an Alberta researcher says, all other oil executives are "merely high-priced employees") wield considerable clout.

In their company, the eastern Canadian may still experience momentary panic, a dizzying slide from the familiarity of shared assumptions. Words, here, have different meanings. The market, the nation—generally discussed in that order—are not the market and the nation as the Dalhousie Four, or Eric Kierans, or even the established Ottawa bureaucrats would understand them. Engaged in faltering dialogue over wellhead price and discovery rates with a bland and thoroughly decent corporate vice-president, one is sealed off from real communication as if by a semantic wall. There is a startling, unsuspected glimpse of another Two Solitudes. The genial man behind the big desk runs a huge pipeline network; he wants to be helpful, but between my questions about the national economic interest and his exposition of the laws of marketing natural gas, there is no point of correspondence. Only twice are we in contact. Once when he says, with considerable candor, "All right, I'll accept that for four or perhaps five years we sold too much cheap gas to the U.S. But it's only quite recently we realized they were running short. I guess they must have been aware of what would happen a long time before we were." The second time, as I am leaving, he has an impulse to say that he is, in spite of everything, as concerned as any easterner that Canada should stay together. I believe him.

But, for that man, gas exports that may conceivably have undermined Canadian development will never have the pejorative meaning they hold for the Dalhousie Four. For twenty-five years he has organized his professional world around the principle that there is one market, a North American one, in petroleum. Nothing is going to change him now. That conversation shows that the use of the phrase "national interest" will often lead to confusion. Men in the oil and gas business suspect it profoundly. Too often, in their experience, national interest has meant the financial and industrial interest of eastern Canada. They appear incongruously seized by a kind of populist fury as they denounce the admittedly iniquitous national freight rates that hamper manufacturing in the West and the "monoposony," or buyer's control, vested in TransCanada Pipelines, which alone carries Alberta gas to Ontario. They resent Ontario Hydro's importuning the National Energy Board to prevent the export of gas that could provide clean power in Ontario. Vern Millard, vice-chairman of the Energy Resources Conservation Board, agrees that East-West conflicts of interest within Canada raise more blood pressure in Calgary, than any difference businessmen there have ever had with their parent industries in the United States. There are, of course, profound roots in history, economics and politics that explain such attitudes. What is immediately relevant is that there is obviously no agreement about goals between national "planners" and those who run oil and gas in Alberta. Nationally and internationally, they are using different codes, and the difficulty has been increased because, for more than a decade, the national government in Ottawa has failed to articulate any clear policy towards resource development anywhere in Canada.

What heightens the sense of unreality is the industry's yearning for a situation in which the forces of the market will have free play. The executives are obviously keenly influenced by oil's lobby for the deregulation of prices in the United States. Even Vern Millard indulges in this economic romanticism. "A lot of the trouble here," he says, "comes from government interference with the market mechanism. The United States side seems to be freeing things gradually—but we seem to be going the other way." To the outsider, the free market notion appears an exercise in doctrinal nostalgia. What influence does the market exert upon the sale of gas by a Canadian subsidiary company to its American parent through a pipeline that is owned and operated by the same parent? It is a relationship that excludes the market. Millard does not explain it. "Any talk of free market forces," says Sten Drugge, resources economist at the University of Alberta, "is a gigantic hoax."

Constitutionally, Canada appears to have the protection it needs. Any long-term contract for the export of natural gas to the United States must be licensed successively by the Energy Resources Conservation Board and the NEB. If the NEB approves a sale the decision must be endorsed by the federal cabinet, though the board may reject licenses without reference to cabinet. The protective shield around Canada's natural gas resources is thus theoretically strong. But the institutions are fallibly human, subject to pressures from both the foreign-owned industry and the Canadian bureaucracy.

Alberta's Energy Resources Conservation Board has considerable authority in the fields of oil, gas, coal and hydro-electricity and a reputation for geological expertise unrivalled in North America. It has a battery of regulatory powers and responsibility for appraising the market requirements for Alberta resources both inside and outside the province, which makes it an important contributor to the formulation of provincial oil and gas policies. But the Calgary-based board is much closer to the industry's decision-makers than is the NEB. And it is profoundly export-oriented. "There have never been any excessive exports from Alberta," insists Vern Millard. The ERCB tends to make doctrinal assertions of the industry's ability to perform well if it is given the prices it wants. Its long-standing claim that an increase of ten cents per 1,000 cubic feet of gas would automatically spur new exploration and add 10 trillion cubic feet to Alberta reserves made even former NEB chairman Robert Howland sceptical.

The National Energy Board, the improbable phoenix that rose from the ruins of the 1956 TransCanada Pipeline scandal, is charged with working out reasonably foreseeable requirements for the use of natural gas in Canada. Then, it must ensure that the quantity exported does not exceed the surplus remaining after Canada's foreseeable needs have been allowed for, having regard to the trends of discovery. Further, it must determine that an exporter charges a price that is just and reasonable in relation to the public interest. In practice, what the board did was produce a formula to protect Canada's future needs: proven reserves must not drop below the rate of production anticipated for four years hence multiplied by twenty-five. Alberta's formula was slightly different—the anticipated production one year hence multiplied by thirty.

Those two duties were perhaps the most onerous of the Ottawa board's functions. A study of the record suggests they have not been well-discharged. Because ultimate responsibility for approval of exports lies with the cabinet, the Liberal governments of the past decade must bear the ultimate blame, but these governments have received ostensibly expert advice from the energy board. The argument that the NEB approved the export of too much gas has been made by many critics, including the Dalhousie Four, and will be developed in this chapter. The case that it exported too cheaply is uncontested today.

The Dalhousie Four say the NEB accepted faulty estimates of Canadian reserves, exaggerated surpluses available for export and underestimated the needs of eastern Canada. It was too optimistic about the proportion of proven gas reserves that could be termed "economic." It approved export-only pipelines, when its guiding theory was that exports should provide economies of scale for Canadian consumers through the use of joint pipes. It pooh-poohed the real environmental advantages of natural gas, accepting at face value the facile claims of oil and coal producers that they could "clean up their act." In 1970, the crowning year of its blunders, the board decided to include half the reserves considered uneconomic in its assessment of supplies, specifically to free more gas for export.

After detailed analysis of the rulings of the decade, Ian McDougall concludes that the board's belated recognition in the summer of 1971 that exports were out of hand and no further gas flows to the United States could possibly be approved was "not the result of a built-in 'Canada First' priority . . . but the unavoidable result of its tradition of placing Canadian interests last and the interests of U.S. consumers first."

Two of his favourite examples in support of this thesis are the 1970 decisions relating to Westcoast Transmission and Alberta and Southern.

The Westcoast Transmission story might almost have been scripted as a textbook illustration for McDougall's critique. Its record combined disregard for Canadian interest with sloppy business practice. The Westcoast pipeline virtually bisects British Columbia, running from the Yukon border south to the American border at Huntingdon. In the Peace River country it connects with the pipe of the provincially-established Alberta Gas Trunk Line Company, where it picks up Alberta gas. Natural gas from Alberta and British Columbia is piped across the international border, where it is picked up by El Paso Natural Gas Company for distribution to points in the American Pacific northwest. The gas flows through Oregon, Idaho. Wyoming, Utah, Colorado, New Mexico and Arizona and is piped to San Francisco through facilities of Pacific Gas and Electric Company.

Westcoast has a bad history in exports. It was criticized as long ago as 1957 by the Borden Royal Commission on Energy. The company, said Borden, was selling gas to the U.S. Pacific Northwest Company so cheaply that consumers in Vancouver were "subsidizing the delivery of gas to Pacific Northwest." All of Westcoast's profits were extracted from Canadian consumers. The exports, effectively, were a gift.

Westcoast's complex transactions illustrate the familial intimacy of trading among multinational corporations. The pipeline company's major U.S. customer was Pacific Northwest, which was soon taken over by the rapidly expanding El Paso Natural Gas. Now El Paso already owned seventeen percent of Westcoast Transmission. Another twenty-seven percent of Westcoast belonged to Phillips Petroleum, which, in turn, held a controlling forty-five percent of Pacific Petroleum, the outfit producing half the gas that entered the Westcoast Transmission pipeline!

Under this new and incestuous complex of corporate relationships, the time came when every party—from field producer to the ultimate distributors of the gas—had some degree of interest in securing a better return from the American consumer. But now the precedents of the bad old deals were invoked by the U.S. Federal Power Commission to keep prices low. Westcoast's new foreign owners had to pay a price for the tough bargains their predecessors had driven with the hapless Canadian firm! After moderate price increases in 1969, Westcoast was back at the National Energy Board in 1970 with an application to export still more gas. The new deals—influenced in part by the FPC's protection of American consumers—were, again, very dubious "bargains" for Canada. The NEB's ruling complained that it did not appear that this commitment of extra gas would even allow Westcoast to recover its basic costs. Having said that, the board granted a license anyway. It did so, its ruling explained, "in view of the urgency of meeting the immediate requirements of the Pacific northwest." Merit was no longer a factor. By 1970 American consumers in the Pacific northwest had become dependent on Westcoast gas, and that fact overrode the board's doubts. Moral: once you commit large supplies of energy to serve a certain market in another country, it is difficult to contemplate turning off the tap . . . ever.

There were, in retrospect, three factors that explain Westcoast's disastrous "bargains." The first was the company's subordinate relationship to distributing corporations in the United States. The second was that executives of the senior American corporations were better bargainers than Westcoast's brass. And the third was that the Federal Power Commission was more effective in defending the interests of U.S. consumers than was the NEB in protecting Canada.

Westcoast Transmission is still in the wars because the New Democratic Party government led by Dave Barrett is not prepared to allow its underpricing to continue losing the province an estimated $100 million a year. There was a time when the combative corporation played an aggressive role in the political life of the province, on occasion embarrassing even the not notably thin-skinned Social Credit Premier W. A. C. Bennett by the ferocity of its campaigning attacks upon what it considered the "socialist menace" of the NDP. That party, long antagonistic to Westcoast's monopoly position in the British

Columbia market, added $4.5 million to the tax bill of the corporation, causing its shares to lose one third of their value in a few months.

In September, 1973, the province promised to implement the recommendation of the British Columbia Energy Commission that the industry should be taken over by a Crown agency that would insist on a realistic price for B.C. gas, seventy percent of which is exported to the United States at just over half its value in terms of competing fuels. Westcoast would lose its monopoly of distribution in the province and be reduced to the status of a simple carrier.

Back in the fire sale era, the National Energy Board, in its solicitude for consumers in California, had approved a huge application from Alberta and Southern Gas Company, a subsidiary of Pacific Gas and Electric Company of California, a corporation which also controls Alberta Natural Gas Company (piping gas from the Alberta border to Kingsgate, British Columbia) and owns Pacific Gas Transmission Company (piping the same gas from Kingsgate to California markets). Alberta and Southern did not get a good price from its U.S. customer in 1970, but the NEB approved the sale anyway. Why? So as not to be "inconsistent with the amity and comity that has come to characterize relations between the United States and Canada in respect of trade in natural gas."

It was not only the poor pricing that made Alberta and Southern a questionable export. There was another factor. The board was sanctioning one more step towards the capacity use of an export-only pipeline. The Alberta and Southern export system, the largest in Canada, had required capital investment amounting to $340 million to install a thirty-six-inch diameter pipeline. That pipeline, which served no Canadian consumer, was planned by its promoters to have a capacity far in excess of their export contracts. The NEB in 1970 was sanctioning its build-up towards optimum profitability.

Moral: it is dangerous to play host to a pipeline you do not yourself need. Like the man who came to dinner, it will never go away. The Carleton University geologist F. K. North says this about export pipelines: "A gas pipeline is the least versatile of fixed capital installations; it dictates the amount transferred, and its destination. It operates twenty-four hours a day until the reserve is exhausted. Unilateral interference with its operations is virtually an act of war."

Was that, one wonders, what the board had in mind when it talked of "amity and comity?" Whatever it had in mind, and notwithstanding its approval of the Alberta and Southern sale, the National Energy Board, as its own ruling shows, knew the risk it was running. "Once a large-diameter pipeline is in place," the ruling observed, "the 'cheap expansibility' available in it gives its owners a very powerful lever in seeking supply contracts and authorizations to develop the system to optimum capacity." A well-built pipeline will last for eighty years. At some historic moment in the next eighty years, or even in the next eight, a Canadian government may be obliged to make an infinitely difficult decision to shut off that flow of gas to California. It will be all the more difficult because of the emphasis the NEB chose to place upon what it called "amity and comity."

Alberta and Southern sold gas to its parent corporation on what is called a "cost of service" formula. That means the deal does not have to maximize the exporter's revenues. Nor does it necessarily have to be related to prevailing market prices, or prices at point of sale. In 1969, a year when the least-cost alternative in the California market was 31.46 cents per 1,000 cubic feet, Alberta and Southern was shipping gas to Pacific at 26.4 cents the thousand. For Canada such a deal makes no sense. But the unpublicized accounting of a multinational resources empire, operating on the principle that one declares one's profits in those places where the taxes are lowest, obeys neither the imperatives of the nation nor those of the revered free market. What the empire may lose on the branch plant swings, it can always regain on the head office roundabouts. The considerations governing the transfers of funds, service charges and management fees within the units of a multinational corporation, including variations in tax rates, opportunities for capital borrowing and government handouts, are subtle and of infinite variety.

But the National Energy Board knew that all was not well. Noting the difference between the export price of the Canadian gas and its lowest-cost alternative in California, the board remarked, "This gap, or cost of service, represents a subsidy by Canada to the United States consumers of the gas." And still, when it had said all that, the board okayed the sale.

Having sifted the ponderous volumes of Energy Board decisions, Ian McDougall concluded: "In all cases a high degree of corporate integration has been pointed to. It has been evident that, because of the high degree of corporate integration, U.S. companies have been able to exert considerable influence over pricing principles followed by Canadian subsidiary companies."

But the fire sale was coming to an end. In the late summer of 1971, faced now with export commitments running 1.1 trillion cubic feet ahead of known supply, the National Energy Board had to call a halt. It rejected natural gas export applications worth a total $1 billion.

Perhaps, at last, now that the exportable "surplus" of gas no longer existed, the Energy Board had learned a lesson. "The danger here is obvious to all," it commented. "An over-commitment to export markets, which appear at this time to be almost insatiable, could deprive the rapidly expanding Canadian markets of access to Canadian gas."

The parliamentary record adds a bizarre footnote. In March, 1973, board chairman Robert Howland conceded to a parliamentary committee he'd known Canadian gas had been underpriced in the U.S., and had not notified the cabinet. The Toronto *Globe and Mail* commented: "It is obvious that Canada needs new prices for the gas and oil sought and found on federal lands, and a new chairman for the National Energy Board." All that is wrong with that comment is its implication that because Howland did not tell the cabinet, the cabinet did not know. All we know about the incident in fact is that the cabinet did not act and it seems, in retrospect, unlikely that any revelation by Robert Howland of what had already become blindingly obvious could have stirred that cabinet to action. Howland, in any event, soon resigned and was eventually succeeded by Ottawa mandarin Marshall Crowe.

On June 7, 1973, Ian McDougall summarized his findings about the Energy Board record before the National Resources Committee of the House of Commons. He termed that record "appalling." Over the long haul, McDougall said, the board had proven itself "industry's best friend and the energy-consuming public's worst enemy." Instead of entertaining pipeline proposals to carry northern Canadian gas to U.S. markets, he urged, the federal government should undertake a profound overhaul of the board's functions and a comprehensive review of Canada's energy needs. Speaking with the confidence accruing from wider public acceptance of his now-familiar analysis, McDougall reminded the parliamentarians that "the board was set up to prevent the very problems that we now have." If it had not mismanaged natural gas resources in the past, a Mackenzie Valley pipeline, he said, would be "out of the question."

If the Energy Board decisions of 1971 are seen as an awakening, a belated attempt to salvage national interest from the embers of the fire sale, it must be remembered that the evil wrought by the earlier decisions is still wounding Canada. Most major exports were committed on twenty-five-year contracts and we shall feel the consequences of some of 1970's blunders until 1995. By then frontier gas, expensively and laboriously extracted from the Mackenzie Delta or the Arctic Islands, may be flowing to factories in Ontario. That gas, at a conservative estimate, will cost three times as much as the remaining supplies from Alberta. Canadian manufacturers of 1995 will feel less than charitable towards those forgotten bureaucrats who long ago committed one third of the remaining accessible supply of cheap gas to the American competition!

Alberta, the alluring target of oil's first great pincer thrust into Canada, will then be a very different place. It is a different place now. The glib salesman's heyday has passed. Though two decades of oil and gas boom locked the province into a resource-based economy, it also produced growth, a relatively sophisticated middle class, a large and questioning student population and two metropolitan cities. Along with disquiet over the inevitable decline in the life index of oil and gas, there is, perhaps for the first time, a lively searching for contemporary options, a generation aware that it cannot build a future on selling depleting raw resources to the United States. It was this new mood that swept out the tired men of Social Credit and brought Peter Lougheed's Conservatives to power in 1971.

Sten Drugge, resources economist at the University of Alberta, is perhaps representative of the province's new men. "In the early years of the boom," he says, "we really had no choices. Oil and gas were seen simply as commodities, their prices a function of what the United States government wished them to be. Albertans were simply price-takers.

"But there's been a real change of heart. Lougheed is asking a fairer dollar, and he will get it. He's insisting that something be done about Canadian transportation rates, which make it cheaper to pipe natural gas liquids or petroleum gases to chemical plants in Sarnia than to ship finished petrochemical products out of Alberta. We think now of natural gas as a factor-input into the petrochemical industry. A consortium of oil companies has shown that a product pipeline from Edmonton to Toronto is feasible. If you drove down the rail rates and made gas cheaper in Canada than it is in the United States, you could have the potential for a world petrochemical business here—and you could make jobs for Canadians. We could build our own refineries on the Athabasca tar sands—it costs no more to pipeline diesel than it costs to pipeline crude oil."

Was the premier, like Drugge, to prove a new man? He was certainly a skilled big-city politician and a vigorous voice for aggressive Alberta regionalism. He indicated there would be no more fire sales in oil and gas, no more wellhead payments of sixteen cents per 1,000 cubic feet to Alberta producers while American domestic contracts were going at fifty-three cents the thousand. The destructive PRIME river diversion scheme was shelved, Lougheed hinting he would bring industrial diversity to northern Alberta rather than attempt to transfer its northern waters to the south. With more than one third of the province's 700,000 workers dependent on the oil industry, the need for diversity was urgent. The premier also introduced a populist stridency into his rhetoric, indicating he would end Ontario industry's "cheap ride" at Alberta's expense and even asserting that the province's oil and natural gas "belong to the people."

But that was only one face of Lougheed. Whatever the rhetoric, he remained close to the province's business elite and to big oil. In his relationship with the industry he was to prove less of a populist than the old Social Crediters from the country towns. The bias emerged in his famous two-price policy for natural gas. Moving to increase the wellhead price from sixteen to twenty-six and then thirty-six cents, he placed Canadian customers outside Alberta on the same footing as American industry; only Albertans were to be protected from rising energy costs. At current royalty rates, the increase appeared to promise a dubious $27 million for the provincial Treasury, but a windfall of some $167 million for the leading gas producers, most of them foreign-owned. Instead of adopting the nationally-oriented two-price policy advocated by economists such as Drugge, the premier was extending the traditional giveaway; he was promptly labelled "the uncritical champion of the foreign-controlled petroleum industry," by provincial NDP leader Grant Notley. Lougheed argued that his gift would encourage exploration by the foreign corporations, but the interest of the major producers, as their renewed lobbying showed, lay not in tackling the hard-to-get foothills reserves so much as in drawing out the balance of Alberta's quick, easy gas. They could sell all they could get on the hungry American market.

It was soon clear that any industry lured to Alberta was likely to be drawn from other provinces. Though Albertans had welcomed Imperial Oil's announcement of a $200 million refinery in Edmonton, that was a consolidation project, permitting the corporation to close older installations in Winnipeg, Regina and Calgary—with a net loss of Canadian jobs.

The issue of feedstock pipelines was more complex. Dome Petroleum and Amoco, a subsidiary of Standard Oil of Indiana, had long pressed for a pipeline to ship ethane and ethylene to Michigan. Ethane is a component of natural gas that normally goes to waste. Ethylene, which can be derived from ethane, is one of the petrochemical industry's more versatile substances. It is used to make film, cleaning materials, styrofoam, paint, antifreeze and a wide range of contemporary products.

But natural gas is not the only source of ethylene. It can also be derived, though more wastefully, from naptha or crude oil. In spring, 1973, a group of companies led by Dow Chemical planned a plant at Sarnia that would produce ethylene by this second method. Some time after Premier Lougheed announced his two-price policy, Dow changed its corporate mind. In July Dow and Dome Petroleum appeared together before the National Energy Board, Dow proposing a $400 million plant at Fort Saskatchewan, Alberta, to extract ethane and ethylene, Dome seeking permission to export 169 million barrels of liquid ethane to Michigan over fifteen years, through a 2,000-mile pipeline that would end in Sarnia.

Such an arrangement has two melancholy aspects. The first is that the extraction process does not require a significant labour force—it is highly capital intensive. The part of the venture that could be expected to spell jobs would be a long way downstream, in Michigan, As the resource economist Sten Drugge sees it, "What it means is that we shall export an industry to Michigan." Had Lougheed introduced the kind of two-price system Drugge wanted—low prices for Canadian gas users, high for foreign—it might have been a manufacturing operation setting up shop in Fort Saskatchewan.

The second, more obvious sorry aspect is that the handful of jobs created for Albertans will be jobs denied to Sarnia. Ontario Premier William Davis had pondered the prospect of a steady transference of jobs from eastern Canada to Alberta. He cautioned the Canadian Petroleum Association: "We are not competing nation-states but two authorities within the national whole; this visits a slightly greater responsibility on both of us.... A natural gas pricing policy that effectively transfers existing industrial activity from, say, Quebec and Ontario to the Province of Alberta can hardly be defined as effective national industrial planning." The oil men listened with respect, even admiration, but knew these words would change nothing. In Windsor, Union Gas president Bruce F. Willson, a former Alberta producer himself, forecast the Lougheed increase would cost Ontario consumers $32 billion over thirty years and render Canadian industry substantially less competitive. He asked a rhetorical question: "Are consumers going to accept a situation where a government, encouraged by a handful of large international oil companies and their industry associations, can actually double the field price of a vitally important commodity without giving any justification in terms of costs of production?" And he answered it: "I hate to answer yes—but, unfortunately, that appears to be what is happening." Davis later decided the Alberta increases must be tested in the Supreme Court.

Three groups would gain substantially from the Lougheed increase. The first would be the major gas producers—Gulf Oil, Shell, Pacific (Phillips), Hudson's Bay (Continental Oil), Imperial (Jersey Standard), Amoco (Indiana Standard), Central del Rio (Canadian Pacific) and Canadian Superior (Superior Oil of California). The second group would be their parent corporations in the U.S. and elsewhere. And the third would be all those American manufacturers who were battling for markets with industries based in Toronto, Hamilton and Montreal.

In June, 1973, two of Drugge's colleagues at the University of Alberta, Dr. Bruce W. Wilkinson, chairman of the Department of Economics, and Professor Frank Roseman, published a devastating analysis of the effects of Alberta's price increases. They, like Drugge, agreed with the stated aims of the Lougheed government—to maximize Alberta revenues from oil and gas endowments, and to develop industry and jobs in the province. But they demonstrated that the beneficiaries of the Lougheed changes would be neither Albertans nor Canadians in general, but the foreign-owned petroleum corporations. With the royalty rate of sixteen and two-thirds percent, the overwhelming benefit of price increases would obviously go to the producers. But even if the government increased the royalty rate this situation would not be changed, because prices would be rising faster than the royalty rates. If the royalty rate were twenty-five percent, the share of increased revenues going into the provincial treasury would still be only eleven percent. And, on top of the special Lougheed increases in gas prices, which provided for a rebate to Alberta industry, gas prices would be rising across the board as a result of the energy crisis. That general rise, affecting Alberta as much as anywhere else, would reduce the disadvantage of locating an industry in eastern Canada rather than Alberta.

But their most detailed analysis exposed Alberta's continuing giveaway to the giant corporations through its system of crude oil pricing. Between 1962 and May, 1973, Alberta oil prices went up a total ninety-three cents a barrel and, in 1973, the pace of price increases was accelerating. Yet production costs declined six cents a barrel during the 1960s because most of the oil was by then coming from established wells. Assuming that Alberta's revised tax on oil reserves, plus royalties, would yield the equivalent of a twenty percent royalty on all producing acreage, Wilkinson and Roseman showed that the net revenue to Alberta from an oil price increase would be only nine percent of that increase, not twenty percent (Albertans would be paying the increase on the oil they consumed themselves). From the most recent increase of twenty-five cents a barrel, Alberta receives only 2.8 cents. "The rest," they say, "is a transfer of Canadian resource wealth to the largely foreign-owned corporations."

Applying this to the ninety-three cents a barrel in price increases since 1962, the economists show Alberta picks up $35 million of the revenues each year and the corporations $357 million. The annual loss to Alberta was $357 million, a result of their failure to obtain the "economic rents" to which the holders of resources are entitled. Applying this rate of loss to the 7 billion barrels of conventional crude still to be produced in the province, without any allowance for further price increases, Albertans will forfeit a further $5.9 billion. If prices rise a further $1.50 a barrel Albertans will lose $13.7 billion.

The economists project this analysis on to a national scale. Since oil corporations pay no more than three percent of book profits in corporate income tax, since eighty-six percent of dividends and retained earnings go into foreign pockets, and since Canadian consumers will pay forty-one percent of the price increases, Wilkinson and Roseman find that "a crude oil price increase does not produce any net gain for Canadians. The higher prices that Canadian consumers pay the foreign-dominated oil industry more than offset the royalties and corporate taxes our governments receive, as well as the share of dividends or retained earnings due to Canadian shareholders in the industry. There is a net loss to the economy equal to 7.73 percent of the price increment. It costs Canadians money to let the oil price rise."

In the design for a new Alberta that was being sketched by Drugge's group of resource economists in that hopeful springtime of 1973, the careful, provincially-managed development of the resources of the Athabasca tar sands occupied a significant place. In protracted negotiations with the subsidiaries of American oil corporations that controlled those resources, the Lougheed government was seeking a measure of provincial participation in the financing and operation of future projects, possibly at the price of nominal royalty rates. What excited Drugge and his colleagues was the possibility that, instead of merely shipping synthetic oil to U.S. markets, the tar sands might become the object of a deliberatively planned program of mixed development, emphasizing built-in refineries and the export of petrochemical products.

But the U.S. energy crisis was operating against that hope. For, suddenly and quite dramatically in the summer of 1973, the tar sands became a central issue in the national debate over petroleum exports.

The tar sands became pivotal because a crisis was on the horizon in Canadian oil supplies. Alberta's reserves of conventional oil were in decline and the Energy Resources Conservation Board, which some considered optimistic, had set the life index at seventeen years. As Alberta oil exploration moved north from the lush southern fields, it was finding wells of steadily diminishing allure. On the northern frontier, the exploration crews were tapping plenty of natural gas but little oil and east coast drilling had not discovered the large oilfields necessary to make offshore wells economic. Large-scale exploitation of the tar sands presented intricate technical problems and, though the potential was agreed to be huge, engineers had placed the sands in the same time scale as the frontier oil—a great prospect for the 1980s.

At the same time, American industry was hitting the panic button; demands for Canadian crude were escalating astronomically from month to month. In March the National Energy Board imposed the first export restrictions and, in May, it was obliged to make "massive" cuts in the orders for crude placed by U.S. refineries for the month of June. It was, and both suppliers and customers sensed it, the beginning of the crunch in the energy crisis. They also knew it would not be a short-run crisis because, on the American side, an awesome supply gap loomed. After protracted negotiations, the major world corporations had just agreed to add 11.9 percent to the prices they paid for crude in eight Middle Eastern producing nations. Washington's own demand forecasts showed the U.S. would need to import 10 billion barrels of crude every day—the output of eight Albertas—by 1980. Though Canada, obviously, could provide no more than a fraction of needed supply, the U.S. pressure for that fraction was urgent and would grow increasingly insistent.

By 1980, the domestic American reserves would have been in decline for nineteen years and, even if the U.S. courts had unlocked the twenty billion barrels estimated to lie under Prudhoe Bay on Alaska's Arctic north slope, the U.S. would need

Middle East oil in quantities that would require a fleet of 200 supertankers capable of carrying 2.2 million barrels each. As the fourth war in twenty-five years erupted in the Middle East, Arab governments stepped up the nationalization of the remaining properties of the giant oil corporations. The threat to cut off oil supply to the West became a potent element in political bargaining in the region.

If the U.S. appeared to be racing towards industrial catastrophe by 1980, the prognosis for Canada was gloomy enough. Major supplies of frontier oil, assuming they existed at all, could not be flowing to market in 1980. And petrochemical engineers such as Edmonton's Jim Ryan were saying that conventional sources would not last a decade at current production rates. "Soon," he was saying in May, "Alberta will not have the productive capacity to supply the needs of the rest of Canada, its growing population and industrial base. If large new supplies of petroleum are not found and made marketable in the relatively near future, Canada will face the same situation as the United States—the forced importation of large quantities of crude oil from overseas. On present trends, Canada will have to increase imports significantly after 1975. Given constant domestic production from all sources and exponentially rising demand west of the Ottawa Valley, Canadian exports to the United States will have to cease after 1981."

A nightmarish notion was forming in the minds of men such as Ryan. It was that in 1980 or very soon afterwards the Canadian customers who had depended on Alberta crude would have to import oil. That would mean competing with American purchasers for overseas oil in markets controlled by American corporations at the very time the U.S. was gripped by pressures to buy up all the crude it could find. "In that situation," Ryan said tersely, "Canada's prospects would not look too good."

Discussion of that horrendous prospect inevitably gave rise to questions about Canadian management of the scarcity. Were the Energy Board's restrictions of exports to the U.S. tight enough? Had the NEB examined the anticipated Canadian supply situation for 1980–81? If it had, should it still have authorized exports amounting to 1,120,717 barrels a day for the month of June, 1973? And why, Ontario's Energy Minister Darcy McKeough was soon demanding, had not the energy board clamped *permanent* controls on Canadian oil exports, reserving for domestic use twenty-five times the consumption projected for 1977—a formula similar to the one protecting Canadian users of natural gas?

In early June, in the midst of all the questioning, the Energy Resources Conservation Board in Calgary dramatically announced that Alberta's proven oil reserves had quadrupled! The basis for this was its first inclusion of the synthetic oil that could be produced from the Athabasca tar sands in the inventory of proven provincial reserves. Instead of 8 billion barrels, said the board, provincial reserves stood at 34.5 billion. Instead of seventeen years, the life index was said to be sixty-nine! If those figures were accepted by the National Energy Board, a vital new element would be introduced into the energy equation.

The tar sands, of course, had been there all the time, a gluey black undercoat to 30,000 square miles near Fort Mc-Murray, 250 miles northeast of Edmonton, and the object of speculation among Albertans for almost two decades. The sands, accessible to stripmining only in limited areas, contain huge deposits of oil in its most intractable form, a motionless tacky black sludge, so viscous it will not flow from a glass held upside-down at room temperature. The National Energy Board has estimated there might be 50 billion barrels of it—a barrel contains thirty gallons—but has never included any in its listing of proven reserves. The industry has talked about as much as 400 billion barrels, or ten times all the proven reserves in North America.

At one time, the Atlantic Richfield corporation proposed to explode a nuclear device under the tar sands in an effort to set the viscous black mass into flowing motion. The technical problems of extracting enough of the material to produce sizable quantities of synthetic oil have been enormous, and it was for this reason that specialists such as Ryan traditionally assigned the tar sands to the same productive time horizon as any remote frontier reserves that may exist. But Great Canadian Oil Sands, a subsidiary of Sun Oil, has been producing 45,000 barrels a day, allegedly at a financial loss, and Syncrude (a consortium of Imperial Oil, Gulf, Atlantic Richfield and Cities Service) says that construction of a $770 million plant at Mildred Lake will enable it to pipe out 125,000 barrels of synthetic oil daily by 1977.

Shell, now the largest permit holder in the region, has unveiled a scheme for a $680 million plant near Fort McMurray to extract 100,000 barrels a day in the early 1980s, plus a townsite for 1,000 workers and their families. Consortia of Japanese, U.S. and Arab corporations are reported to be exploring the sands.

Present technology being applied to synthetic oil production involves a vastly destructive system of strip-mining; Shell, for instance, estimates it must rip up 200,000 tons of earth a day to meet its 1982 production targets. Corporate officials investigating the more sophisticated underground recovery methods warn these will be "economic" only when the oil sells at $8 a barrel (present Alberta crude averages from $3.60 to $3.75 a barrel).

The Alberta board was conscious of the strategic timing of its announcement, but its chairman, Dr. George Govier, insisted the volumes of synthetic oil were "firmly proved" and that it would have been "unrealistic" not to include them. Dr. Govier, predictably, did not hesitate to use the tar sands announcement as an occasion to renew the provincial pitch for a policy of 'carry on, exports'.

Announcing Alberta's approval of the Syncrude plan in September, Premier Lougheed promised to set up a Crown agency that would ensure twenty percent Canadian ownership of the project. Albertans, at last, were to have a piece of the action. But, said the premier, the foreign corporations controlling eighty percent would not pay any royalties until the project was showing a profit. What's more, the Syncrude deal was contingent upon a demand that the price of the synthetic oil would not be subject to regulation by Ottawa! The foreign corporations would be free to charge energy crisis prices for the Alberta resource. Even Donald Macdonald could hardly approve such a crude power play.

Yet the tar sands potential could ultimately prove crucial in a new and more rational resources policy for Alberta and the nation. In the view of Wilkinson and Roseman "by far the greatest hope for expanding secondary industry in Alberta must rest on the potential base provided by the tar sands. Each plant capable of producing 100,000 to 125,000 barrels per day will require perhaps four to five years to construct. And, once in operation, about 1,000 men per plant will be needed." Despite the uncertainties and the enormous environmental costs of tar sands development, Alberta might be wiser to ensure it receives the economic rent from a careful program of development on the sands than to continue to support the lobby for hasty development in the Arctic.

"Perhaps," Wilkinson and Roseman speculate, "this is a way of retaining the political support of the many oil companies in Alberta with interests in the North. Alberta will gain much more in the way of employment, industrialization and revenues from the tar sands than from the development of the Arctic . . . . Certainly national long-run employment possibilities will be greater from the tar sands. Alberta and the federal government should be cooperating to ensure that the tar sands development is given preference and that work proceeds under provisions ensuring maximum benefits for Canada."

If the Calgary board is correct in its estimates, Ryan's prognosis for Canadian oil must be substantially modified; the anticipated swing from Alberta to federal primacy in petroleum development may be delayed; and northern gas and oil pipelines may begin to look markedly less attractive.

Big-scale production remains years away. The chain of extraction plants could call for an investment of the same proportion as the Mackenzie Valley pipeline. Syncrude's 1977 production target is still received with some scepticism. The blackmail on pricing cannot be accepted in Ottawa. Extraction of one million barrels a day from Athabasca is still a long way off.

For the short run, then, the blunder of too-easy gas exports will continue to be repeated with Alberta's crude oil. For the short run, the oil problem for Canadians will be one of supply as well as of pricing. In the Mackenzie Delta and the Arctic Islands, natural gas discovery is proceeding on a far more hopeful pattern than is the finding of oil. The gas that is discovered, of course, will be costly stuff. The cheap stuff still flows to U.S. markets under the long-term contracts negotiated in the fire sale era.

The point is not a novel one for Ian McDougall. "We've

got our national priorities all wrong," he says. "We should put an immediate freeze on exports from the southern part of the western sedimentary basin (Alberta). Any future gas exports should come from the North, though no pipeline should ever be designed for exports alone. Export sales from the north could then subsidize further domestic exploration in the south, with public involvement perhaps through a corporation set up on Pan Arctic lines." The former Liberal cabinet minister Eric Kierans proposes a more conservationist approach: keep northern gas in the ground, he says, until we know that Canadian industry needs it. Yet, as recently as July of 1973, the National Energy Board found it necessary to undertake the ritual of hearing applications from Amoco and other corporations to increase gas exports to the United States!

Perhaps the tragic fire sale in Alberta could have taken place only in a highly regionalized federal state that had not even staged the pretence of formulating any comprehensive energy policy. It happened in a vacuum of national policy—a paralysis, even—in the absence of any agreement about goals. Canadians today are as divided on the environmental aspects of gas exploitation as they are on export policy. In Calgary, for instance, I repeatedly heard Ontario Hydro described as a kind of agent provocateur of East-West conflict because it had opposed gas exports in the interests of cleaning up its big Hearn plant—and the atmosphere of Toronto. Albertans from Vern Millard to Robin Abercrombie, economist with Alberta Gas Trunk Line, to Premier Lougheed himself have described the Hearn plant as a "bad use of the resource." Was it? It is difficult to see sinfulness in dramatically reducing the air pollution of Canada's second largest city because some American factory is thereby deprived of increased supplies of cheap Alberta gas.

One answer to the mystery may be that Alberta is promoting coal as the answer to its own future power generation needs and as a commodity to be sold to hydro utilities in the East. After a series of hearings in which the major oil and gas producers were conspicuously represented, the Energy Resources Conservation Board in April, 1973, recommended "that as a matter of general policy it subscribes to the use of coal rather than gas as the energy resource for future thermal power plants." The board's report laid heavy stress upon the need to

106

maintain the export trade in natural gas. Coal, of course, is making a comeback in the American midwest and many of the major oil corporations are now involved in large-scale strip-mining. It may soon be possible to transmit coal through pipe-lines on a major scale.

If, as the Conservation Board recommends, Alberta em-barks on expanded coal production both for its own thermal plants and for sale to eastern Canadian utilities, thousands of square miles of the foothills will be destroyed. This will happen at the same time as the stripping necessary to exploit the oil in the Athabasca tar sands. A consultants' report by Intercontinental Engineering of Edmonton has already warned the prov-ince that years of environmental study are needed before the tar sands stripping goes ahead; otherwise, the consultants said, damage will be "enormous." Ominously, the report urged Al-berta not to permit the use of "more than ten percent of the minimum monthly flow" of the Athabasca River for washing out the treacly oil. The delicate Athabasca system, almost ruined by the Bennett Dam on the Peace, threatened for years by the PRIME water diversion scheme, appears in jeopardy again. Simultaneous expansion of stripmined coal and the tar sands project contain the makings of one of the most intense environ-mental controversies seen in Canada. One of the Dalhousie Four's criteria for bungled resource development is a disregard of the environment, and Alberta appears likely to qualify on this count as well as the rest. For Sten Drugge and those who would reorder priorities in Alberta, the environmental approach will be as important an indicator as the installation of onsite refining. If these programs are not planned in the provincial interest, if the tar sands project is rammed through by the majors with the object of providing the swiftest possible service for the United States market, the development could prove as calamitous as James Bay.

It is, after all, a quarter century since the pincers of oil closed around this province. Business and government are operated by a generation that is post-Leduc, by people who do not remember a time when the majors were not a presence in their lives. The conventional attitudes of foreign-owned corpor-ations have become accepted as naturally and uncritically as nursery rhymes or the Mosaic Law. The candid American author James Ridgeway wrote recently of Canada that "the U.S. has come to regard the place as a sort of resources storage bin into which we dip as we feel the need." In Calgary, uniquely in Canada one feels, this remark would occasion surprise rather than anger. Oil men who say there is only one North American market are not advancing a theory but reflecting the experience of their years in business; the national interest aspect of economic decisions that will have an effect upon Ontario is an unfamiliar abstraction to them. In contrast to James Bay, the project of a managerial elite pushed through in the face of mass indifference, ignorance or hostility, the conquest of primary-producing Alberta by the petroleum industry appears to have been almost an act of participatory colonization.

That is only a subjective clue; in the next chapter, we shall examine a material one. During oil's twenty-five-year occupation of Alberta, the corporations themselves, adapting to world changes in the economic environment, assumed new forms. Moving beyond that "high degree of integration" Ian McDougall had discovered to be influencing the pricing policies in natural gas deals, the majors were reaching into new types of enterprise, ceasing to be the oil companies and becoming the energy corporations, controlling together an empire in resources that would equal the wealth of one hundred Albertas.

Chapter Six

The Energy Empire

"The producer of crude in one country who sells for
export, and the refiner in another country who purchases,
are usually both subsidiaries of the same parent and
giving effect to a common purpose. Such transactions
are obviously not at arm's length and the overriding
objective is the best interest of the international company,
which may not necessarily correspond to the best
interests of either of the countries where some portion of
its operations are conducted."

– "Gasoline Marketing in the context of the Oil Industry,"
Report to the Government of Alberta, December, 1968.

Were North American economic life not dominated by large
corporations, this in itself would be no guarantee that contemporary problems could be solved, merely that solutions to them
could be objectively discussed. This is as true of the energy
crisis as of other crucial questions. Jim Ryan, with a good
teacher's gift for vivid analogy, is sure, for instance, that "if the
United States as a matter of policy decided to become self-
sufficient in oil, it could do this merely by putting a stop to driving. If this were done, the demand in the U.S. would decrease
from 24 million barrels a day to approximately 14 million barrels a day, the projected U.S. productive rate in 1980." There
would be no energy crisis.

In a world governed by philosophers, Ryan's statement
might be the takeoff point for an important debate, in which
logic might be ingeniously deployed both for and against the
proposition to stop driving. In the North America we live in,

such an argument would be a waste of time. We know the United States will not stop driving. Even if we have not examined the energy situation in any profundity, we can make that assertion with confidence. We can predict, with as much confidence, that before long the North American motorist will pay one dollar, or two dollars, or even five dollars, for every gallon of gasoline he buys. Within our experience and folklore, it is axiomatic that, for large corporations, the control of scarcity can be at least as profitable as abundance.

The nature of these corporations, the price of the gallon of gasoline and the development of Canada's frontier resources are closely related. Questioned about the corporate structure of the oil industry, an investigator who has studied it for more than a decade immediately thinks about three service stations at the main intersection of a prairie town; the fourth corner is empty. "Chances are," the investigator says, "there never will be a fourth station. That town's market is shared by three major oil companies through franchised operators, who are simply expedient pawns. Because of the way the market has been carved up, the only person who would try to open a fourth service station would have to be an independent and he would have to be out of his mind, because the major companies have the capital resources and the necessary controls on supply to drive him into the ground. Furthermore, if independent people ever get to control more than ten percent of the gas stations in a province, the major companies get extremely agitated—it throws their market planning out of whack."

The investigator paused significantly, as if preparing to deliver a new economic law: "An oil company that controls markets," he said, "is in a much better position than you might think." The events of the spring and summer of 1973 provided dramatic confirmation of this thesis when hundreds of independent operators, pinched for supplies from refineries owned by the big corporations, were closing their gasoline stations all over Canada and the United States thereby strengthening the grip of the giant companies upon the market.

Gasoline stations, of course, are simply the homeliest facet of oil's pervasive presence in modern society. Another facet is the division of the Calgary oil business between the thirty or so senior men who know what is going on and the remaining executives our investigator terms "simply high-priced employees." A third facet is the tightly-knit alliance of eight super-corporations working to monopolize the energy resources of the world.

The connections are not easily traced, and not merely because the clubby freemasonry of the oil industry's insiders is unwilling to have them traced. In the mid-1960s, the Alberta government commissioned a Committee of Enquiry under Kenneth A. McKenzie, an Edmonton Q.C., to undertake an exhaustive report on gasoline marketing. A diagram appended to that report charted how thirty corporate officials linked eight subsidiaries of major foreign oil companies, four other oil companies, four international pipelines and nine Alberta pipelines. Each one of the top thirty served at least two of these entities as a director, many served more. One Imperial Oil director, for instance, was also a director of three of four major pipelines.

Yet even the commissioners found understanding oil an exercise of infinite complexity. They compared it rather wittily to the fable of The Blind Men and the Elephant:

> It was six men of Hindustan
> To learning much inclined,
> Who went to see the elephant
> (Though all of them were blind)
> That each by observation
> Might satisfy his mind . . .

The blind men of Hindustan picked up a predictable diversity of impressions. The sage who fell against the animal's side pronounced it "nothing but a wall"; but one who felt the tusk thought an elephant "very like a spear"; for the one who touched the trunk, it was snakelike; examination of other anatomical regions evoked comparisons with a tree, a fan and a rope. The fable concludes:

> So, oft in oil's commercial wars
> The disputants, I ween,
> Rail on in utter ignorance
> Of what each other mean
> And prate about an elephant
> Not one of them has seen!

Observed the McKenzie Commission: "Very few persons in the industry have the opportunity to see or comprehend the whole elephant. The colossal size of the industry almost defies comprehension." In an attempt at comprehension, the commission compared the magnitude of the world oil giants with Canada's largest industrial firms in 1966. The largest of these, Alcan Aluminum, was fifty places down the chart from Standard Oil of New Jersey, the largest corporation in the world with assets of $14 billion. Jersey Standard, now calling itself Exxon, owns seventy percent of Imperial Oil, the largest corporation in Canada. Despite the legendary skill of oil corporations in the enjoyment of tax concessions and corporate welfare-bumming (Shell, for instance, the world's second largest oil corporation, paid no taxes on its extensive operations in Canada in the period 1964–69, a period in which the company made more than $500 million in profits) the committee found that one subsidiary paid more than $100 million in Canadian taxes in 1966 alone. "Yet," they said, "this subsidiary is only one of several hundred subsidiaries controlled by its international parent, which, in turn, is one of the seven giants referred to as the cartel."

Those designated as international petroleum cartel companies by the U.S. Federal Trade Commission are Standard Oil Co. (New Jersey), Royal Dutch/Shell Group, Mobil Oil Corp., Texaco, Inc., Gulf Oil Corp., British Petroleum Co. Ltd., Standard Oil Co. of California.

Traditionally, these seven monster corporations, together with the government-backed French Group, controlled the exportable oil of the world and the prices of crude oil and refined products throughout world markets. Sometimes operating singly, they often combined in major joint ventures such as pipelines. The McKenzie Commission found this "an outstanding characteristic of the seven cartel companies," and commented that "this cooperation is most apparent near the top of the pyramid where the degree of joint action and common purpose is almost suggestive of monopoly rather than oligopoly." Cartel members carved up national markets between themselves.

For comparative purposes, McKenzie noted that the 1965 revenues of the Alberta government were $491 million, of the Canadian government $8.9 billion and of the cartel companies $48.2 billion. The cartel was earning one hundred times as much as Alberta. Combined revenues of cartel corporations exceeded the combined revenues of Britain, France, Germany and Italy and the gross income of the cartel per employee was between $40,000 and $50,000, about six times the average actual salary, including directors. Looking at the ownership of all the oil in the non-Communist world, the committee found that: 61.3 percent was owned by joint companies within the cartel; 26.9 percent was owned by individual cartel companies; 10.3 percent belonged to independent oil companies; 1.5 percent was state-owned.

In the wry understatement of the McKenzie Commission, "The economic power of the cartel companies is immense."

In the 1950s and early 1960s, the cartel controlled one of the wealthiest empires in human history. By 1970 Standard of New Jersey alone controlled crude oil reserves of 50 billion barrels and natural gas reserves of 126 trillion cubic feet. The empire John D. Rockefeller had built by securing exclusive concessions on rail freights, though formally disbanded in the American trust-busting era of 1912–13, had regrouped in a strength that even the old monopolist had never dreamed of. From New York's Rockefeller Plaza, Standard directed the flow of crude into seventy refineries in thirty-seven nations, with a total run of 4.8 million barrels a day. It owned 184 tankers, had another 142 under charter and had placed orders for twelve supertankers of 250,000 tons each. Through its ninety-five percent interest in Creole Petroleum Corporation, it controlled half the oil production of Venezuela, which contributed sixteen percent of the parent corporation's income. Standard was also important in Canada, Saudi Arabia, Libya, Iraq, Iran, Syria, Lebanon, Africa, Holland, Indonesia, offshore Malaysia, Singapore and offshore Australia. Its American coal reserves were estimated at more than 6 million tons and it was increasing its holdings in coal, ore processing, uranium and real estate, selling liquefied natural gas from Libya to Italy and Spain, researching hydrogen fusion in association with General Electric and buying a one-quarter interest in the Trans-Alaska pipeline, while its Canadian subsidiary, Imperial Oil, prepared to mount a sustained political lobby for a gas pipeline down the Mackenzie Valley. Its directors had strategic interlocks with dozens of America's biggest corporations, including Morgan Guaranty

113

Trust, J. P. Morgan, Trans-Arabian Pipeline, Caterpillar Tractor, Prudential Insurance, Carborundum and, in Canada, with International Nickel Company and the Royal Bank. As the seventies opened, Jersey was North America's largest single supplier of oil and gas, had amassed the largest coal reserves in the United States and was busily fabricating nuclear fuels.

But the sixties had been the bonanza years. They were the imperial heyday, before the massive holdings of the cartel corporations in the producing countries had spurred serious resistance. The cartel, then, was operating on an infallible formula for classical profiteering. It was an essentially simple device—an artificial price structure that would enable the cartel to gouge the petroleum consumers of the entire Western world.

What was the market price of oil? The worldwide price of oil was the amount that was high enough to produce a profit on Texas crude, where production costs were then among the highest in the world. The price of all oil was a function of Texas prices. At the time the McKenzie Commission had the cartel under the microscope, it cost two dollars to produce a barrel of Texas crude. At the same time, it cost less than seven cents to produce a barrel of crude in Kuwait. Texas oil and Kuwait oil sold at the same price on world markets! Since the greater part of the cartel-controlled empire, from the Middle East to Venezuela, was functioning on the peonlike labour standards of the underdeveloped world, the opportunities for profit-making were, of course, unparalleled. The cartel's own profit statements reflected the enormous disparity between American and colonial labour and production costs. In a year, for instance, when Jersey Standard earned six percent on its domestic assets, it made fifteen percent in Venezuela. While Gulf was earning ten percent on operations in the U.S., it was pocketing thirty-three percent from Kuwait. Just as the price of natural gas produced in Alberta was a function of what the American government wanted it to be, the price of crude oil all over the world was a function of what the American oil industry wanted it to be. The extortion had been going on for decades, first formalized by the industry's original big three— Jersey Standard, Shell and BP—in the Achnacarry Agreement of 1928. The big three were later joined by four other American cartel members—Standard of California, Texaco, Gulf and

Mobil—in basing the prices of oil from all sources on the price of high-cost Texas crude plus transportation costs from Gulf of Mexico ports, and all seven were soon completely interlocked in joint production combines and joint marketing arrangements. The cartel members, as a result, enjoyed tremendous, extra-constitutional influence with Western governments. When BP's Near Eastern interests were threatened, British paratroops dropped on Kuwait. When intrepid Peruvian nationalists ventured to expropriate oil concessions belonging to Jersey Standard, they were promptly overthrown by an American-backed military coup.

Canada provided a copybook example of the artificiality of oil pricing under the pattern established by the cartel, which included the Canadian national oil policy. Under this policy, western Canadian oil is burned only by Canadians west of the Ottawa River, while their countrymen east of that line burn crude imported from Venezuela and the Middle East. Canada exports to the American West about ten barrels of oil for every seven imported into the Maritimes and Quebec.

At one point in the sixties, mathematicians of the Canadian Refinery Section of the Dominion Bureau of Statistics were startled to have to record that the oil that had left the wellhead in Kuwait at six cents per barrel and the oil from Alberta that had a production cost of $2.25 were reaching their respective markets in Montreal and Toronto at an identical price! Much of the oil used by Quebeckers comes from Creole Petroleum, Jersey Standard subsidiary and Venezuelan counterpart of Imperial Oil. This trade was at its height of profitability before the indigenous government was able to exert taxation and price pressures upon Creole, which currently pays a sixty percent royalty to the government. For years, the crude was leaving Venezuela at a price close to $1.45 a barrel and arriving in Montreal at more than $3. It was the same oil, and the same barrel. But by the alchemy of mid-ocean transactions between Creole, an interlocked tanker company in Nassau and Imperial Oil, it was yielding the Jersey Standard empire more than 200 percent in profit. Such artificiality reverberated to all Canadian consumers through the mechanism of the national oil policy. As the pressures of people in the underdeveloped world impelled cartel subsidiaries to hike their prices—Venezuelan

prices have increased six times since the beginning of 1971—
the subsidiaries of the same cartel companies operating in Alberta hiked their prices to match. Canadian industries, in the process, lost much of the natural advantage of operating in an oil-producing nation and Canada's balance of payments lost needless millions in a giveaway that parallelled the Alberta gas fire sale. And, in the period before the Latin government's long-anticipated increase in royalty rates, it was important for Jersey Standard to maximize Venezuelan output and get it to market in a hurry.

There was a beautiful symmetry about the pricing and marketing operations of the big seven cartel in its global heyday. Alberta's McKenzie Commission made a careful study of the process in order to demonstrate how the cartel affected a national oil industry. They found six important aspects to the complex process:

1. Importing nations could buy oil from cartel members only at prices that were acceptable to the cartel.

2. The refineries of the importing nation belonged to the cartel.

3. The oil being imported had to be carried in tankers or through pipelines belonging to subsidiaries of the cartel companies. This gave the cartel the opportunity to fix the carrying charges.

4. Cartel subsidiaries owned a majority of domestic production within the importing nation. This output was transferred to the refining divisions at prices that conformed at least roughly to the prices of the imported oil controlled by the cartel.

5. Nationally-owned oil companies, if there were any, produced such a tiny fraction of the nation's output that they, too, had to conform to cartel pricing.

6. The international oil companies outside the cartel controlled such an insignificant proportion of the total business that they, too, were obliged to conform to cartel practices and price structures.

There was no way the cartel could lose!

The world trading pattern described above is the operation of the global oil cartel in the classical period of its unimpeded power. Since the cartel corporations are now the masterminds of the pincer thrust around the Canadian North, it's important to know their operation. But changes in the world economic and political climate have forced important modifications upon the cartel—its northern thrust, indeed, is in some measure a response to setbacks elsewhere on the world scene. To see that thrust in global perspective, we must review both the setback the cartel encountered and its dynamic response.

In the cartel's golden noonday, its relationship with the governments of the major oil-producing countries was a quasi-imperial one. The countries were rich in energy resources, but little else, and though their rulers retained a measure of political independence, they lacked the capital, the technology and the marketing that could put the resources to profitable use. The cartel came along with the wherewithall to put the resources on the market, took the oil and provided a measure of indirect subsidization for the indigenous government, which had less bargaining power than even the province of Alberta enjoyed in the early years of Premier Manning. The benefits of resource exploitation were generally enjoyed by an infinitely smaller segment of the population than was the case in Alberta; the majority, in fact, continued to fester in desperate poverty. The local elites were isolated from their underprivileged countrymen and locked in dependency upon the cartel. In the subservient mythology of the times, the cartel corporations were assumed by both their own executives and the local governments to be playing the role of benefactors. Thus in 1951, the London-based Anglo-Iranian Oil Company pulled out of Iran rather than pay to a reform nationalist government what Aramco (a consortium of Jersey Standard, California Standard, Texaco and Mobil) was already paying to King Saud of Saudi Arabia. Soon afterwards, after political manipulation in which the Central Intelligence Agency was reported to have been involved, a reshuffled consortium of cartel companies returned to Iran.

Though cartel operations were never labour-intensive, they invariably generated sufficient economic activity to broaden the local elite. A middle class sympathetic to Third World ideologies— Arab nationalism in the Near Eastern countries, anti-colonialism in the Latin world—was finding its place in the ranks of the powerful. The cartel corporations would become its inevitable target. In nation after nation, new leaders from

117

the professions, universities and military elites were agitating for a share of the wealth—through fairer taxation, higher royalties, a share in pipeline ownership or the expropriation of reserves. In 1960 the foundation of the Organization of Petroleum Exporting Countries (OPEC) provided an international lobby for nations seeking a better share of their own oil wealth. Though slow to gain recognition, OPEC became significant because its economic policy succeeded in uniting Arab and Latin nationalists with feudal sheiks—almost all the governments hitherto at the mercy of the cartel. By the late sixties, through threats of cutting off supplies, OPEC was steadily forcing up taxes and royalties and increasing national shares in the ownership of pipelines and reserves. The status of the cartel corporations was diminishing in eleven nations. No longer sole landlords, they found themselves in uneasy partnership with ambitious colonels and zealous populists in the administration of pipelines and, in some cases, became customers of nationalized oilfields. It's true that in the panicky awareness of American resource depletion the cartel would have no trouble passing all the increases along to the consumer. But the panic was helping OPEC more than it was helping the international corporations.

If local participation in oil exploitation was changing the world pattern of cartel operations, so was the emergence of a reindustrialized Japan as one of the great energy-consuming nations. Caltex, a combine formed by Texaco and California Standard, quickly became Japan's largest supplier, but eighty-seven percent of the 3 million barrels a day the Japanese were importing by 1970 was Middle East crude. Japan thus found itself caught in an uncomfortable squeeze between the cartel and OPEC. The cartel had an early lead because of its massive exploration in the Pacific offshore, which was scarcely deterred by a setback on the uninhabited islands of Taioyutai, claimed by both Japan and China. Declaring it "absolutely impermissible for any foreign aggressor to poke his finger" into the shallow seas belonging to China, that country proceeded to formalize an alliance with OPEC that is potentially important for Japan and for the world.

One morning in May, 1973, the pumps ground to a halt at hundreds of desert oilwells in Libya, Iraq and Kuwait, and did not resume for twenty-four hours. At a marathon press conference later, the Libyan Colonel Muammar Gaddafi talked about the use of oil as a "weapon of Arab self-defence." His context was a political outburst against Israel and the United States, but what made the shutdown an ominous portent for the cartel was the fact that it happened just four days after the breakdown of an attempt by OPEC and the cartel companies to negotiate an increase in the price of oil made inevitable by the earlier devaluation of the American dollar. A settlement was reached at the beginning of June. OPEC, in the past, had frequently threatened a boycott in supplies; May, 1973, was a demonstration that these pumps could be stopped on the word of command. In June, Gaddafi nationalized a company owned in Dallas "because the United States deserved a strong slap in the face."

And that was but the first slap. Soon five cartel giants— Jersey Standard, Texaco, Mobil, California Standard and Shell —were struggling to salvage as much profit as possible from their once-great empire in Libya, now subject to fifty-one percent nationalization. More slaps, clearly, were on the way as oil became a crucial bargaining factor in the search for a settlement of political differences in the war-plagued Middle East.

Canadians, like the oil consumers in other Western nations, are voiceless in this test of economic wills. Future supplies and future pricing of Middle East oil are dependent on the issue of a conflict between frustrated Arab leaderships and the profiteering cartel. Whatever price the producing nations get, the cartel will get more from the ultimate consumers. Cartel oil from Texas and Alberta will perhaps become a function of Middle East prices. If the Carleton University geologist F. K. North is correct in asserting that the Persian Gulf Basin, with reserves understated by an amount exceeding the total known reserves of the rest of the world, is likely to be the world's main oil supplier until well into the twenty-first century, then it is time for the governments of consuming nations to push aside the cartel and take over the negotiations with OPEC themselves.

What OPEC still lacks is the manipulative power that comes from controlling the market—the service station at the prairie crossroads. "A company that controls markets," as the investigator said, "is in a better position than you might think." OPEC may have recognized this. A few days after the Libyan shut-down, the Quebec government disclosed it was talking to Saudi Arabia about Arab participation in a huge development on the south shore of the St. Lawrence that would include a pipeline, refinery system and deep-water port. The possibilities did not lack intrigue. One was that OPEC, through such a port and pipeline, might plan to challenge the cartel operators on their own home ground in the United States. Another was that, by the mere use of such a threat, OPEC might win co-option into the cartel's own marketing network and open up, at last, the service station on the empty fourth corner. It would be in cartel tradition to merge with the competition.

But that is speculation. What is now historically demon-strable is that with the emergence of OPEC as a counter-cartel with bargaining power, the world monopoly in oil has been loosened in less than a decade, though the pricing monopoly has not. Between 1965 and 1973, OPEC made important gains on the cartel in both Venezuela and the Middle East. Since 1970, OPEC has doubled the price of Middle East crude.

It is not, however, this shift in the world balance that is of prior importance for those with an interest in preserving Can-ada's sovereignty. The force that has to be looked at closely from this point of view is not the waxing of OPEC but what may be taken for the waning of the cartel. From the standpoint of Canada's future, a cartel rebuffed in the Middle East may be more immediately menacing than a cartel luxuriating in stable control of world markets. Nothing that has happened has re-duced the enormous profitability of the cartel, because every time the Arabs or Venezuelans win higher prices, the cartel slaps a bit more on the top and then hitches up the price of its product throughout the rest of the world. Its member com-panies, with record 1972 profits bulging in their pocketbooks, have never been better equipped to finance the acquisition of resources all over the world. Whatever the potential for oil and gas may prove to be on the Pacific rim, Indonesia, the North Sea and dozens of other offshore and frontier regions, that potential already belongs to the cartel. That pincer operation around the Canadian North is but one front in an enormous world sweep. And it is not only in the geographical sense that the cartel is spreading out. All the time it has been battling

OPEC and simultaneously drilling for oil and gas in one hundred regions, the cartel has been spreading into disparate fields of energy supplies, undergoing a metamorphosis that makes the concept of an "oil company" obsolete. The oil company died years ago and the energy corporation burst out of the crysalis. In the fading decades of the fossil fuel age—our children's lifetime— the energy corporation will certainly be in position to profit from every fuel it uses up.

In his book, *The Last Play*, the American journalist James Ridgeway set out to document "the struggle to monopolize the world's energy resources." He stated his theme succinctly in this chilling sentence: "A handful of corporations are in a position to determine the development of the remaining fossil fuels, the rate at which they will be produced, and the uses to which they can be put." It is a large claim; yet it cannot be called inconsistent with the pattern of large-scale resource development we have seen in Canada in the last half-decade. When the Dalhousie Four professors analyzed the Alberta gas fire sale, they pointed to "the high degree of corporate integration" as a key factor in the process. The more closely one examines their examples of bungled resource projects, the more conscious one becomes of corporate relationships that cut across normal divisions of specialty and trade. Ridgeway's concept of a many-faceted energy business seeking profit from each twist of scarcity, far from being a fanciful one, can help illuminate some of the murkier connections now being revealed.

If the cartel, then, stood to lose an empire in the Middle East, it would seek to conquer new empires by winning control of the oil and gas resources in still undeveloped parts of the world, and by consolidating its dominance in an increasingly integrated energy business. To retain their dominance in the Japanese oil trade, Jersey Standard, Mobil, Texaco and California Standard plunged into a hectic program of exploration in the Pacific. The cartel needed an alternative to Middle East supplies. They doubled production in the shallow seas off Indonesia and the rich Java Sea basin and that region became the source of eleven percent of Japanese supply. Jersey discovered substantial oil off Australia and, with the encouragement of a pliant government in South Vietnam, extended its refining in Southeast Asia. At the same time, the six U.S. corporations exploring the China Seas began promoting the idea that the world's richest deposits of sulphur-free oil and gas might lie in the subsoil of the shallow waters between Japan and Formosa. In the North Sea off Britain, Jersey Standard and Shell, in a characteristic joint venture, bid $50 million in 1971 for tracts of sea that would double the area of exploration in that region. In 1972, Jersey Standard, Gulf and the Bechtel construction company of San Francisco proposed in Tokyo and Moscow that they should participate in the exploration, by a consortium of thirty Japanese corporations, of the Soviet continental shelf facing Alaska. Reviewing the expansionism of the early seventies from the special vantage point of the American dissenter, James Ridgeway observed that the corporations had also "reopened old base camps and made resource colonies of those safe, white islands of colonialism created by the British in the nineteenth century—Australia, Canada, South Africa, the Appalachian region of the United States." The policy towards Canada Ridgeway termed "simple enough . . . . As fuels are depleted in the United States, thereby driving prices upward, the American petroleum and mining industries, which dominate the Canadian resource economy, will find it economically feasible to open up the Canadian North by the end of the century, just as the railroads opened up the Canadian West in the previous century. The abundant supplies of oil and gas in the Canadian North will be drawn into the United States to meet our shortage. This is euphemistically referred to as the continental approach, and involves establishment of free trade zones. All that means is that the United States seeks formal recognition of current practices, where it takes what it wants."

Though polemically expressed, this prescription parallels the one advanced by U.S. Treasury Secretary George Shultz at a press conference in May, 1973. "We know there are large sources of energy in Canada," said Shultz, "we would like to be the recipients of some of that." He added that "they would like access to our markets. We have a lot with which we can work together." The Toronto *Globe and Mail* reporter present followed the quotation with this parenthesis: "A broad spectrum of Canadian leaders . . . have emphasized the need for a strong export-oriented manufacturing sector to absorb Canada's rapidly-growing labour force. At the same time . . . some leaders have argued it would be politically and economically unwise to export large amounts of oil and natural gas to the United States. But Mr. Schultz seemed to leave the impression that it might be all or nothing."

While its drilling crews fanned across the world, the cartel and its allies were promoting a wave of mergers and integrations that would transform their business. Some of these, such as the merger on New Year's Day, 1970, of BP Oil Corporation and Standard Oil Company (Ohio), were of an essentially traditional nature. The oil strike in Alaska provided its rationale. BP Alaska, British Petroleum's wholly-owned subsidiary, held leases to Prudhoe Bay oil reserves estimated at 5 billion barrels, which was more oil than BP could ever bring to the American retail market. Standard Ohio, generally called SOHIO, was strong on marketing but short on reserves. For BP, the merger was a way to put its eventual product into the corner service station. In this case, the Prudhoe Bay reserves having been locked in the ground through court actions, the benefits to the merging companies will be delayed. But, when they come, they will come at premium prices. And, in the even longer term, when all the reserves have been drawn from Prudhoe, BP will still be in business in North America energy since its new partner SOHIO, founded in 1863 when John D. Rockefeller built his first ten-barrel refinery in Cleveland, now controls subsidiaries diversified in coal, oil shales, chemicals, plastics, motels and food service industries.

That process of integration has been accelerating since the mid-1960s, when the U.S. Internal Revenue Service issued a significant series of private rulings. These rulings permitted oil and mining corporations to buy up coal companies without paying any taxes on the money used in the purchase. For cartel members, this was one of three incentives for getting into coal. Another was profitability, since major American coalfields in the mid-sixties were yielding profits of almost one dollar a ton while the industry remained heavily subsidized by government. A third incentive was to prevent the coal industry from building refineries that would turn coal into gasoline through hydrogenation, the hydrogenation process developed by the German I. G. Farben chemical complex. In the 1930s, Farben and Standard Oil of New Jersey signed their cartel agreement under which all American rights to the hydrogenation process passed to Jersey Standard. Jersey and Shell Oil then formed a world combine, which granted Imperial Chemical Industries (ICI) an exclusive license for coal hydrogenation throughout the British Empire. In return, ICI agreed to limit production and buy its oil from Jersey and Shell. The two cartel companies had no interest in marketing the process themselves. There was, they knew, more coal in the world than oil, and if the coal industry took up hydrogenation on a mass scale it could conceivably destroy the supremacy of the oil business so carefully organized by the cartel. Oil itself must win control of coal.

Gasoline is not the only useful substance that can be produced from coal. It can also be processed into a synthetic form of natural gas, equally serviceable for heating or electric generation. Britain has produced natural gas from naptha for decades. In North America, the cartel that was drawing profitable natural gas in huge quantities from its oil-producing areas frowned on the production of substitute gas. The cartel changed its mind only after U.S. federal regulators, succumbing to a lobby by the oil corporations for higher gas prices, allowed prices to rise. Once this happened the cartel proclaimed a "shortage" in natural gas and set about the gasification of coal in a big way. By 1980, predicts Jersey Standard, 100 million tons of coal, a tenth of anticipated United States output that year, will be destined for gasification, with the substitute gas selling at even higher prices than natural gas pipelined from the sedimentary basins.

Canada today, it should be noted, also pursues policies promoting integration and concentrated ownership in the energy business. Under the Liberal government's so-called tax reform, corporations may charge the interest on funds borrowed to buy shares in other firms against existing profit. Petroleum corporations may deduct for tax purposes four dollars for every three they actually spend on exploration and development costs. Under existing policies, as Eric Kierans has pointed out, "government itself finances half the cost of acquisitions and mergers."

Tax concessions, subsidies, gasification and new processes, however, were not the only considerations spurring oil corporations to expand swiftly into coal in the sixties. Perhaps most

124

important for them was the opportunity it would provide to control the prices of competitive fuels. If a small group of big corporations could establish control of oil and natural gas, coal and nuclear fuels, the public would be at their mercy. The majors would have cornered the entire energy market and substantially reduced the competition for the fuels dollar.

Earlier, we saw how major corporations could measure gas prices against those of Bunker oil and organize a series of "matching" increases that would create an incessant ladder of rising prices in both. In such near-monopoly conditions, a seller withholding supply could extract an exorbitant price and this, the Union Gas counsel had claimed, "appears to be the strategy of the entire industry." Corporations controlling all major energy supplies would be ideally situated to apply such a strategy. Corporate tactics did not change much over time. In 1973, Darcy McKeough, the tough-minded Energy minister in the Ontario government, would note with alarm an amendment to Alberta's Gas Arbitration Act that would make it mandatory "that the arbitrators relate natural gas prices to the equivalent prices of other energy sources."

The integration push dates back at least to 1963, the year Gulf bought out the Pittsburgh and Midway Coal Company. Soon afterwards Continental Oil, twelfth largest petroleum corporation in the United States, placed a $63,875,000 down payment in a complicated transaction that would lead to the acquisition of Consolidation Coal Company, the largest coal producer in the U.S., with an annual output of 60 million tons and eleven percent of the total market. The rush was on. Soon Ashland was buying Archer Mineral, Standard of Ohio, the Old Ben mines, and Occidental had acquired Island Creek and Maust Coal and Coke. Continental was after nuclear resources as well as coal supplies. Through its 54.9 percent Canadian subsidiary, Hudson's Bay Oil and Gas, Continental had negotiated with Toronto mineowner Stephen Roman the purchase of his Denison Mines, the largest single uranium reserve in Canada. In one of its rare assertions of economic stewardship, the Trudeau government blocked the sale. If it had gone through, almost all of Canada's major uranium reserves—and this country has close to one quarter of the non-Communist world's assured reserves—would have passed into foreign hands. The

Trudeau regime ruled that future foreign ownership in Canadian uranium production would be restricted to one third of the whole, but it excepted all the companies already in operation. It was, of course, a classic instance of locking the stable door after the horse had bolted.

Rio Algom was already sitting on 100,000 tons of uranium ores at Elliott Lake, Gulf was in a consortium at Wollaston Lake with the German Uranerzbergbaw, and the big American Kerr-McGee oil firm held Elliott Lake reserves jointly with a Japanese consortium. Even Roman's Denison Mines was in joint ventures with Phillips Petroleum of the United States.

Oil was buying coal companies in a big way. It was buying reserves—a subsidiary of Jersey Standard snapping up the biggest in the United States. By the beginning of the seventies, forty percent of the listed tonnages belonging to America's fifteen largest coal producers were in the hands of the oil industry. The petroleum corporations were also snapping up leases. Continental acquired permits and leases to 38,000 acres, Kerr-McGee Oil to 55,000, Atlantic Richfield to 51,000, Sun to 36,000, Jersey Standard subsidiaries to 15,000 and Texas Alberta Oil to 5,000 acres.

Canada, of course, was the target of a parallel integration; by 1972 one quarter of total coal output was coming from mines controlled by these and similar companies. The traditional pattern has been for eastern Canada to import about 17 million tons a year from the U.S., while western Canada exports to Japan. The proportion of steam coal imported by Canada was not expected to decline appreciably before 1980 and when resource economist W. B. Ganong, working for Ontario's Advisory Committee on Energy, looked at the situation in early 1973, he felt obliged to warn of the 1980 prospects: "Vulnerability to possible oligopolistic pricing practices from U.S. supply areas will still be present . . . the potential for instituting pricing practices detrimental to the public interest is present to a high degree." Drawing upon Ganong's researches, the committee under Dr. John J. Deutsch cited "the surprising degree of horizontal integration by energy companies. The long-term implications of this trend," it found, "could be significant for energy prices."

In the late sixties in the United States, then, oil, gas and coal corporations were plunged into a swirling maelstrom of merger and reorganization.

By 1970, the energy industry had emerged, with big oil still in command. Of the fifteen leading coal producers seven, controlling twenty-eight percent of the total output, were in the hands of oil, as was one quarter of total production of uranium and coal combined. With unfamiliar names such as Gulf General Atomic and Jersey Nuclear, seventeen of America's top twenty-five petroleum companies had acquired an interest in nuclear fuels and four of them were engaged in all stages of production—from uranium exploration through mining, milling, fuel fabrication and reprocessing. One oil corporation alone, Kerr-McGee, controlled more than one quarter of the U.S. uranium supply. However badly stalled the U.S. nuclear program might be by administrative and technical blunders, oil knew that the uranium would surely be needed one day. When that day came, oil planned to command the pricing.

Parenthetically, the newly placed emphasis on the extraction of coal by the cartel corporations has been faithfully echoed by their Canadian subsidiaries in Alberta. The hearings leading to the April, 1973, report of the Energy Resources Conservation Board, which chose coal as the favoured material for future thermal power generation, was dominated by the submissions of the cartel subsidiaries, all placing heavy stress on the use of coal, which they do not produce, in preference to natural gas, which they do. A key sentence in the board's report declares, "Several of the participants also contended that it was in Alberta's public interest to utilize its coal resources for thermal generation, thereby freeing gas reserves for higher priority uses and for extraprovincial markets." The subsidiary spokesmen justified their arguments on the basis of coal's lower cost. But it appears likely that extensive stripping of the foothills and plains and, for the longer term, even deepcast mining in the plains, will be organized in the interests of keeping Alberta's diminishing gas reserves flowing down pipelines to the United States. The interventions of the cartel subsidiaries demonstrate that it is not only through ownership that the big seven can retain control of the formulation of policy in energy resources. Direct pressure will sometimes do the job. Historically, of course, Alberta's new plunge into coal is a regression. As F. K.

North has noted, "The hazards of dependence upon coal are well-known: distasteful acquisition, inefficient usage, militant unions, lacerated landscapes, derelict townsites. The most critical obstacle is an economic one. North Americans have virtually completed the transition from a coal-powered economy to one powered by oil, gas and hydroelectricity. To convert back again would be politically gauche and economically almost tragic."

By 1970, the emergence of energy corporations was a fact of economic life. To profile such a company we need not always refer to the pervasive influence of Jersey Standard. The number two cartel company, Royal Dutch-Shell, will serve, with its 1970 total sales of $10.5 billion and net income of $882 million. Shell, despite its impressive headquarters in The Hague, is not as Dutch as its name suggests: shareholdings are forty percent British, twenty-one percent American and only nineteen percent Dutch. Shell, which has important interlocks with United States Steel, Caterpillar Tractor, the Iranian oil consortium, Dunlop rubber, Rootes motors, Lord Thompson's London *Times* and Morgan Guaranty Trust, operates more than 500 subsidiary corporations in 105 nations. Its 415 tankers totalling 23.6 million tons constitute the largest fleet in the world; it provides fourteen percent of the world's oil and invests more abroad than the rest of Great Britain. It owns 35,000 miles of crude and product pipelines and 11,650 miles of natural gas pipelines and its refineries process 252 million metric tons of crude annually, 11 million of them in Canada. In combination with Jersey Standard, Shell controls almost half the European pipelines carrying crude from the Mediterranean to refineries inland.

When Shell's more than 500 subsidiaries, many of which control their own networks of subsidiaries and operating companies, are listed, it becomes apparent that only a minority are occupied in the extraction, refining and marketing of oil. There are chemical companies, exploration outfits, engineering services, geological study groups, industrial gas manufacturers and liquefied petroleum companies, manufacturing companies and marketing groups, mining and metal companies, research units and transportation companies from Trinidad to Tonga. This is a modern energy corporation.

128

World powers as concentrated as Shell, James Ridgeway argues, are reducing governments to impotence and cannot be restrained from manipulating one energy source after another in the pursuit of profit. When applied to Canada, the implications are awesome. It is not merely that the capital requirements of major Canadian energy projects, conservatively estimated by Ontario's Advisory Committee on Energy at $60 billion for the remainder of this decade, threaten the nation's balance of payments and jeopardize the expansion of labour-intensive secondary industry, the only type of expansion that will permit Canadians to break the chronic cycle of high unemployment in our country. An equally serious consideration is the inflationary consequence of having the prices of the dominant fuels established by a world cartel—how many millions of dollars and thousands of jobs has cartel control of world fuel prices cost Canada so far?

Big oil's millions in campaign contributions helped elect the discredited American president Richard Nixon. That did not stop the industry holding even Nixon's government to ransom. Cartel corporations would be no less tough than OPEC's negotiators in squeezing extra dollars from the pockets of U.S. consumers. Higher U.S. domestic prices, corporate lobbyists insisted, would increase exploration and discovery of domestic crude—thereby reducing the dependency on OPEC supplies that was proving damaging to America's balance of payments. The shortages of January, 1973, the lobbyists claimed, proved that the industry must have higher prices! At the same time, Nixon's Cost of Living Council was warning him that higher oil prices would help push the inflationary spiral out of control. On March 7, Nixon decided that inflation, at least for the moment, was the greater evil. He clamped price controls on the petroleum industry—controls he knew would necessitate increased imports.

Canada is the only major oil exporter to the U.S. that is not a member of OPEC, and Nixon had conditionally lifted the import quotas on Canadian crude back in 1971. When Ottawa imposed a compulsory cut in crude exports to the U.S. in 1973, the federal government stressed that this was a stopgap measure, not a long-term policy of restriction. The assurance of long-term Canadian supply strengthened Nixon's hand in defying the cartel; but it did not help the Canadian consumer. Denied higher profit from increased wellhead prices at home, the multinational corporations were free to jack up their fuel prices in the Canadian market.

Anyone who questions the emergence of an energy industry in the late sixties need consult only the membership of Canadian Arctic Gas Study Ltd., the consortium currently promoting the Mackenzie pipeline development. The members include Columbia Gas System (Delaware); Northern Natural Gas (Nebraska); Pacific Lighting Corp. (California); TransCanada Pipeline; Atlantic Richfield (New York); Standard Oil of Ohio; Natural Gas Pipeline of America (Chicago); Canadian Pacific Investments (Montreal); Imperial Oil (Jersey Standard); Shell; Mountain Pacific Pipeline; Bechtel Construction; El Paso Natural Gas and Southern California Edison Co.

Here the energy industry comes together to create a powerful lobby—cartel corporations, mon:polists in pipeline transmission and gas and electricity supply, investment companies and engineering concerns such as Bechtel of San Francisco. Bechtel had been involved in the construction of ninety percent of the pipelines in Canada, managed the development at Churchill Falls and is developing James Bay. Together with the development-minded senior bureaucrats in such federal departments as Energy, Mines and Resources and Indian Affairs and Northern Development, and Liberal politicians such as ministers Donald Macdonald and Jean Chretien, they exert unremitting pressure for such projects as the Mackenzie Valley gas pipeline.

W. O. Twaits, chairman of Imperial Oil, once described by the former Liberal cabinet minister Eric Kierans as "the most powerful man in Canada," is one of the lobby's more predictable spokesmen. In one recent pipeline oration, he emphasized that "the scale of the market needed to justify development of reserves requires, in addition to a Canadian market, access to close export markets in the U.S. Just as we recognize that the transmission of electric power is limited in distance, so we must recognize that there are economic limits on the pipeline distribution of oil and gas and that, in order to achieve economic unit cost, operations must of course be of a very large scale." This argument, based on the economies of scale provided by the American market, is precisely the one used to justify the

130

Alberta gas fire sale, with which Twaits' corporation was so conspicuously and profitably associated.

If there are any limits at all to the exploitive ambitions of cartel subsidiaries, and it is doubtful that there are, those limitations surely fall away when the cartel executives join forces with an energy consortium as multi-faceted as Gas Arctic-Northwest Project Study Group. All resources are grist to its mill—the nuclear fuels and minerals along with the oil, gas and coal. Whatever resource is there to be profitably exploited, one of those energy corporations, or one with which they are allied through interlocks and common financing, will want that resource. Corporations such as the ever-present Bechtel, the biggest construction outfit in the world, serve as a catalyst to an ever-widening circle of exploitation in which Canada's development needs rate scarcely a moment's thought.

There is no auditor-general in the resources field to present the Canadian Parliament with an annual statement of national gain and loss. If there were, he would point out to the nation that while, in the period 1947–1972, petroleum corporations spent $18.7 billion in Canada and earned only $18.2 billion, they removed in the process oil and gas reserves with a value of something like $45 billion, which is more than $2,000 for every man, woman and child in Canada. Even that is less than half the story. Having taken out oil and gas worth $45 billion, these corporations today control reserves in the ground valued at more than $50 billion. To the nation's losses in gas and oil the auditor-general of Canadian resources would add the lost electricity, the consumptive price of exported waters and the inestimable environmental values that never show in corporate or governmental accounting. Ripoff, surely, is too mild a word for plunder on this gargantuan scale.

The auditor-general of resources would also point out that every project of the type criticized by the Dalhousie Four creates an infrastructure of services that become the launchpad for a new round of exploitation. When the roads, electricity and water are in place adjacent to the Athabasca tar sands to service the Syncrude consortium, Alberta can promote the exploitation of the region's titanium, iron, zinc, copper, nickel and chromium reserves. When Bechtel opened up Churchill Falls for Hydro-Quebec, it bared the mineral wealth of Labrador and when it has built its dams on the James Bay rivers, it will leave the servicing for a new spurt of mineral exploitation to replace the economic activity that once existed in the broken, stripped-out towns of the Abitibi region.

Hydro-Quebec, of course, is only the "shadow" beneficiary of a project such as Churchill Falls. Behind Hydro-Quebec and its Bechtel managers stands the giant Brinco group, an amalgam of the Rothschild-backed Rio Tinto Zinc Corporation and the American Bethlehem Steel Corp. Now that the services are in and the dammed river is providing plentiful cheap power, it will be Brinco that will strip mineral wealth out of Labrador. Though Brinco was a mere fifty-seven percent partner in the Hydro development, it secured exclusive rights to mineral exploitation in the region.

Rio Tinto Zinc is part owner of British Petroleum, one of the oil cartel's big eight. Rio Tinto also controls Rio Algom Mines, Canada's largest producer of uranium. Rio Tinto is interlocked with the Anglo-American Corporation of South Africa, which controls that continent's great uranium mines. Rio Tinto Zinc is looking at the possibility of using Churchill Falls power to enrich Canadian uranium for the export market. In Australia, Rio Tinto is in a joint venture with the American-owned Kaiser Industries to dominate aluminium and iron ore production, as well as to mine coal. With control of seven of Canada's eleven uranium mines, plus deposits in southwest Africa and Australia, it is now exploring for uranium in the United States and is involved in Spanish and Rhodesian copper, Australian tin and Nevada's borax deposits. Together with the American-owned Kerr-McGee oil firm, the interlocked firms of Rio Tinto and Anglo-American dominate the world uranium market. Though Rio Tinto, with annual sales of $1 billion, is not a large corporation by cartel standards, its literature states that it aims to "discover and exploit" the resources of the world. It has made a convincing start.

With something approaching a monopoly in uranium and an important stake in one of the big oil firms, a corporation such as Rio Tinto appears well-equipped to join the cartel companies in squeezing maximum advantage from the energy crisis. Its affiliate, Brinco, will apply similar dynamics to the finite supplies of Canadian minerals. Successive sellouts in the resource field will lay down the infrastructure for a further round of ripoff in minerals. "During the next twenty-five years," the Science Council of Canada has reminded us, "known reserves in Canada of copper, gold, lead, mercury, natural gas, petroleum, silver, tin and zinc will have been used up." It is not difficult to guess by whom. The pincers now in the grasp of the energy corporations will ultimately close around all Canadian mineral reserves unless Canada, for the first time, asserts a significant measure of political control.

United States experience suggests that this will be an exceedingly difficult act. In analyzing the American energy crisis, U.S. author Ridgeway concludes: "The policies that produced the energy crisis are a function of the corporate social state. They represent part of the process towards centralization of economic and political power into the hands of a few organizations, some business, some governmental, some a combination of both. The overall effect is to lessen the ability of the citizens to influence the events that shape their lives, to remove power from their grasp."

Chapter Seven

The Continental Bearhug

"Are Canadians to pay billions of dollars to discover, produce, and transport materials for use by peoples of another country; materials that Canadians themselves do not need (yet) but which their descendants will wish had been preserved for their use? Are Americans to be asked to pay for production and delivery systems that will lie entirely in another nation's territory and be under that other nation's political control? Or are Canadians to surrender effective sovereignty over, say, twenty percent of their territory, by allowing all the capital fixtures, all the ore carriers, all the ice-breaking LNG tankers, to be under the American flag?"

— F.K. North, professor of geology, Carleton University.

For Robert Descher, chief geologist with Elf Oil of Calgary, it was no simple matter to convince the tiny Eskimo community of Sachs Harbour of his company's need to move half a dozen Rollogan land vehicles across Banks Island a few days after the permitted work season. Questions thrown at him during the hamlet meeting were blunt, pointed and unyielding. What made it especially difficult was that these questions were informed by rather more certainty about the likely condition of the ice, the location of the fox dens and the temperament of the calving caribou than he or the federal land use official beside him could muster. The tone of the exchange is apparent in the hamlet record.

Alexandria Elias: The shutdown time was April 30, you

know that. Why don't you take your stuff over the ice to Desalas Bay?

Robert Descher: I don't think it is possible to go over the ice, as the tires will get cut up. We believe also that the barges will not get to Desalas Bay until September.

Alexandria Elias: Closing time is April 30—you should know that.

Before the meeting was over, Descher was firmly reminded that there was a 4,000 gallon oilspill still to be checked near Barnord Bay, and, though the meeting reached no conclusion on his proposal, the hamlet learned later that the Rollogans were indeed to be moved through Desalas Bay.

Sachs Harbour's mood in springtime, Descher found, was Tuktoyaktuk's mood in the fall. There, earlier objections by the hamlet council had led to the cancellation of Elf's summer program of seismic blasting. In October, the councillors at Tuk made it clear they did not approve of Elf's winter program for blasting in the Bathurst Peninsula, where Tuktoyaktuk hunters shot caribou from October to March and trappers snared the Arctic fox and snowshoe hare from December through May. A survey documenting hunting and trapping interests had been compiled from random interviews with seventeen of the community's seventy-five households and a petition asking the federal authorities to save the hunting grounds was under way. The area superintendent from the Department of Indian Affairs and Northern Development had laboured strenuously through hours of discussion to be reasonably persuasive, but the Eskimo councillors remained disconcertingly alert, unruffled and indisposed to compromise. Robert Descher could hardly have been surprised by the subsequent November announcement from Ottawa that oil exploration in the 600-square mile district would be suspended one year, so that the effects on the peninsula's wildlife might be studied.

Yet there was surprise in those developments, for Sachs Harbour and Tuk are small communities and Elf Oil, Robert Descher's employer, is part of the French Group, one of those eight giant corporations in the worldwide cartel that has virtually monopolized the marketing of petroleum products for close to thirty years. Tuktoyaktuk versus the French Group was a

David and Goliath encounter and the hamlet's winning round cannot be attributed entirely to the strength of its historic claim on the Bathurst hunting grounds or the resilient fibre of its local democracy. There is, the councillors themselves point out, another perspective to the affair. In the first nine months in which the hamlet council was asked to comment on land use permits in its region, it opposed only three of thirty-four applications. Not even Ottawa can deny that that is a cooperative record; a hamlet that has said yes to thirty-one sets of explorers in its backyard can hardly be faulted when it says no to the possible loss of its fish and game.

What should surprise us more than the hamlet's one-year reprieve, surely, is the physical presence of the French Group on Canada's Arctic shores, along with Imperial Oil, Shell, Gulf, Mobil and the rest. One or other of the cartel partners is now a physical presence in almost all the Canadian communities north of the sixtieth parallel. We have seen how the majors, after skimming off the cream of Alberta's oil and gas, moved on to mount a pincer thrust upon the frontier regions. We saw how the same corporations, having been forced into tough bargaining positions with their Third World resource colonies, transformed themselves into a new corporate organism called the energy business. Now we see them assuming physical possession of Canada's frontier regions—the Mackenzie Delta, the Arctic Islands and the Atlantic offshore.

In their taut vigilance over the caribou and the Arctic fox, the Inuit people of Tuk and Banks Island have responded to a set of new realities still unperceived by many Canadians in the south. The continental policy in energy resources, when viewed from Tuk or Sachs Harbour, is no longer an idea, something for Canadians to consider, accept or reject, but an accomplished reality. The process of resource development to service the United States that was documented by the Dalhousie Four in various periods and regions is no longer a question of local projects undertaken at the initiative of provincial interests, but a dominant fact of the national economy. As James Ridgeway puts it, "The purpose behind the American march into Canada is the capture of natural resources." To complete the closing of the pincer around the frontier, the cartel needs only approval by the National Energy Board and the Canadian cabinet for the delivery vehicle that will plug frontier resources into the United States industrial system forever.

This northern takeover has been under way for years, with cartel corporations snapping up cheap exploration permits to eighty percent of the Mackenzie Delta and the Arctic Islands. Imperial Oil, the largest corporation in Canada, is also the largest permit-holder in the Mackenzie Delta-Beaufort Sea region. It has been there since 1966, spending some $90 million on exploration and development, and has already contracted to export $4 billion worth of the region's natural gas to the United States over twenty years. Gulf, Shell, Mobil and the French Group have not been far behind the Exxon subsidiary.

Off the Grand Banks of Newfoundland, Imperial, Amoco, Standard Oil of British Columbia and Skelly Oil are drilling the continental shelf in a joint hunt for an undersea oilfield they hope will some day yield 200 million barrels. There are Mobil rigs on bleak Sable Island off Nova Scotia and there will soon be more in the Bay of Fundy. In New York, Nova Scotia Premier Gerald Regan offers his province as a repository for superports and refineries to service New England, slyly reminding U.S. businessmen that environmental groups fighting oil spillage and pollution "are more heavily organized in the United States and have weapons available to them such as injunctions that aren't available under the Canadian constitution."

In August, 1973, Quebec, the four Atlantic provinces and the governors of six New England states met in Prince Edward Island to form a permanent lobby pushing for Canadian energy exports. The declared intention of this lobby is to harness the energy resources of eastern Canada to service the "crisis" in the northeastern U.S. The national interest was downgraded throughout the meeting and Premier Regan set the tone for continuing collaboration with the declaration that, from a development point of view, eastern Canada and New England "are really one region."

The permits and leases, then, have been sold, the seismic camps and drilling rigs are physically emplaced on the frontier and, in some cases, even the gas has been found. All that is required to connect it to the energy-starved U.S. industrial system is the delivery vehicle—the pipeline. The 1974 hearings about the wisdom of installing the northern delivery system will take place not before the Parliament of Canada but before the National Energy Board. The irrevocable national decision that will be under discussion will be whether Canada, like Alberta twenty years ago, should commit its frontier resources to effective regulation by the continental market or whether, in an unprecedented assertion of national priorities, we will insist that the timing and extent of resource exploitation be measured to fit the needs of Canada's own development. Those pleading for a quick approval will argue, as they did in Alberta twenty years ago, that an immediate export program will provide "economies of scale," guaranteed to "open up" the North swiftly, and provide Canadian consumers with something of a free ride. Those opposing it will point to Canada's growing needs—the National Energy Board says Canada will need 2.1 trillion cubic feet of natural gas, an amount equalling Alberta's total 1972 production, by the year 1980—and emphasize that, once another country has come to rely upon energy supplies flowing through a vehicle for which it provided billions in capital investment, any change in the arrangement suggested by the resource-producing nation is "tantamount to an act of war." Once our energy becomes integrated into the American productive system, they will argue, we can never turn off the tap.

What will be immediately at issue in those 1974 hearings—and this is significant—is the pipeline to carry natural gas, a carrier servicing companies with gas to sell and other companies wanting to buy it, sometimes the same multinational corporations. It will be forty-eight-inch diameter steel pipe running 2,500 miles from the Arctic Circle to the North Dakota border, costing an estimated total of $6 billion and delivering 3.3 billion cubic feet of gas to southern markets every day. One prong of the pipeline will begin at Prudhoe Bay on Alaska's north slope and swing southeast. Near Inuvik it will meet an eastern prong carrying gas from Beaufort Sea regions and form a trunk line pushing up the Mackenzie Delta through Norman Wells and Fort Simpson and diverging again near the Alberta border, one link flowing into the Alberta trunk system and south to California through existing pipes, a new installation crossing the prairies to Emerson, Manitoba. From there the gas will eventually flow east to serve Ontario and Quebec and south to serve United States markets. The Canadian Arctic Gas Study promoters say optimistically that the first part of the system, carrying Mackenzie Delta gas, could begin transmission in 1978 and be at capacity in 1980–81.

But, according to some pipeline promoters in industry and government, the gas line is only part of the package. A parallel oil pipeline is contemplated and a railway has been discussed. Another gas pipeline from the remote Arctic Islands is also being considered. Prime Minister Pierre Trudeau threw in a $100 million highway from the Alberta border to the Arctic, without knowing what the route would be or the effect on wildlife and fish, and catching off guard his senior officials in Northern Development, who first heard the highway announced on the radio. Trudeau talked about a $10 billion Mackenzie transportation corridor he promised would be "mind-boggling"; it was an occasion that found the prime minister indulging unashamedly in the distinctively Canadian parlor game of "northern vision" rhetoric, in which comparisons of the latest project with the eighteenth-century fur trade and the building of the CPR are mandatory. Jean Chretien who, incongruously, is responsible for both Indian Affairs and Northern Development, is a rhetoric buff. "We are on the threshold of great events in the North," he likes to say. "We are in the midst of an adventure of social and economic impact rivalling the construction of the Canadian Pacific Railway." As F. K. North has pointed out, "the words Arctic and northern have been admitted to the pantheon of magic words."

It was, of course, John Diefenbaker who popularized the game in his northern vision years, which produced little useful development in the North. But the mythology has lingered and there remains a vague general impression of the Canadian North as a treasure chest in resources so opulent and extensive that they have the capacity to "solve" the deepening North American energy crisis. The proven realities are nothing like that.

The Canadian treasure chest theory is an illusion. Suppose that, tomorrow, it were possible for Alberta to forbid the sale of any crude oil and natural gas to Canadians, so that the entire provincial output of conventional oil could be shipped to the United States. The crude oil would represent less than one-eighth of the quantity the U.S. must import and the natural gas would represent about six percent of total U.S. consumption. If we could make a gift of our entire conventional oil reserves, it would not add more than a few years to the U.S. reserve life for oil. There is no prospect whatever that Canadian petroleum resources, from conventional or frontier sources, can ever meet the American deficit in energy supplies.

The only conventional oil and gas that has been reliably measured is that in western Canada and the reserves of both these resources went into decline in 1972. Reserve statistics assembled by the foreign-dominated Canadian Petroleum Association are consistently and highly misleading, since they equate the sour gas of the foothills and the most intractable pools with easily-accessible gas. But the industry's estimates of potential in the frontier regions are the rankest guesswork, based on study of petroliferous regions in other parts of the world, and there is no requirement that Canadians should believe them. Even such perennial optimists as the National Energy Board and Energy Minister Donald Macdonald have indicated they do not. The reputable Canadian Society of Petroleum Geologists estimated in 1973 that Canada's recoverable ultimate potential supply might be 85 billion barrels of oil (seventeen times as much as has been discovered to date) and 577 trillion cubic feet of natural gas (more than seven times what has been discovered to date). That is their estimate of all the oil and gas that might, potentially, exist and includes the tar sands and all the wells that, because of depth or remoteness, could be too expensive to exploit.

What is more immediately relevant is that the highly-skilled explorers of the giant corporations that have been at work in the frontier regions for almost a decade have so far found very little oil. "It doesn't look at all good for oil," says the University of Alberta petrochemical engineer, Jim Ryan. "They're finding some gas—they know where to look for gas. But with oil you've got Imperial Oil's two strikes at Atkinson Point, and that's about it. Maybe that's why the majors are diversifying so fast."

Ryan does not know, the corporations and government do not know and we do not know how much oil there is north of sixty and on the Atlantic shelf. What we do know is that the north of this continent has one beautifully concentrated field of conventional oil and gas wealth, and that is at Prudhoe Bay on Alaska's Arctic north slope. This marvellous formation provides little clue to the rest of the North because, though Prudhoe is geographically in the Arctic, it is geologically an extension of the Brooks Range mountains.

For Ryan, Prudhoe is "a unique thing, the one classical structure as perfect as the example you would find in a textbook. But," he says, "the fact that you have found an oil-bearing basin should not be taken to mean that you have found a Texas. There are twice as many possible oil-bearing basins in the world as there are basins that contain oil."

F. K. North is more emphatic. The claims of huge potential oil reserves north of sixty have meaning, he says, only if they are prefaced by the qualification "assuming that every area of sedimentary rock in Canada is as petroliferous as Texas." There is no prospect of any North American self-sufficiency in oil and "if we ponder them dispassionately and not as propagandists, the odds are quite unacceptably long against any of the basins containing more than a fraction of the reserves prophesied for them."

But we do know there is natural gas; enough, according to Imperial Oil, to reach that threshold needed to make the Mackenzie Valley gas pipe economic, even if Alaska supplies were not forthcoming. The recent maps of the Department of Indian Affairs and Northern Development are stippled with the star shapes representing suspended, dry and abandoned and operating gas wells, with the black circles that spell oil remotely spaced. That is why it is significant that, although its propaganda supports the mythology of a treasure chest in resources, the petroleum industry, so far, has put its money only into a pipeline designed to carry natural gas. The industry's propaganda machine no doubt throws in the innuendo of huge oil potential as another element that will weaken resistance to the approval of the pipeline. (The machine is untroubled by consistency. During the lobby for higher gas prices in Alberta, for instance, it claimed repeatedly that the higher prices would stimulate discoveries sufficiently to increase the province's reserves by 10 trillion cubic feet. When prices went up, the industry dropped the theme of increased reserves and began to frighten Ontario householders with the prospect of an energy shortage if the Mackenzie pipeline was delayed.

In promoting the northern adventure, the propaganda machine, snugly based in downtown Toronto, rarely mentions elements of difficulty and cost. With present technology, we have seen, it is questionable even in Alberta whether the sour gas in the foothills is worth drawing out of the ground. There will, inevitably, be more such marginal sources in the Arctic environment and offshore. The more hazardous, remote and costly exploration and drilling become, the more imperative it becomes to make discoveries on a grand scale— ideally, on a ·Prudhoe Bay scale. H. E. Quellhorst, supervisor for the Grand Banks consortium that keeps two giant semi-submersible rigs drilling year-round in the face of drift ice and bergs, has been quoted as saying, "We're playing in the big leagues here. As a rule-of-thumb, an offshore field has to be able to yield at least 200 million barrels to be worthwhile. In all the shore-based exploration done in Canada to date, only fourteen oilfields of this size have ever been found." A field of 50 million barrels, which might be profitable in Alberta conditions, would be a dead loss under the sea. A 12,000-foot well that would cost $350,000 to drill in Alberta's Whitecourt area would cost about $2 million on the Grand Banks, Quellhorst says. The same consideration is true for the Arctic Islands, where every phase of the operation would have to contend with ice floes, treacherous open water, Arctic storms and permafrost. Given the hazards and the expensive protection drilling demands, only a large pool would have value: the same quantity of oil scattered through a number of smaller fields would not be worth drawing from the ground.

Having considered these hazards, North says, "We should therefore give very serious consideration to an utterly heretical conclusion: that the reserves we have any expectation of finding are not worth looking for. The expense and danger involved in the search have scarcely any chance of being justified by the reward. . . . The most sensible forecast that can be made is not that Arctic or Atlantic oil will have solved North America's fuel problem by the mid-1970s, but that the search will have been abandoned in failure before that time arrives. The failure need not be literal to be decisive; it may merely reflect success insufficiently spectacular."

All the resources known to exist in the Arctic, argues North, including the dry natural gas, "have no value whatever to this generation of Canadians. Canadians, as consumers, will not need to exploit any remote source of any of these materials during this century, unless we go on selling our easily-accessible resources to the United States. It is the Americans who are interested in resources from the Arctic, not Canadians . . . . This is the crux of the whole matter." United States industry needs the gas now, the cartel corporations, as Imperial's deals show, can get profitable export contracts now, and the lobby is therefore anxious to get on with the Mackenzie pipeline now, before Canadians have had time to compare it to the melancholy pattern of the Alberta gas fire sale, or relate it to their future options as a manufacturing nation.

The lobby is a smooth one. Everything it does is smooth, from the promotional movies designed to scare Ontario householders about the coming energy shortage to the early commitment of $20 million for social, environmental and wildlife studies conducted under the control of the Arctic Gas Studies consortium. Its liaison with the politicians and civil servants of the federal government is also smooth. Under the management of William Wilder, an influential financier, and Vernon Horte, former president of TransCanada Pipelines, the Gas Arctic Group presented in the months before the Energy Board hearings on the pipeline an image of purposeful and unflustered preparation.

One reason for the emphasis on studies is that the Gas Arctic planners are anxious to avoid the blunders of the American lobby pushing for the trans-Alaska oil line down an 800-mile pipe to the ice-free southern Alaska port of Valdez, where the north slope oil will be loaded on tankers for delivery to the U.S. Pacific coast. That pipeline was stalled for years by conservationist appeals to the U.S. courts; Gas Arctic people cite it, therefore, as an instance of poor corporate planning and insensitivity.

It was that, but the apparent bungling derived from the curious fluidity, even openness, apparent in the battle for and against the Alaska pipe. Out of that flux, admittedly, came the confusion and prolonged litigation that kept the miles of pipe in stockpiles at Prudhoe Bay, but also came the Alaska Native Claims Settlement and a set of royalty regulations that will benefit future generations that live in the state. From the point of view of oil corporations, Alaska was a messy example, but for 60,000 native people and future generations it is arguable that the protracted negotiations produced a closer approximation to justice than anything Gas Arctic is likely to achieve.

The methods of the Canadian pipeline lobby are in many respects the antithesis of the Alaska struggle—quieter, smoother, more neatly interlocked with government and the northern bureaucracy, and virtually closed to the public. The corporations and the federal bureaucracy present a common front, interested primarily in development on corporate terms and sealed off from any real interchange with the northern peoples. In Alaska, the corporations joined forces with the native people's lobby for a settlement of their land rights, as part of a deal to get the pipeline approved. Once the oil flows, the residents will draw their agreed share of royalties, and the state will receive a return that is more than derisory. Alaska seems less likely to become a social disaster than the Northwest Territories.

The state of Alaska, certainly, is no less susceptible to pressures from the cartel corporations than the Canadian federal authority. But, from the protracted horse-trading process that produced the Alaska settlement, the government in Juneau salvaged some effective powers. Where the cartel corporations were collecting leases at nominal fees in the Canadian North, Alaska obliged them to enter competitive bids in a one-day auction that realized $900 million from oil leases for the state treasury. It is part of the continuing suppleness of the American system that corporations do not always win. Where the legislature in Juneau prescribed a twenty percent royalty fee on Prudhoe Bay oil, Ottawa, using land-use regulations drawn up in secret in the Diefenbaker vision days of 1961, asked only five percent for three years and ten percent thereafter!

Andy Thompson, a wiry, stiff-bearded University of British Columbia law professor who has denounced these wrist-tapping regulations in speeches across the North, calls them "a resource giveaway unparallelled in any country in modern times." In almost one billion acres of leased northern land and a roughly equal amount offshore, the cartel is happily inheriting the "northern vision" legacy. For a $250 filing fee and a payment of one dollar an acre, the oil companies secure permits granting them twelve years' exploration rights. If oil is found, the permit may be extended twenty-one years and, if the oil should be drilled in commercial quantities, the permit is extended a further twenty-one years. Thus, a corporation's one dollar can secure an oil-bearing acre for a possible fifty-three years!

When production starts, the royalties on the output will be five percent for the first three years, less than one third of those charged in the cartel's homeland in the lower forty-eight states. Thompson worked out a comparison. Since the Mackenzie pipeline is expected to carry one-half Canadian and one-half Alaska gas, he assumed that equal quantities of gas from the two sources flowed down the common pipeline for a period of three years. At the end of that time, Thompson found, the government in Juneau will have collected $144 million; Canada will have received just $36 million. Over a decade, Thompson argued, Canada would give away to the cartel corporations enough to settle the land claims of the 30,000 Indian, Eskimo and Métis people of the Yukon and the Northwest Territories, and provide the seed money for diversified economic development within both territories.

When those regulations were drafted, as now, there was no public involvement. As Diefenbaker's Northern Development minister, Alvin Hamilton permitted the Oil and Gas Land Regulations of 1961 to be debated only within the boardrooms of cartel branch offices and government departments. The government, in Thompson's words, "gave the oil industry carte blanche, telling them to write the kind of regulations that would create incentives for northern development." The Trudeau administration, working along the same cosy insider lines, theoretically reviewed the giveaway rules about two years ago. No changes were suggested. Thompson's charges were reinforced in 1973 by Newfoundland Energy Minister Leo Barry, who pointed out that Ottawa's regulations were far more generous to the cartel corporations than those governing North Sea exploration, which had caused a giveaway scandal in Britain. Perhaps the most tragic aspect of the federal regulations, three times more generous to corporations than those in effect in Alberta, is that eighty percent of the promising acreage in the North and offshore has already been leased under the existing system.

The pipeline consortium can look forward to even kinder treatment from the federal "regulators"; the gas line is unlikely to pay any taxes at all. The experience of Vernon Horte will be valuable here. TransCanada Pipelines, of which he was formerly president and which is the monopoly carrier of Alberta gas to Ontario, racked up $368 million in profits after 1958 without paying a cent in federal income taxes.

It is not only with respect to royalties that the Alaska experience can be instructive for Canadians. The many-faceted political struggle over the oil pipeline gave birth to the Alaska Native Claims Settlement, which provides 40 million acres of land, $462.5 million in federal treasury funds and $500 million in future oil royalties for the state's 60,000 Indians, Eskimos and Aleuts. In return, the natives surrendered their aboriginal title to the remainder of the state's 375 million acres. It is by no means a perfect settlement. The cash total, which looked so imposing in the settlement terms, soon proved what Alaska's candid Attorney-General John Havelock calls "a drop in the bucket" against the enormity of the economic and social problems in an immense country that had been, for the United States, a neglected resource colony, and, for the native Alaskans, a sprawling rural slum.

That said, the settlement, which provided twelve large native corporations with the first seed money for the economic development of their regions, was an infinitely more hopeful and challenging event than anything that has happened to the 30,000 Indian, Eskimo and Métis people of the Canadian North. To fly from the north slope of Alaska to the Canadian North, I found in the fall of 1972, was a journey from day into night, from self-confidence and rudimentary social planning to frustration and social despair. The Alaskan natives were already achieving a variety of emancipation in the period in which the Trudeau government was sowing despair with the cruelly terminationist White Paper of 1969 inspired, a member of Trudeau's cabinet told me, by "a civil servant who was determined to get the government out of the Indian business."

While Emil Notti, a contemplative Athabasca Indian whose people had been ravaged by tuberculosis, pneumonia and alcohol and who had emerged as perhaps the most universally respected native leader in Alaska, was calling the settlement "unprecedented, but not generous" and musing that "if, only if, the money is well-invested and managed, kids now one and two years old will benefit," thoughtful Canadian natives in Inuvik, Yellowknife, Whitehorse and Old Crow in 1972 could see only the most clouded of futures for their one and two-year-olds. The villagers of Sachs Harbour and Tuktoyaktuk might have been less ready to approve thirty-one out of the thirty-four exploration permits in their country had they possessed a one-tenth part of the political muscle I had witnessed in the Iniupiat Eskimo settlement of Barrow, Alaska's largest municipality and the world's richest Eskimo village. In Barrow, village meetings were planning the people's first land selections and borough councillors were talking about property taxes and pollution laws for the corporations at Prudhoe Bay, which falls within their jurisdiction; at the same time, native brotherhood leaders in Whitehorse and Yellowknife were still seeking recognition of their land claims, their counsel struggling to restrain the incursions of exploration crews onto traplines, social disintegration spreading so swiftly that Nellie Cournoyea, the industrious Inuvik civil rights worker, exclaimed one day that "every other person in town is cracking up!"

However discredited, corrupt and even quasi-criminal American institutions may appear from the outside, they retain a flexibility that has not been attainable in the Canadian North. The Alaska settlement arose out of a singularly American horse trade—at a given moment in history, the oil industry and the native people recognized a common interest in clearing up the issue of land titles. From the first meeting of minds between Hugh Gallagher, a British Petroleum lobbyist with a Byronic zeal for native causes, and Charlie Edwardsen, the north slope Eskimo militant, a campaign was orchestrated that changed the minds of influential senators, representatives, labour leaders and oil men and even harnessed the sympathy of Vice-President Spiro Agnew before the deal was won. This type of lobbying is, certainly, an eminently fallible and corruptible form of political action, but it does provide room for manoeuvre. Between the diverse pressures of oil, conservationists, the state authority, the native people and local business, the American federal authority was obliged to play a role of mediation. In Canada. there is no such obligation. Federal authority has formed a common front with industry in the interests of swift development, and a native brotherhood leader can rarely get to talk to

147

an oil company president. The only friend the native organizations have had has been the northern courts, which issued 1973 restraining orders freezing land transactions in 400,000 square miles of the Northwest Territories. After the Supreme Court of Canada's divided decision in the 1973 Nishga case, which had the effect of strengthening morally the native claims to aboriginal rights, the Trudeau government's intransigence relaxed. But it was then very late, the bitterness very deep. In contrast to the Alaska natives, who had been fully consulted in a legislated settlement, the Canadian brotherhoods, it seemed, could only progress when they appealed to the humane northern courts.

In June, 1973, one of the few representatives of white authority generally respected by the peoples north of sixty was the object of an unprecedented attack by the Trudeau government. It filed with the Federal Court of Canada an application to remove the issue of the frozen land titles from Mr. Justice William Morrow of the Northwest Territories Supreme Court, a living symbol of Canadian justice in the North. Arguing that the question of land title in the Territories was out of his jurisdiction, the Trudeau government wanted the freeze lifted through the use of an Ottawa-based court of equal constitutional standing to Morrow's own. Mr. Justice Morrow reasserted his authority until such time as it was rejected by the Territorial Court of Appeal.

In a twenty-nine-page judgment, Judge Morrow declared the federal move "the first time in the history of Canadian jurisprudence, the first time since Confederation, that one superior court has been placed under attack by another superior court judge of equal status." It was his duty, the northern judge said, "to let the people within my jurisdiction and their Parliament know what is happening, so they will have their judge's side of the story .... The federal government is undoubtedly anxious about these proceedings, having such a substantial property interest in the lands involved—but then, so do the Indians." In the Commons, Flora MacDonald, Conservative critic on Indian affairs, commented that the Trudeau government was attempting to maintain a colonial system in the Territories.

It is this Trudeau-corporate alliance that speaks with condescension of insensitivity in Alaska! One day in Whitehorse, I checked over the Alaska settlement with able James Wah-Shee, twenty-seven-year-old elected leader of 7,000 status Indians in the Northwest Territories. In every particular—in its initial land freeze, in its formula providing land, plus cash, plus a share of royalties for the native people, the Alaska deal provided what he wanted. Because the corporations had already taken the best eighty percent of the land in the Canadian northwest, he felt, royalties would be of paramount importance. One point was very emphatic: "No settlement . . . no pipeline." And, said Wah-Shee, the brotherhood would need twenty months of research before they would be prepared to negotiate. So the Mackenzie line must not be rushed.

Six months later, Wah-Shee was making the same points before the Commons' Northern Affairs Committee. This time he emphasized the urgent need for the federal research grants that must precede negotiation of land claims and said he wanted to "gently explode the great Canadian myth of the northern dream." That dream, he said, was "false because the premise is faulty; Canada does not own the Northwest Territories and no amount of political, economic or resource expedience will move us, the owners of the land, at a pace faster than we are prepared to go." With varying degrees of firmness, non-status groups, still unrecognized as land claimants, were making similar demands. The Inuit, unrecognized by Ottawa, were preparing with Peter A. Cumming of Osgoode Hall Law School, author of the authoritative *Native Rights in Canada*, a sophisticated program that would harness Eskimo skills in land use planning. But Ottawa was painfully slow to move, and another adviser to the Inuit, the University of Toronto geographer Carl Francis, was concluding that even the cartel corporations, having experienced political instability in the Middle East, were becoming more aware than the government about native land claims because "they've no wish to be stopped by the land freeze, or to build a pipeline in the midst of a civil war."

In two important respects, then—royalties and native rights—the monolithic Ottawa-Gas Arctic front, for all its vaunted efficiency, has not performed as well as those who negotiated the Alaska deal. In the long run, even from the narrow standpoint of corporate self-interest, these omissions will hurt the

149

promoters, since they demonstrate that the project offers little to those who live in the North, or to Canada's tax and royalty revenues.

The efficiency of the pipeline consortium, in fact, like that of the men involved in earlier resource deals examined by the Dalhousie Four, has nothing to do with the project's ultimate consequences. It is an efficiency in wheeling, dealing, arm-twisting, and promotion, selling the project to uncritical politicians and getting it licensed so Canadian gas can flow to U.S. markets. Promoters rarely deal with the long view.

Until the spring of 1973, no breach appeared within the federal-corporate alliance promoting the Mackenzie pipeline. Those who opposed the project, almost all of them outside government, did so for a variety of reasons.

Economists such as the former Liberal cabinet minister, Eric Kierans, who planned to lead a specialized commando of interveners at the National Energy Board hearings, felt it would jeopardize Canada's industrial future. The investment of $60 or $70 billion in one decade in huge energy projects would push up the value of the Canadian dollar, rendering our manufactured goods less competitive and increasing our unemployment. The Trudeau government's emphasis on promoting resource sales was, he felt, a national tragedy because it ruled out the possibility of a future as a sophisticated industrial nation, consciously programming resource exploitation to service job-creating manufacturing at home. He considered the pipeline a utility serving corporations that would receive ninety-five percent of the resource wealth extracted, Canada getting five percent. "The wealth," he stressed, "is not the pipeline but the resource itself, and the important thing is to control the resource. The way to do that is to declare all natural gas not yet contracted for export as 'needed for Canada' and then keep it in the ground until we do need it."

There are the physicists who understood the process by which resources are depleted, like Dr. J. Tuzo Wilson, principal of Erindale College at the University of Toronto and a world authority on geophysics. "Surely," he told Canadians in 1972, "a cautious individual would be concerned to husband his resources lest he soon be left without . . . . The only conclusion I can draw from this is that we should sell nothing abroad, but proceed very slowly and cautiously to develop supplies to meet our own needs. This will give us the time to do the research required to find in usable form the other sources of energy that in the life-times of some now living will be absolutely imperative."

There are the political figures such as New Democratic Party leader David Lewis and the former Liberal cabinet minister Walter Gordon.

Walter Gordon expressed the growing doubt of many Canadians that such a vast project in the North could be entrusted to the cartel corporations. The corporations that controlled the prices of oil and natural gas, he argued, should not be conceded control of Canada's Arctic resources. It was not, he said in a speech at Calgary, a matter of private enterprise, the economic system he favoured. Too much of the Canadian economy was already controlled abroad by monopolies and oligopolies and "neither of these . . . can qualify as free enterprise in a truly Canadian sense."

And there are scientists specializing in the North, who stressed repeatedly that we do not have enough knowledge about the ecosystem to justify digging a huge trench in the permafrost and ramming in one million tons of steel piping. The permafrost itself remains something of a mystery. The frozen mix of soil and water is often sealed and insulated by the tundra of slow-growing lichens and moss. When the tundra is ripped away, the ground melts and erosion may ripple through the sub-surface in patterns still not understood. When giant earth-moving machines start to smash through 300 rivers and streams, we do not know what will happen to the land or the freshwater system, to the char, salmon, lake trout and whitefish and twenty-nine other species of fish, to the Canada geese, swans, ducks and endangered whooping cranes and Peregrine falcons, the roaming caribou, the fur-bearing mink and lynx. Where will the fish spawn when Bechtel construction gangs scoop out the riverbed gravel? Where will the Arctic fox den when the earth rumbles under heavy drills? Scientists still do not have the answers.

"We do not have enough basic knowledge to design good management methods and technologies," says Dr. Kenneth Hare of the federal Environment Department. We do not have a wildlife census, says McGill biologist Dr. Max Dunbar. We need ten years to study the natural disturbance a pipeline might cause, says Carleton biologist Dr. John Lambert.

Dr. J. B. Sprague, zoologist at the University of Guelph, summarized the problems in 1972. "Our ignorance of Arctic aquatic systems is profound; the danger of irretrievably destroying natural resources is great; basic ecological research should be completed, and effective management procedures established, before extensive northern development is undertaken. The last aim could be quite reasonably achieved by beefing up ecological research by a factor of something like ten times, and holding off any massive Arctic exploration for something less than a decade."

Law groups, such as the legal working group associated with the Canadian Arctic Resources Committee, expressed concern about the lack of public hearings on such projects as the Mackenzie Highway, pipeline construction guidelines and on land use regulations, and about the absence of monitoring of major projects. The people and the environmentalists were being excluded from pipeline planning.

These critics opposed the Mackenzie project on diverse grounds. Some wanted it stopped, others felt that, under proper control and with unhurried timing, it could benefit Canada. But all agreed that it must not be rushed. None of their arguments impressed the federal-corporate common front. Energy Minister Macdonald wrote to assure U.S. Interior Secretary Rogers Morton that he was getting on with the job, and Energy Board chairman Robert Howland deplored the idea that pipeline-builders should be "compelled to meet standards which entail unrealistically high-cost components."

But, in the spring of 1973, dramatically, the first cracks appeared in the front. The critics found themselves reinforced from the least expected quarter—the federal bureaucracy itself. The leak of two confidential reports to newspapers by civil servants showed that even within the development-oriented federal bureaucracy, the accelerating ripoff in energy resources was fuelling slow-burning resentment. One report, "Canada's Commercial Policy and Energy," was concerned with cheap energy sales to the United States and revealed that the Americans had used trade talks to ask for "a substantial degree of control over fundamental Canadian policies."

Though eighteen months old at the time of the leak, it was an authoritative document, prepared under the supervision of James Grandy, deputy minister of Industry, Trade and Commerce and submitted to Energy Board chairman Robert Howland on November 22, 1971. It warned that United States energy demands would mean a "transfer of control" over Canadian policies to the government in Washington and would lock this country into a subordinate economic relationship with the U.S. that was "unacceptable."

The report, amazingly, echoed the analysis of Eric Kierans. It said Canada was allowing the U.S. to buy Canadian resources too cheaply and was failing to use these resources to develop a strong Canadian economy. It urged a two-price system for these resources—high for U.S. customers, low for Canadian consumers. It wanted "a very high priority" for using indigenous energy resources "as a tool of industrial development in Canada."

Parts of that report sounded like a quotation from the critique made by the Dalhousie Four. "The financial return to Canada on gas and oil exports is significantly below what could be achieved for natural gas and to a lesser extent oil," it said, "because the commodities are being sold to the U.S. at prices below the opportunity price and because of the very high degree of foreign ownership of the Canadian industry."

In addition to charging the highest possible export prices, Canada, the report stressed, should act to "ensure that a larger share of the gains accruing from exploitation of Canada's energy resources are captured by Canada and Canadian interests and not by foreign interests." This "would seem to require increased government intervention."

Without changes in Canadian regulation, the civil servants warned, Canadians would have to pay substantially higher prices for natural gas because of rising U.S. prices. And the prices Canadians paid for oil would increase significantly as a result of strong pressures from Venezuela and the OPEC countries affecting eastern Canada, and the pull of American prices in Ontario and the West. The report charged that the cartel companies supplying oil to Canada "have been charging artificially high transfer prices to reduce taxes paid in Canada and move taxable income to tax havens."

Revealed for the first time was an aggressive new American attitude towards Canadian frontier development displayed by U.S. government negotiators in a November, 1970, briefing to a Canadian trade delegation. The United States, the report says, was requesting "a substantial degree of control over fundamental Canadian policies respecting imports, exports and pipeline movements of Canadian oil." It did not detail how the United States would exercise this control—conceivably it could be by treaty, as on the Columbia River—but it did say that all the Americans offered in return for this quasi-imperial control of the Canadian trading system was a change in the method under which the U.S. controlled its oil imports from Canada. Under the far-reaching economic domination the Americans were seeking, the report noted, "each time Canada wished to extend a pipeline or build a new one, further concessions could be requested by the United States."

It was a prescription for national surrender. It demanded the total absorption of Canadian energy resources into a continental system controlled in the United States.

It is conceivable that the leaking of that report was not entirely displeasing to Energy Minister Donald Macdonald, since its principal recommendation, a two-price system in oil and gas, was an idea the minister himself was beginning to talk up in May of 1973. But there was no doubt of his baffled chagrin over that month's second leak, which he found totally embarrassing because the whole flimsy rationale for his pipeline-now policy was peeled to shreds. This second thoroughgoing report, completed in October, 1972, by a task force of civil service economists under the supervision of the Department of Finance, frontally attacked the pipeline as a project undertaken to service the United States. Its chief recommendation was a throughput tax of ten cents per 1,000 cubic feet of natural gas exported by the pipeline, which would yield Canada some $125 million a year.

Macdonald blustered when that one leaked. It was only, he first claimed, "a very preliminary report." No, he would not publish it. Then he claimed that further confidential studies would negate the conclusions the economists had reached. But the bluster came too late; the damage had been done.

The task force had produced a document of historic portent. Working from terms of reference established by the government policymakers themselves and being therefore privy to project policy requirements that had never been disclosed, the economic mandarins, using sophisticated input-output models, had sifted the consequences of the pipeline in considerable detail and with allowance for a number of significant variables in the economic background projected for the 1970s and 1980s. Having done all this, the government economists reached conclusions substantially consistent with those of such vigorous pipeline critics as Eric Kierans. Their careful and objective projections, informed by the best and most recent data government could provide, were loaded with authority. For the first time, it was possible for Canadians to see the pipeline installed and at work on the national economy.

The Mackenzie Valley pipeline, the mandarins said, "will not make a major long-term contribution to the Canadian economy in terms of employment or personal income." It would be, at best, "a mixed blessing."

Specifically, the mandarins found it necessary to point to these hazards entailed in the project: an increase in the exchange rate of the Canadian dollar that would hurt exporting industries; upward pressures on Canadian energy prices once the northern gas was flowing to its markets in the United States; increases in the costs of interest for other Canadian borrowers; widespread inflation.

In setting out the terms of their assignment, the mandarins indicated the direction they had received from the cabinet policymakers. Their introduction implied two decisions that had not been reported to Canadians. There was, they said, "little doubt" that the gas reserves from the oilfield at Prudhoe Bay on Alaska's Arctic north slope would "move to the American market via a Mackenzie Valley pipeline" and that its availability would be determined by the production schedules of Prudhoe Bay oil, which would itself go to market through the trans-Alaska pipeline and Pacific coast tankers. They were also to assume that "most, if not all, of the natural gas transported by the pipeline will be marketed in the U.S."

Their analysis was to be based upon a number of given assumptions. These included: that the Canadian section of the forty-eight-inch diameter pipe would cost $4.5 billion and would move 1.2 trillion cubic feet per year; that Canadian expenditures on the pipeline corridor—including a highway, transport and communication facilities and government-funded research—would be more than $200 million; that "almost all of the long-term social and environmental costs will be borne by Canadians . . . a disproportionate share of these costs will fall on northerners, many . . . already facing the stresses of converting from their traditional way of life to that of a wage economy"; and that "once an application for the pipeline is approved, control of its timing will largely move out of government hands. At that point it will be difficult if not impossible to adjust the timing to accommodate other major capital projects which may be desirable in the same time frame."

Starting from such assumptions, the mandarins began to measure the pipeline's general economic impact, first for the construction stage, then for the period when it was in operation.

The impact of the construction phase on the Canadian economy would depend on the state of the economy in general. If the nation were enjoying full employment, as some projections have suggested is possible for the late 1970s, "any increase in net incomes will be negligible." Between 5,000 and 6,000 workers would be directly employed each season of the two-to-three-year construction phase and, of course, if the employment levels in the country were high, these workers would simply be drawn away from other jobs. Since the jobs will not last long, "construction . . . could have a destabilizing effect on employment trends in the economy." Requirements for direct labour would be confined to the West and indirect jobs would be created in those industrial centres where employment is high in any case. Impact on the Maritimes could be "negligible" or even "negative" if the pipeline detracted from offshore developments.

If, on the other hand, the Canada of the late 1970s were suffering "massive" unemployment, the pipeline would achieve its maximum impact, affecting 105,000 workers, or one percent of the labour force, in each of four years. In a situation of chronic joblessness, the pipeline could bring important temporary benefits in employment and incomes, though these benefits would create additional problems for the export sector.

Financing the $4.5 billion Canadian portion of the pipe, the mandarins said, would inevitably strain Canadian and world financial markets, especially if it coincided with other large-scale resource projects such as James Bay, pushing up interest rates and inflationary pressures. Increasing demand for the Canadian dollar would result in higher imports and lower exports, and the shift in the balance of trade might be as much as $1.6 billion over the three years of construction. The plight of Canadian exporters would be compounded by further increases in domestic inflation.

If the pipeline were built in a period of full employment it would bring few benefits in jobs and incomes. If it were built at a time of substantial unemployment, it would bring maximum temporary job benefits at a cost of nightmarish problems in the export sector.

Once the pipeline was in operation, it would move $1 billion worth of gas over the U.S. border every year. "Only a small portion of this amount, however, represents incomes to Canadians." Under existing tax arrangements we would collect only $366 million, less than one-quarter of one percent of the nation's potential Gross National Product in 1980. "Even without the pipeline," the mandarins pointed out, "most of this $366 million would have been generated in a fully-employed national economy." Once in place, the automatically-monitored pipeline would create only 150 or 200 permanent jobs. The promoters had talked of 600. The 150 jobs would not necessarily be a net addition to employment.

As for the pipeline's effect on Canada's industrial structure, the mandarins said, "A highly capital-intensive, export-oriented long-term project, by its nature, reduces to some extent the capital available to other more labour-intensive industries elsewhere in the economy. By generating a continuing high demand for Canadian dollars to pay for the pipeline service, it tends to make other Canadian products . . . more expensive for potential foreign customers." The delivery of high-priced northern gas to U.S. markets could lead to "pressure from existing suppliers for higher domestic prices of gas and other energy products." The

157

government should order a study of this impact on Canadian energy prices and slap on a two-price system.

Instead of endorsing the pipeline consortium's self-image of superior efficiency in comparison with developments in Alaska, the mandarins were prepared to learn something from the Alaskan experience. In terms of federal tax revenues "the government cannot expect to receive significant corporate income taxes ... corporations are able to deduct from taxable income an amount substantially greater than the depreciation normally charged .... TransCanada Pipelines Ltd., the largest gas pipeline in Canada, has not paid any income tax since it began operations in 1958." Whereas the state of Alaska would gain $300 million a year from the trans-Alaska pipeline, including a levy for native peoples, Canada could hope for only $73 million in taxes. Of that, $48 million would come not from the pipeline but from withholding taxes on interest and dividends paid to foreign investors.

The pipeline was clearly for United States benefit. Canada, which was to be used as a "land bridge" to the U.S., should get far more than the $50,000-a-year rental proposed for the pipeline right-of-way. A throughput tax of ten cents per 1,000 cubic feet should be imposed.

"For Canada to accept anything less than the maximum possible return," the government task force concluded, "would be to subsidize the U.S. user at the expense of the Canadian taxpayer." That sounds familiar. It is Ian McDougall's critique of the Alberta gas fire sale, blown up to national dimensions.

The two secret reports, considered together, constitute confirmation from some of the best sources in the land of the sell-out critique mounted by Kierans and McDougall in the face of the consortium's smooth promotion and the euphoria of "northern vision rhetoric."

John Helliwell, the University of British Columbia economist conducting the most extensive independent analysis of the project undertaken anywhere in Canada, summed it up neatly for the Commons' Resources Committee. It was his calculation that United States consumers would receive 96.8 percent of the net monetary benefits of the natural gas carried by the Mackenzie pipeline. The Canadian treasury would get 2.3 percent.

With the throughput tax suggested by the mandarins' report, Helliwell said, Canada's share would jump to 26.7 percent.

Dr. Helliwell said his complex, computer-based economic models showed that after the completion of the pipeline there would be a net loss of Canadian jobs because the construction would have attracted workers from existing jobs that would disappear before the pipeline was finished. During the operation of the line, purchases of Canadian gas by U.S. consumers would thrust the Canadian dollar up to $1.04 U.S., making Canadian exports prohibitively expensive in the United States. Over thirty-three years' operation, Dr. Helliwell said, U.S. industry would save $10.8 billion through its purchases of gas from the pipeline.

Using weighted averages, he calculated that seventy-five percent of the permits for Mackenzie Delta gas are owned by American-controlled firms. "The purpose of building the pipeline now," commented New Democrat Tommy Douglas, "is for U.S. companies to sell Canadian gas to U.S. consumers. For Canada it is an economic absurdity."

Social disintegration will be further accelerated under the impact of pipeline construction. Reporting to the government of the Northwest Territories in May, 1973, Pat Carney, a northern consultant generally sympathetic to resource development, predicted rising urban tensions in Inuvik, Fort Simpson, Norman Wells, and other communities. Only construction jobs, she reported, were being created for native people. In a March visit to Painted Mountain, the only producing gasfield in the Territories, she found not one native employed in the operating phase! Welfare rolls and unemployment payments would continue to grow. "In some communities, a sharp escalation in the cost of serviced land is pushing or threatening to push native people out of town."

The development, Pat Carney predicted, will increase alcoholism, sophisticated crime, welfare, social dissension, family breakdown, child neglect and psychiatric problems. "During the transitional phase of the development, racism—as a function of economic discrimination—will increase."

Donald Macdonald, like his Liberal predecessors in another pipeline hassle, is minimizing the role the Canadian Parliament must play in determining the Mackenzie issue. The

National Energy Board Act, he argues, makes that body the proper forum, despite its melancholy conservation record to date. Whatever the forum, there are now too many Canadian interests involved for the country to be stampeded into fast approval. In the anticipated eighteen months of hearings, the economists, geologists and petrochemists, the engineers, worried biologists and wildlife men and the Indian and Eskimo land claimants will, one hopes, all be heard, along with the hamlet councils from Sachs Harbour and Tuk.

The pincer squeeze is tight now. Searching for oil in the Canadian frontier regions may be, F. K. North has suggested, an economic gamble. But it is a gamble the cartel corporations can easily afford—they are doing the same thing in at least fifty nations. And they are confident that they will get, at least, Canadian natural gas, the gas that will save American industry $10 billion and earn the cartel many billions of dollars in due profits.

For Canada, the process of economic takeover has assumed a character of finality with the Mackenzie pipeline proposal. NAWAPA was a poor, bungled foray in contrast. Today all the projects reviewed by the Dalhousie Four appear as but a curtain-raiser to the formidable emplacement of cartel corporations on the Canadian frontier. And in Washington, as the leaked disclosures of 1970 showed, the political power stands ready to assume control of Canadian resources. The continental energy pool in resources, which was once only an idea, is becoming an economic reality.

Chapter Eight

The Last Wild River

"The Churchill is our last great wild river."

— Gerald Malaher, former director,
Manitoba Wildlife Branch.

One afternoon in the strangely balmy March of 1973, Dr.
Robert W. Newbury sat among stacked files and photographs
in his cluttered basement office at the University of Manitoba,
wondering if they would be seized by men with a warrant from
Sidney Green.

Newbury is a Canadian authority on the special science of
shorelines. The photographs showed reservoirs, rivers and dams.
An unruffled giant in open shirt and blue jeans, Newbury, you
feel, is not a man who would easily panic.

But he was under great pressure that afternoon. For more
than a year he had led a federal-provincial task force studying the
environmental effects of diverting the Churchill River through
Southern Indian Lake into the Nelson. Suddenly Green, the
provincial minister of Mines, had announced that Newbury's
task force was to be wound up. Green had received, but not
yet read, an interim report on the group's progress over one
year. Because Newbury had publicly criticized the diversion
plan, his report Green said, would be "subjective." So the shore
study would be completed as an "in-house" job within the
Mines Department. The geologists and engineers working for
Newbury were asked to carry on, but declined. They didn't
think the in-house study would be serious work.

Now Green wanted the data amassed by Newbury while
Manitoba was helping fund the study. It was a tall order.

Shorelines had been his career. He'd studied them for his doctoral thesis, Canada's geological survey, two royal commissions. How, now, could he isolate from his lifework that segment owing its existence to funds authorized by Sidney Green? And why did Green want it?

The answer to that lies close to the heart of Manitoba's Churchill-Nelson controversy. Diversion supporters say switching 20 million acre feet of Churchill water 250 miles across northern Manitoba into the roughly parallel course of the Nelson will assure the province's electricity supply. Critics say the scheme will destroy the Churchill, ruin the fishing-trapping economy of 3,000 natives and create irreparable environmental damage.

But scientists didn't know enough about what happens to the natural systems of rivers jerked out of their courses and impounded lakes to make a conclusive assessment. If you flushed twelve feet of Churchill water on top of Southern Indian Lake, as Ed Schreyer's New Democratic Party government proposed, how long would nature take to re-establish a balanced system? A year? A decade? Many decades?

Newbury and his fifteen-man team of geologists and engineers addressed themselves to that. From spring, 1972, they examined and classified sixteen shorelines involved in dams and diversions in the region of the Canadian Shield. They observed, calculated and classified the rates of natural recovery and devised an entirely new system of measurement. In the second year of the study, they would apply the system to the Churchill, Southern Indian Lake and the Rat and Burntwood rivers, tributaries that would carry Churchill water south from the lake to the mainstem Nelson. This is the job they were not allowed to finish.

The first year had produced startling results. When Newbury's findings from the sixteen projects were applied to the Churchill, the case for diversion would be significantly—even conclusively—weakened.

Contrast these two statements. In 1970 the Manitoba Hydro task force recommending the Churchill diversion said of Southern Indian Lake: "It may take from ten to twenty years or more to establish new equilibrium conditions in the reservoir when the water level is considerably raised. This is the time required to establish new shorelines and new equilibrium for the living species." That March afternoon, Newbury said: "We found a yardstick for measuring the physical impact of such projects. Our data shows that shores of projects undertaken fifty years ago have barely begun to readjust. These projects have a legacy many times Hydro's planning horizon of twenty years. At the small Ogoki diversion into Lake Nipigon, undertaken by Ontario Hydro during the war, the river is still thrusting an endless stream of silt into the lakebed. The Ogoki diverted 3,000 cubic feet per second for twelve miles. Manitoba Hydro proposes to divert 30,000 cubic feet per second for 250 miles. And that shore is permafrost! I can guarantee it will be a century at least before there are stable conditions again."

Hydro's twenty-year claim was supported only by the engineering assumptions of the day. Newbury's projection of one hundred years was based on a year of careful fieldwork. The research Green killed was original work, following no established procedures. It produced a scientific method new in the world. The phlegmatic Newbury threw up his hands. "My God," he said, "I didn't know myself exactly how we'd finish it."

Axing that study was not Green's first attempt to choke debate on the Churchill. He had already silenced the Manitoba Water Commission, set up in 1969 as a watchdog on water development. Before long Hydro chairman David Cass-Beggs was refusing information to the commission; Green was rejecting Newbury's request to subpoena witnesses at formal hearings. Newbury quit. His university colleague, Professor Cass Booy, settled for information meetings. "If you keep on asking for hearings, the commission won't even hold public meetings," Green warned him.

Booy compromised, hoping, he says, the commission could act as an honest broker between Hydro and the public. But the public meetings proved only an exercise in governmental public relations. Green revised the terms of reference, permitting the commission only to "facilitate the implementation of government policy already decided upon." In October, 1971, he fired Booy. "Oh, it was brutally done," says Booy. "Green was absolutely ruthless about it. I heard it on the radio before he phoned to tell me."

There was no forum for debate. Even the Legislature was denied a root-and-branch discussion. When the Clean Environment Commission registered unanimous dissent, Green told them it "wouldn't make a goddammned bit of difference," and it didn't. Legal aid for the native victims of the diversion, set up by the former government, was now cut off.

Green never did seize Newbury's files. But he had, earlier, suppressed critical letters, or quoted them out of context. In 1971 he interpreted a water commission letter as "approval in principle" of low-level flooding, ignoring its qualifying rider that "this must not be interpreted as meaning we agree that there should be any flooding. That decision is only to be made at the conclusion of the required studies."

But the studies were never concluded. Soon after Green licensed the diversion project in December, 1972, lawyers acting for the people of South Indian Lake filed with the Manitoba Court of Queen's Bench an application for an injunction to delay the project on the very grounds that the facts were not in.

Sidney Green, a city lawyer still popularly identified with "socialist" ideas, a nimble sophist in debate and relentless in-fighter behind the scenes, was proving the ablest and toughest front man Hydro ever had. But his manoeuvres were only a chapter in the Churchill story, which has haunted Manitoba politics since the early sixties.

An observer preoccupied with the notion of retributive justice might almost imagine that the great river itself was fighting back, casting some primeval curse on men who would tamper with its natural harmony. The Churchill has marred careers. It hurried Walter Weir, the smalltown undertaker who succeeded Duff Roblin as Conservative premier, to political oblivion. It sent Kris Kristjanson, Manitoba's pioneer hydro developer, to premature professional exile. It exposed the contempt for public opinion manifest in Hydro chairman David Cass-Beggs. And it cast in shadow those humane and rational qualities in Ed Schreyer that, in 1969, had seemed to promise a new openness in Manitoba's government.

If the Churchill could diminish its adversaries, it can also enhance its friends. Robert Newbury, at least, made creative use of provincial monies. His discovery that the laying-waste of Southern Indian Lake will last one hundred years cannot ever be lost. From it has sprung an idea equal to some of the Churchill's grandeur, an idea that will be applied elsewhere. "I think," Newbury says now, "we shall move from these findings to new design criteria. Hydro projects have always concentrated destructive energy, instead of distributing the forces of readjustment. If, with cascade dams and other devices, we can work out energy re-distribution in a natural harmony, we may be able to develop design criteria that will have environmental thinking built in."

Walter Weir's government had not been much concerned with harmonies. It wanted to flood Southern Indian Lake to a depth of thirty-five feet, an unpopular decision that contributed to the NDP's surprise victory in 1969: Schreyer had promised he would flood no more than twelve feet.

Even then, the economic case for the Churchill diversion —and it is real—had become an article of faith with the officials of the publicly-owned Manitoba Hydro. Their long-term plan was to plug the Nelson with a string of dams. Pouring the Churchill's waters into the Nelson, they learned, would increase the Nelson's potential by one third. For them, that was reason enough.

The Churchill and Nelson dominate northern Manitoba, their watersheds covering half a million square miles. The Nelson, which flows from the eastern slope of the Rockies across the prairies to Hudson Bay, has a watershed four times larger than that of the northerly Churchill; all streams entering Lake Winnipeg contribute to the Nelson's flow. It is rapidly becoming a controlled river, punctuated by dams and timber-clogged reservoirs. The Churchill remains wild and clean.

Manitoba's demand for power, rising even faster than the seven percent per year projected by Hydro, is greatest in wintertime, when the Nelson's flow is low. The Churchill diversion, engineers say, will meet the winter peak demands of the early 1990s. The Nelson dams alone would provide enough until 1990. But if the Churchill is plugged into the Nelson, adding 1,900 megawatts to the system, the province's $3 billion development program will meet the needs until 1994. Four years will have been gained before alternative sources of power must be introduced.

Considering economics alone, it sounds a reasonable proposition. The entire Nelson River development, with five major dams costing an average $500 million, the Churchill diversion and the regulation of Lake Winnipeg, is a $3 billion program. The diversion itself is expected to cost a mere $109 million. In the swiftly-rising cost projections for the Nelson program, the Churchill diversion appears as a minor item. That does not imply that the program is a sound one. In his definitive cost-benefit analysis prepared in 1970, the Michigan resource economist Gunter Schramm pointed out that hydro construction costs were soaring at the very time thermal power plants were becoming markedly more efficient. Declared Schramm: "What we can conclude with some confidence, and what Manitoba's power planners should have concluded in 1966, is that the capital costs of new hydroplants will gradually rise, while those of thermal plants will have an overall tendency to fall or remain constant, if moderate inflationary pressures continue."

Even in 1966, concluded Schramm, the Nelson project was "a much less attractive development than available alternatives." He quoted a former Manitoba Hydro chairman: "Hillary was asked, 'Why did you climb Mount Everest?' He answered, 'Because it was there. The Nelson has dared us to harness it.' You and I? We have accepted that dare? As a justification of the project," commented Schramm, "perhaps that is all there is to say."

Manitoba's projections ascribed no dollar value to the Churchill, Rat and Burntwood rivers or to Southern Indian Lake. They did not measure the resource losses of the region's Indian people. Unsurprisingly, then, their projected balance sheets looked like clear gain.

But Schreyer and Green introduced an inconsistency. When elected, they denied that economic aspects could be considered alone. They also denied that the people of South Indian Lake should be flooded out of their homes. Their decision to allow no more than twelve feet of flooding complicated both the economics and the engineering. It is now seen necessary to add a costly program of regulating Lake Winnipeg to the Churchill diversion. Instead of storing water for winter release to the Nelson in Southern Indian Lake, they will store it in Lake Winnipeg. Cost estimates leap with every survey. With $60 million in contracts already let, Hydro says the work on Lake Winnipeg has passed the point of no return.

Green, ironically, justifies his drive for "low-level" flooding at Southern Indian Lake as a thoroughly reasonable, Schreyer-esque compromise. But the compromise carries little conviction. If diversion is really the golden key to Manitoba's future Hydro propagandists claim it is, then, surely, the Conservatives were right and it should be done the way Kris Kristjanson, a no-nonsense developer in the nineteenth century mould, always wanted it done—at least cost and greatest depth.

The debate, so far, has scarcely considered the Churchill itself, which few Manitobans know. Gerald Malaher, who built the province's Wildlife Service, is one of the few. Forty years ago he snowshoed after beaver poachers by its placid lakes and racing rapids. A passionate, almost spiritual outdoorsman now confined to cities by the frailties of his years, Malaher trembles in his outrage when he contemplates the destruction of the wild river.

What Newbury has tried to measure, Malaher has experi-enced—the teeming life of the Canada goose nesting grounds, the estuary's beluga and seal, the sense of an ageless human presence in 180 archeological sites, the self-renewing fish and fur economy of the native people he knows and respects. The undeveloped, unpolluted Churchill is Malaher's natural world. His canoe has nosed through miles of its backwaters and lakes.

The writer Sigurd Olson, who led some of the canoe expedi-tions of the famous Voyageurs' group including Pierre Elliott Trudeau and the late Blair Fraser, spoke of the Churchill, in a note to Malaher, as "one of the most beautiful regions of Canada . . . usable, accessible, its waters warm compared to the frigid rivers and lakes of the far North. Fishing is excellent and there is much wildlife . . . . If the South Indian project is abandoned, future generations will bless the vision of the deci-sion-makers of today."

The region's fascination for the outdoorsman and a recent road link south suggest to Malaher an altogether different future for the Churchill—as an increasingly accessible recreational haven, developing alongside the mines and the self-reliant native community of South Indian Lake. Of 3,000 Indians affected by the diversion, the 600 at South Indian Lake, descendants of the most aggressive hunters from the reserve at Nelson House who ranged far in search of hunting grounds, will be the worst hit.

"They're people," says Malaher, "who don't know what social assistance is." Newbury calls theirs "incomparably the finest native community in the province." They use aircraft, a modern system of registered traplines and cooperative marketing. In the year ending April, 1972, South Indian Lake Co-op Fisheries Ltd. grossed half a million dollars from the sale of whitefish, equipment and supplies. The seventy families were averaging $4,000 incomes from fishing and trapping. Investments in equipment of the 131 members ranged between $15,000 and $20,000. These people spurned government offers of cash "compensation" and opted to fight for survival through the courts.

Long before Newbury's dismissal, it was known that Southern Indian Lake was scheduled for ruin. Earlier studies had effectively visualized the diversion's impact on the Churchill, the lake itself, the Rat and Burntwood, despite the environmental pretensions of Hydro propagandists.

The Churchill will choke at Missi Falls, 250 miles from the rivermouth on Hudson Bay. When the river is at its summer peak, only about one-seventh of its natural flow will seep down the spillways into the old riverbed. The rest of the year, only local drainage will trickle in. The flow to the old channel cannot be increased to much more than one-seventh of the natural rate of 35,000 cubic feet per second because Hydro's license will not permit fluctuations of more than two feet in the reservoir created behind Missi dam.

Attenuated flows dribbling into the lower Churchill's broad channel will spread thinly over the bottom. In winter it will be a thin sheet of ice. The pattern of small summer flood and winter freeze-up will never allow the emasculated river to carve a smaller channel to match its reduced flow. And the dam will end the scouring renewal that comes with spring breakup.

Naturally, the surging spring current thrusts ice over the banks, stimulating the growth of young vegetation. With this young vegetation, the nesting Canada goose nurtures its young. What will happen in northern Manitoba's largest nesting grounds cannot be predicted. The impact on the whales and seals breeding in the estuary and on the water chemistry of Hudson Bay is also uncertain. What effect the combined changes in spring breakup from the Churchill and James Bay projects will have on Canada's weather system has not been gauged.

The upstream Churchill, recoiling from the dam wall at Missi, will swoosh into Southern Indian Lake, raising its level twelve feet and swelling its area by one-eighth. The South Indian Lake village, though not inundated, will be sliced in two, the natives obliged to move to higher ground.

Their concern will be economic survival. In the first year after diversion, scientists agree, the fish will be fat. Inflowing nutrients from the Churchill system will enrich, temporarily, the chain of life.

Then the cycle of ruin will begin. The Churchill's current will slash into the lake's 300-mile shoreline and its mixture of clay and permafrost will start dissolving in the water's rush. Ninety percent of that shore is permafrost and clay. All summer it will melt in the brown waters. Crumbling soil, tree trunks, floating islands of peat moss and churning debris will turn the water to thick brown soup. In late fall, this oozy sea will freeze. At next spring's breakup, new debris will make it more turbid still.

Whitefish will die, denied the shallows over sandy gravel in which they spawn. The beavers' sturdy lodges, half below the old surface level, will be swamped. The moose population will be trimmed by drastic changes in the shoreline vegetation.

The desolation does not end at Southern Indian Lake. It sweeps on into the Rat and Burntwood. For 200 miles after it has left the reservoir, the Churchill's flow will thrust itself between their banks, grotesquely swelling their levels. The Rat, which normally carries 3,000 cubic feet per second, will be assaulted by ten times that flow. The current will tear earth from 200 miles of new banks like a horsehair comb, building up silt and debris to be spewed through the Burntwood into the mainstem Nelson, no longer a river so much as a Hydro sluiceway.

There's no assurance Hydro's push will end with the Nelson and Churchill. Given the geometric growth of its demand curve and its projection that the Churchill adds only four years to Nelson power, Hydro may reach farther into the unspoiled

North. Only the Seal River system remains, draining most of the province north of Southern Indian Lake. Hydro's 1970 task force said, "It has been pointed out that ultimately a diversion of the Seal River . . . might be used to compensate for reductions in the available flow from the Churchill."

"If they go for the Seal," says Gerald Malaher, "they'll have to flood many times more land, they'll have to create a stretch of water reaching more than 300 miles from Nelson House to the Territories."

But why should they go for the Seal? Why should Ed Schreyer's stolidly reformist administration be indulging in a kamikaze rush for remote northern bridgeheads? What weird dynamism impels such developmental adventures? They are entirely out of character with Schreyer's generally cautious approach to political change and economic development. Schreyer, after all, is no glib promoter in the mould of a Bennett or Bourassa. He is, on the contrary, one of Canada's more attractive political leaders, a working premier of considerable concentration and resilience, a pragmatic gradualist of modest demeanour who would not promise a great deal but would deliver all he had promised. Schreyer strode confidently into the election campaign he had called for June, 1973, as he was entitled to do, since most of his NDP government's programs had been generally considered successful—except for the Churchill diversion.

A provincial leader who is capable and also possesses the inherent good taste and political discretion to avoid extravagant claims is clearly well-equipped to win people's trust. This is Schreyer's strength. Once I questioned him about a complex series of taxation changes that had the net result of adding $22.40 to the annual income of a father of four earning $10,000. Wasn't that a pretty limited rate of social progress? Schreyer's response I found both forthright and chastening. "The pace," he said, "does not disturb me. I admit it is slow and gradual. But as long as it is manifest, as long as there is no movement towards an aggravation of the inequalities, I am not disturbed. The changes we have made have brought improvement in degree but not in kind. Operating as a province in the context of a nation makes it difficult to make fundamental changes. You really have to make those changes at the national level;

otherwise you will have a province functioning out of proportion. It is extremely limited."

At the time it struck me as a posture of admirable sanity, as did his freely-stated reservations about the process of growth, his preference that Winnipeg remain small rather than swell cancerously into a second Chicago, and that the north burgeon slowly rather than be scarred by rip-and-run developers. None of this appears, at first sight, consistent with Schreyer's involvement in the Churchill disaster, which some of his political critics believe results from the successive pressures of David Cass-Beggs, Sidney Green and zealous developers in the Hydro bureaucracy.

My own view is simpler than that. It is that Schreyer's keen sense of the limited possibilities of provincial power has inhibited him from imposing a political judgment against the supposedly expert opinions of Hydro's engineers and economists. That would not be uncharacteristic. In Schreyer's four-year-term he was confronted with only two opportunities for decision-making that verged upon fundamental change. One such decision would have been to kill the Churchill project. Another would have been to have adopted a set of proposals advanced by the former Liberal cabinet minister Eric Kierans that would have ended the ripoff in Manitoba's north by giant mining corporations. In both instances Schreyer, in keeping with his modest view of the limitations of provincial power, refrained from effecting any major change. The result, on the Churchill, is a compromise that satisfies no one. Instead of drowning the houses of South Indian Lake, the premier will bring water up to their doors. Comparing his mode of destroying the Churchill with that proposed by the former Conservative government, he can congratulate himself with the achievement of "an improvement in degree."

Manitoba Hydro, fiercely committed to the diversion, continues to frighten people with threats of rationing and brown-outs and does not appear ready to consider the competitive costs of nuclear generation. Historically the province has drawn cheap power from the water resources that today provide ninety-five percent of its electricity. Before the nuclear period, it had no easy access to other energy sources and, while neighbouring Saskatchewan moved into thermal generation and

Ontario into nuclear power, Manitoba remained locked in dispute about various hydro-electric options, a hangover from the period when there were always new rivers to dam and remote lakes to flood.

But the diversion project could have been stopped. Sidney Green licensed the diversion before receiving the required permit from the federal Transport minister. Ottawa's jurisdiction over navigable waters, the environment, native peoples and migratory birds provided openings for federal intervention—had there been the will to intervene. Manitoba could have joined Saskatchewan in developing a mixed thermal-and-hydro system to serve both provinces. A more committed, popular provincial government could have challenged frontally Hydro's growth doctrines, promotion and rate structure.

These opportunities were lost. And the American energy shortage added a new urgency. Speculation about the Seal is not prompted solely by internal planning. American money is needed for the $3 billion Nelson program, American appetite for Canadian energy is growing and neighbouring Minnesota's nuclear program is having troubles. "The Americans," says Malaher, "are not going to be satisfied with seasonal exchanges of power. They're going to want firm, long-term contracts to buy Nelson power."

Talk of a secret export deal was a recurring theme in Winnipeg before the June election campaign. Liberal leader Izzy Asper, shopping for a vote-winning program, accused Schreyer of deception, telling the people the Nelson development was needed for the province's needs while negotiating "massive" power sales to the U.S. If Manitoba planned to sell to Minnesota for fifteen years, Asper warned, it should not reckon on ever getting it back from such a "power-thirsty" nation.

Asper was talking about direct energy sellouts. There is another kind. It stems from the assumption that increasing hydro consumption and rising living standards are the same thing—a proposition disproved by Canada's postwar history. The assumption, nonetheless, leads utilities to promote sales very aggressively. Ignoring environmental costs, they promote new uses for their product—neon signs, twenty-four-hour office lighting, heated pools, electric shoeshiners and electric toothbrushes. One part of the Hydro propaganda promotes such

172

gadgetry. Another part scares the customers with threats of future "brownouts" if hundreds of millions are not invested in dams and diversions.

If promotion fosters artificial demand, so does the rate structure. A manufacturer, using thousands of times more electricity than a householder, buys it much more cheaply. If the first kilowatts cost him four cents, a doubling in his consumption will bring a two-cent price and another doubling will cut it to one cent. He gets his electricity wholesale.

Most rate structures are calculated in such a way that the tertiary (cheapest) rate per kilowatt is slightly higher than the cost of fuel used in thermal generation. Though Manitoba has no thermal power, its structure still follows the pattern of thermal economies. "Incredibly," says George Bowman, chairman of the Manitoba Energy Council, "nobody has examined how much these factors are responsible for the seven percent annual load growth assumed to be necessary here." As the rate is currently structured, "the more electricity industry uses, the more the rest of us have to pay for it."

This brings us back to the Dalhousie Four. They gave the Churchill diversion star billing in their national critique of bungled energy deals. It was, they argued, undertaken for a short-run saving—four years. It was pushed on provincial initiative, without regard to the environment, the native peoples, other provinces or the national economy. It was undertaken, at least in part, to service U.S. industry. Ottawa's involvement was "unimposing." The only possible short-run beneficiaries were citizens of southern Manitoba and the United States.

Even that is doubtful. Consider an elderly Winnipeg homeowner who married at the end of World War I. Using most electricity when his children were young, he was paying for the construction of small power stations along the Winnipeg River, the oldest dams in the system, now producing the cheapest power. But each new station makes electricity more expensive. His children married now, the homeowner is using less power; but he helped pay for the big dam at Kettle Rapids. And now he is required to help pay for the Churchill River diversion.

This old Winnipeger already subsidizes Manitoba industry, preponderantly the branch plants of American corporations: Winnipeg, after all, is the prototypical branch-plant city. By contributing to the Churchill scheme, he will assure industry of adequate power supplies for part of the 1990s.

Whether that power subsidizes the branch plants in Manitoba, through the rate structure, or flows directly to the parent corporations in the U.S., through exports, will be of scant concern to him.

The foreign-owned corporations will be the largest beneficiaries. And when, in 1994, the Churchill-Nelson system is insufficient to sustain Hydro's magic load curve, that old man's son may be required to pay for the diversion of the Seal, or the costly transition to a more contemporary system of power generation. That son and succeeding generations will never see the wild Churchill River.

This is why Ian McDougall made this long-range assessment: "One of Canada's greatest potential recreation areas is being foreclosed. One of its finest native communities is being destroyed. This project is an enormous rape."

The Churchill diversion is a sellout primarily engineered, promoted and realized by Canadians themselves. The captains of U.S. industry did not even have to ask that Manitoba's last wild river should be destroyed in their service.

Chapter Nine

James Bay

"They gave me some sugar and some tea and told me they were going to build an airstrip in my section."

— Indian trapper Philip Cox.

A study of large-scale resource development is not a reassuring exercise for those who believe in Canadian democracy. My record so far has shown a pattern of complicity between energy corporations and governments. The public is rarely involved in the big decisions relating to energy. Communication between the promoters of a project and its victims is fragile at the best. At the worst, which is exemplified by the James Bay hydro-electric project, there is virtually no communication at all. This project attains non-communication in the ultimate degree, a condition we can illustrate by considering three of the individuals touched by the development, the Indian trapper Philip Cox, the Quebec politician Robert Bourassa and the businessman Pierre Nadeau.

Philip Cox is a Fort George Cree, fiftyish but lean and supple. He has been a trapper all his life and his profile is a weathered prow, his steady eyes a stoic window on years of solitary endurance at the northern limits of the boreal forest and there is in his demeanour that reserve, that self-containedness, often seen in self-reliant men who have survived by surmounting ordeals.

One September morning in 1971, as Philip Cox strode through his huge trapping section from Duncan Lake towards the south bank of the La Grande River, he came across a survey gang from Hydro-Quebec. They were young technicians and they hailed him in a friendly way. "They gave me some sugar and some tea and told me they were going to build an airstrip in my section."

Philip Cox, characteristically enough, did not remonstrate with the gang. His reaction, as he moved on towards the river, was one of incredulity. Once before white men—mineral prospectors from Toronto—had demonstrated an interest in the section of bush that had been worked by his family for more than a century. Nothing had come of it. It was only later, talking it over with neighbours in the inland village of Fort George, that he learned that Hydro-Quebec wanted that airstrip to service construction of the 450-foot LG-2 dam, which was to be the key installation of the entire James Bay project. Officially, no one consulted Cox. He received no letter from the provincial government, from Hydro-Quebec or the James Bay Development Corporation. No compensation was offered.

Months later, Cox and I squatted by the big black stove in his windowless home in Fort George, his children coughing and stirring under thick blankets, while he showed me a cheque for $650 from the Hudson's Bay Company. That was the price of thirty-eight beaver skins taken from his trapline in the winter of 1971–72. That season had also brought him twenty lynx, the best of which sold at $45 the skin.

Cox smoothed a crumpled map over the linoleum floor to show me his section, a huge tract between Duncan Lake and La Grande that was marked with a thick blue line. He had learned as a boy that the section had been in his family more than a hundred years and, in his mind at least, their "right" to it had received official sanction in the thirties. After a period in which the beaver population had been dangerously reduced by over-trapping, the provincial government had reopened trapping on a quota system after consulting Indian families and including their traditional sections on official charts.

On Cox's map, there was a large X near Duncan Lake. "That," he explained, "is where my grandfather died. He had been starving that winter. He walked out of his trapping camp to hunt in the bush one morning and he never came back." Cox paused. "I know what it's like. I have starved out there myself." We squatted through a silence, as if Cox were alone, enduring again the ordeal in the bush near Duncan Lake.

Robert Bourassa is a thin, bespectacled, sleek-haired politician whose most engaging attribute in his late thirties remained his ability to project an impression of perpetual boyishness. Endowed with a crafty intelligence, a Harvard training in economics and excellent family connections in the business establishment of Quebec, he demonstrated as Liberal premier of his province an opportunist's facility for cutting corners with the truth. Elected in 1970 with the help of the skilled political manipulator Paul Desrochers and the entirely spurious promise of creating 100,000 jobs, Bourassa found himself losing credibility within one year of taking office. In the spring of 1971 Quebec's unemployment rolls were still rising, as were separatist sentiment and the terrorist activity of the FLQ. It was then that Bourassa hastily ordered the officials of Hydro-Quebec to dust off an old scheme to harness the rivers flowing into the east of James Bay for power generation, a scheme that had been rejected by Rene Levesque as Natural Resources minister in the earlier Liberal regime of Jean Lesage.

Bourassa's jerky rhetorical style is, at the best of times, strangely suggestive of a spindly doll manipulated by some unseen puppeteer high over the rostrum and the extravaganza of April 29, 1971, in the Quebec Coliseum was, in fact, the most flamboyant manipulation of Paul Desrochers' eventful career. April 29 was the first anniversary of Bourassa's assumption of power, and as he gesticulated before a partisan audience of 5,000 cheering Liberals the young premier was striving to recover the strong man image that had been eroded in the FLQ crisis, in which he had appeared so indecisive while the repressive sentiments in the country had been so effectively harnessed by his Liberal big brother in Ottawa, Pierre Trudeau.

When the auditorium darkened at Desrochers' signal and Quebec actor Roland Chenail shouted that "The world starts today," rockets, missiles, jets and giant turbines flashed across the wide screen. Chenail's voice declaimed in hyperboles the coming adventure of James Bay: enough electricity to "solve" the energy crisis of the northeastern United States, five, perhaps seven, great rivers dammed; sixty miles of dikes, ten mammoth dams, eleven generating stations or more, 500 miles of northern roads, 20 million cubic yards of rock blasted out of place, huge new lakes, airports, a seaport on James Bay, 125,000 jobs for unemployed Quebeckers! The audience of hypnotized Liberals let out a visceral roar.

Bourassa rose, thin shoulders twitching. He quoted a letter he said he had just received from Hydro-Quebec President Roland Giroux: "Hydro-Quebec recommends to the government of Quebec that the project for the hydro-electric development of James Bay be undertaken without delay." It was, shouted the frail young premier in the spotlights, a turning point in history! It was the project of the century! It was the beginning of "the economic liberation of the Québécois!" The mesmerized Liberals cheered again.

It was, at that point in history, a daring fantasy. Bourassa, Desrochers, even Hydro-Quebec's technicians then knew virtually nothing of the James Bay rivers. The premier talked that day of reordering the systems of five great rivers and their tributaries and generating 14,000 megawatts at a development cost of $6 billion.

They were talking of country that was virtually unknown; and what was known offered little to encourage the hydro engineer. There were really two parts to the scheme. One involved the Nottaway, Broadback and Rupert (NBR), the three river systems flowing into the southern bulge of James Bay. The Nottaway and Broadback, said Bourassa, would be blocked in their courses, their waters funnelled through lakes and canals into the Rupert, where a ladder of power stations would be constructed.

The skimpy research that Hydro had completed was centred on the marshes, shallow lakes and swamplands around NBR. It seemed improbable country for building hydro dams, which call for considerable "head"—fall in the level of a river—and a base of solid rock. Early in the NBR phase, Ottawa contractor Terry Godsall, who had supplied heavy equipment for surveys and dams at Hydro's earlier Churchill Falls project, decided the thing was impossible and pulled out. "Hydro was attempting an engineering impossibility," he said later. "They were drilling in quicksand. They just weren't hitting solid rock."

About the rivers farther north—the Eastmain, La Grande, Great Whale and Caniapiscau—Hydro knew nothing. They flowed through uncharted wilderness. The country they covered was 500 to 1,000 miles north of Montreal. But it seemed probable they had a greater potential for power generation than the slow-falling southern rivers and, in May, 1972, Bourassa told the National Assembly that La Grande would be the focus of the first development on James Bay. The Great Whale and the Caniapiscau, plus a tributary of the Eastmain, would be engineered into La Grande in a scheme to generate 8,000 megawatts at a development cost of about $5.8 billion.

Northwest Quebec had never been white man's country. For hundreds of years before Henry Hudson sailed into James Bay in 1611 the bush had belonged to a few thousand scattered Cree Indians who lived from hunting and trapping, the bleak tundra of the Ungava peninsula to a few Eskimo settlements. Yet Bourassa's Bill 50, establishing the James Bay Development Corporation, made only passing reference to the native population. The project began before any real consultation. When Indians complained that the land and the animals that provided their subsistence were to be destroyed, they received from corporation officials what Lionel Chevrier, the old Liberal politician appointed by Bourassa as head of a "negotiating committee," would later admit was "a runaround." It was not until October 25, 1972, that Indian and Eskimo leaders got as far as the premier's office.

That was a revealing encounter. Bourassa, flustered because meeting the natives was delaying a scheduled lunch-hour cabinet meeting in his office, was cold and hasty. He answered the eloquent pleas of leaders who argued the project would destroy their way of life with the remark that "this is not a special situation for you." All over the province, he said, "when we build roads or highways, we have land which is expropriated because this is a public service."

Eskimo Thomasie Kudluk told Bourassa, "We, the Inuit, depend on the wildlife, animals that breathe and smell .... You are destroying my land. You are destroying my wildlife that I depend on for food. What would you think if I went down to your land and destroyed your garden where you grow your vegetables and your food? If I destroyed even a little garden, what would happen to me? Now you are coming up to my land and destroying everything. We do not want our land destroyed .... We have many children growing up now .... We want them to know the wildlife as we have known it ...." The premier interrupted that he was due at another meeting. As the natives were shepherded out, an old Eskimo said, "If I do something wrong up north, I am sent to jail in the south. The premier did something wrong here today and he should be put in jail in the north."

In the months that followed, Bourassa demonstrated that it would take more than the fears of natives to dim his extravagant zest for the project of the century. In July, 1973, just two years after the passage of Bill 50, the premier found, on his fortieth birthday, the "opportune moment" to visit the James Bay country for the first time. He flew to the site of LG-2 and shook hands with the dam workers in what Canadian Press called "almost election campaign style." He described the project as "the new frontier for modern Quebec," but he did not meet Philip Cox. Between the premier and the Indian trapper, lines of communication did not exist.

Pierre Nadeau was granted but a brief tenancy of his precarious niche in Quebec's history. But though he is a virtually forgotten man today, his swift rise and fall reveals something of the dynamics of a hastily-improvised resource development.

Nadeau was the vice-president of a loan company and a relatively inconspicuous figure in Quebec's self-made business elite when he received a pressing invitation to Robert Bourassa's hotel suite in Montreal. There, the premier urged Nadeau to take over the management of the James Bay project. In the spring of 1972 Nadeau was comfortably installed in the broad-loomed Montreal command post of the president of the James Bay Development Corporation—a lean, craggily handsome, forty-seven-year-old tennis buff with the powers of a colonial governor over a territory two-thirds the size of France. Urbanely receiving visitors, he apparently saw nothing incongruous in his appointment; when asked if he had visited the James Bay bush, he would readily concede that he had not.

His appointment, which had not been universally popular, soon triggered a power struggle within the Quebec bureaucracy. Nadeau faced a powerful antagonist in the provincially-owned power utility, Hydro-Quebec. Since the years of Jean Lesage's quiet revolution, in which private power companies were nationalized, Hydro had become a mighty institution. It was the biggest French-language employer in Quebec and the pride of the nationalist-minded technocrats who had been attracted to Lesage and his Resources minister, Rene Levesque. A song by chansonier Georges Dor had popularized the dam-building at La Manic and, for many, Hydro had become a symbol of modern Quebec achievement; Levesque's personal popularity in Hydro had survived his switch in allegiance to the separatist movement. Self-confident and expansive, the utility inevitably had its detractors, including some who were close to the premier. They complained that Hydro was not sufficiently accountable to the public, that it was fast becoming "a state within the state." Bourassa's decision to separate the James Bay project management from Hydro was seen as a political move towards curbing the utility's powers.

If that was the premier's purpose, it failed. In mid-1972, while Bourassa toured the world's investment houses in an effort to drum up capital for James Bay, Hydro's Robert Boyd and Roland Giroux were telling legislators that only Hydro's control of the project could ensure the necessary investment would be forthcoming. Bourassa succumbed, Boyd replaced Nadeau as head of the James Bay energy corporation, and by 1973 Hydro's borrowing ($500 million) was exceeding that of the provincial government.

But Hydro's supremacy would prove short-lived. Within months the utility was becoming a junior partner in James Bay management, as key posts fell to the Bechtel Corporation of San Francisco, supported by the adroit Paul Desrochers. Bechtel, the biggest construction outfit in the world, had built most of the pipelines in Canada, managed the construction of Hydro's dam at Churchill Falls, and was engaged in giant resource projects from Suez to offshore Siberia. The firm had a reputation for tough, tight project management even if, as Terry Godsall puts it, "they left a few carcasses bleeding in the bush." And Bechtel had important corporate connections with the investment house of Morgan Stanley, which floats bonds to raise capital for big projects, and Hanna Mining, a giant in mineral exploitation. Hanna, in turn, was allied with Rio Tinto Zinc, owned by the Rothschild interests, which controlled Brinco. Brinco, in its turn, controlled the Churchill Falls (Labrador) Corporation, in which Hydro-Quebec was a junior partner. Before long Bechtel managers from the United States were moving into the key jobs on the James Bay project. As Bechtel's share of project fees rose to a reported $250 million, Montreal unions and student groups protested the U.S. corporation's strangle hold and the serious loss of prestige for Quebec engineers.

While criticism mounted, Bourassa was describing James Bay as the spawning ground of "a purely Québécois civilization." Pierre Nadeau was forgotten. But the question that had ruffled him in discussions with reporters continued to haunt the controversy.

Why, an irritated Nadeau had asked, in the midst of so much expansion, was everyone asking him about 5,000 Indians? "Can't we cohabit with 5,000 Indians in twice the size of England?" Nadeau had demanded. "We're not out to destroy all the lakes and beaver and caribou. We want to give the Indians a choice between the traditional life, which is disappearing anyway, and taking training courses to be bulldozer operators and craftsmen."

What Nadeau and his successors never understood is the Indians' knowledge that the choice is no choice at all, merely a rationale to legitimize the destruction of their subsistence economy.

In the age of large-scale resource development, evil intentions are not required to wreak havoc in a way of life; a simple failure of imagination will do it. It should be apparent that men such as Bourassa and Nadeau, callous as they would appear in the development of the James Bay fiasco, did not set out to injure the Cree people of northwest Quebec. What became equally apparent was that such men were not well-equipped to see the Indians as they really were. As Liberals and technocrats, these two were exhilarated by the achievements of modern technology. As ethnocentric white men, they equated employment with wage labour. In their narrow understanding, an Indian drawing $80 a week from a menial bush-clearing job was employed. Philip Cox on his trapline, the hunters in the goose camps on the islands near Fort George and the groups of Indians drawing nets of whitefish from the summertime La Grande were not employed because their lifestyle eluded the simple classifications of wage labour.

Nadeau's idea that a young Cree might find his personal fulfilment in tearing up the bush from the back of a bulldozer overlooks and insults the Cree's sense of the relation between man and nature. In the goose camps near Fort George in 1972 one met "educated" young Indians who had come home from exile in the white man's world—students fleeing high school in Moosonee, a teacher who had quit, a surveyor who'd worked for Hydro-Quebec—because, as they put it, each needed to "get my head together." For them the rhythm of life in the bush was the only assurance of sanity in a world going crazy.

In the camps, they would break the thin shore ice at dawn and set up their well-carved decoys and crouch in familiar trenches to wait for the distant pencil lines of geese spearing north over the treeline and, as the great birds neared, they would call to them from deep in the throat, shooting them surely and cleanly when almost directly overhead. At dusk snowmobiles would draw home tub-shaped wooden sledges laden with geese, which would be taken to a teepee with fragrant spruce boughs on the floor where village women were cleaning and dressing geese, wasting no part, before the meat was shared out among the people, as it had been for hundreds of years. Bourassa and Nadeau were perhaps not aware that the Cree did not hunt for kicks but maintained a respect for their prey, recognized their interdependence with the geese and the caribou, and saw a good day's hunting as nature's reward to men who live by this immemorial code.

In Fort George, the largest and most "urban" settlement of the entire region, there could be no more adaptable Indian, even by Nadeau's standards, than Josie Sam Atkinson. Josie Sam is a businessman, franchised by the Shell company to sell gasoline and motor oil to Fort George. He is a politician—a diligent and articulate band councillor. He is a householder, with a princess telephone in the kitchen of his government-designed house. But on days when the geese fly before the spring break-up the Shell pump stands idle while Josie Sam is away in the camps. He has no illusions about what Nadeau's choice will mean for the village. He does not believe for a moment that the presence of free-spending gangs from Hydro-Quebec and a stepped-up cashflow in the Shell station can mean a better life for his children.

"Money," he says, "is a thing that comes and goes. Remember the DEWline—that brought money into the North; but where is it now? The village, the country, the food and the animals are here. They don't come and go. We depend on the animals and fish and they depend on the country. If we lose the country, we lose everything—everything that matters to us." Chief Billy Diamond, energetic young leader of the Rupert House band, put it more forcefully in the natives' inconclusive 1972 encounter with Bourassa: "Social effects on the Indian people," the young chief told the flustered premier, "will be greater than in any other project in the world. We have a project when the people are not socially developed. You are pulling them back fifty to seventy-five years and their future is nothing but beer and destruction."

Northwest Quebec was a wilderness only on the white man's maps. For the Cree people who trapped along its riverbanks and made its forest trails and knew the rapids where the whitefish spawned, it was a garden. They developed decades ago a viable system of land use. Even after the federal government had introduced compulsory schooling and broken the pattern of seasonal family migration to traplines and hunting and fish camps, the Cree evolved new economic patterns in which wage labour and welfare payments played a part, but in which food from the bush remained essential for subsistence.

All this is scientifically supported. The Quebec anthropologists Harvey Feit and Ignatius La Rusic had studied Indian land use over decades and shown how, by a complex system of rotating hunting and trapping grounds, the Cree had introduced a viable pattern of hunting rights and conservation that preserved the species that brought them subsistence. Wintering in the Mistassini bush, the young Toronto anthropologist Adrian Tanner reported that seventy-five percent of the winter food was meat from hunting. "I found here," he declared, "one of the few aboriginal populations still in control of its culture. It is not in the sorry state of most of Canada's northern Indian communities today." The Cree economy, he urged, must be preserved if the tragedy of dependence and social disintegration were to be avoided.

But, ironically, the most telling testimony of all came from the task force of McGill University anthropologists under Dr. Richard

Salisbury that the James Bay Development Corporation itself had invited to report on the native economy. Salisbury's scholars introduced mass survey techniques into Fort George, where they listed the game catches and cash earnings of one third of the adult male population, and assembled the first authoritative economic profile of the region's 6,000 Cree and Eskimo people. Wild game, they reported, provides sixty percent of total food supply and ninety percent of all protein. Basic sustenance of the northern settlements came, seasonally, from geese, rabbits and fish. The pattern of remote settlements such as Rupert House and Mistassini was true with only minor qualifications for the 1,289 native people of relatively "urban" Fort George.

In that village, said Salisbury, hunting and fishing brought in 421,189 pounds of meat in a year, 84,838 pounds of it white-fish. Estimated cash value of the meat was $525,000. When receipts from trapping furs, wages, pensions and welfare payments were reckoned in, the community had annual cash earnings of $1,543,100, representing $5,130 for the average household of 4.8 persons. If that average household had to buy all its food at the Hudson's Bay store (the only store in town) its annual spending on food, rent, heat and light would come to $4,260. There'd be little margin to pay for snowmobiles, outboards, canoes, guns, fishing tackle, house maintenance, storage freezers, gasoline or ammunition. The Cree would be virtually im-mobilized.

Dr. Salisbury concluded: "If all needs were met using cash, basic subsistence covered in our estimate of $4,260 per year could not be met. Not all a family's needs can be met by cash alone. Yearly catch records, wage and income figures and the conclusions reached for meat consumption and wild food values have clearly shown hunting is still a vital part of the Fort George economy and a necessary subsistence activity." When that conclusion was in, Bourassa and the James Bay developers could no longer shelter behind ignorance or uncertainty about what the loss of hunting, trapping and fishing caused by the project's destruction of rivers and forests would mean to the Cree.

What might have been news to Bourassa was, of course, already understood by the leaders among the Cree. By a cruel irony, the project had been launched in a time of relative plenty.

185

Beaver were abundant and the caribou were returning in numbers to the northern regions. Fort George chief Robert Kenatawat and a party of hunters in a chartered DC-3 had assured his village of winter meat by shooting ninety caribou in a day and a half near Great Whale.

Kenatawat, Josie Sam Atkinson, Billy Diamond in Rupert House and sensitive Philip Awashish, who had trained in engineering at McGill and then discovered that the best way to stay sane was to return to his people in the Mistassini bush, realized quickly that the Hydro project was a death sentence on their way of life. For the first time, they saw, the Cree and Inuit of the scattered communities faced a common challenge. They must come together if they were to survive.

In June, 1971, Philip Awashish and Billy Diamond chartered aircraft to bring leaders from throughout the region to a three-day meeting in the little schoolhouse at Mistassini. The chiefs decided to cable Indian Affairs Minister Jean Chretien, their constitutional guardian: "We, representatives of the Cree bands affected by the James Bay hydro project, oppose these projects because we believe that only beavers have the right to build dams in our territory ... we request the minister to use his legal jurisdiction to stop any attempt at intrusion...." Chretien was to claim later that he never received the message.

The first Cree protest was under way. And there can be no doubt that the delegates at Mistassini were speaking for their people. Happily for the historical record, the Quebec anthropologist Ignatius La Rusic spent that summer wandering through the Waswanipi country, taking his tape recorder to meetings of the people in tiny settlements. Here, in my very free translation, is a fragment from one of those meetings, introduced by La Rusic's own humane commentary:

"It would be wrong, however, to believe that the Waswanipi are thinking only of their own welfare when they assess the damage likely to be created by eventual flooding. At one meeting an old woman created enormous concern when she asked: 'Are all the dead people in the graveyard going to be under the water?' And when the answer was positive, the people all reminded themselves of the care with which they had chosen the burial grounds in order that the family tombs—though scattered all over the Waswanipi territory, they were meticulously and affectionately remembered—were always positioned so they could never be flooded.

"Beyond that, perhaps the saddest comment of all came from an old woman who listened attentively as the chief outlined the effects of the project with the aid of a map showing the districts earmarked for flooding. She said, as much to herself as to the others, 'Poor fish!' "

Nadeau's corporation, meanwhile, began to distribute propaganda favouring the project through the villages. The first distribution was a truncated version of a federal-provincial task force report on the environmental effects of the project. It was, unhappily, in a bastardized Cree. In Rupert House on February 21, 1972, Annie Diamond, the chief's sister, attempted to read the document to a village meeting but found it unintelligible; the dots between the vowels had been omitted and the words made no sense. A man in the audience shouted that "it should go into the fire" and the people, gathering pamphlets in their arms, rushed to stuff them into the wood stove. Others were taken out into the snow and, in something of a carnival air, burned in a ceremonial bonfire. Later, the Waswanipi began mailing copies back to the corporation with polite little notes in Cree, regretting that they were unable to understand the report.

What followed, in Lionel Chevrier's words, was "the runaround." The Indians of Quebec Association repeatedly attempted to set up negotiations, to talk to Bourassa, to appeal to Chretien. The federal minister, maintaining an uneasy posture of public neutrality, came through with $250,000 in research funds. Dr. John Spence, the dynamic McGill biologist, organized the many-talented scientific James Bay Task Force. And the Indians of Quebec Association assigned Montreal lawyer James O'Reilly to prepare an application for a temporary injunction to stop construction by the James Bay Development Corporation affecting one quarter of the land area of Quebec. By the time that application opened before Judge Albert Malouf of the Quebec Superior Court, Spence's scientists had assembled the most massively documented case against a major resource development ever advanced by Canadian native people. Through seven long months of expert testimony, Judge Malouf would hear the most comprehensive critique of the project that could be mounted on social, economic, and environmental grounds.

The political system, having proved effectively closed to them, the natives of northwest Quebec had turned to the courts to plead for survival.

Whatever the Indian reaction, Quebeckers and Canadians at large had received the announcement of the James Bay project with a kind of numbed incomprehension. It sounded too big, too impossible, to get one's mind around. Fort George, Great Whale and Fort Chimo were a long way from populous urban Canada and, for a long time, it seemed that nobody much cared. With the honourable exception cf the Montreal writer Boyce Richardson, the English-speaking media appeared to ignore James Bay, mustering more interest in Brazilian genocide in the Amazon jungle than in the fate of such countrymen as Philip Cox. Except for the left-of-centre tabloid Quebec-Presse, the French-language press displayed a parallel apathy.

In popular terms, it was not until the spring of 1973 that things began to move. Almost a year to the day after my meeting with Philip Cox I was sitting in the crowded auditorium of Université du Quebec's Pavillon Lafontaine in Montreal, where chansonier Gilles Vigneault, the symbol and beguiling voice of Quebec's cultural renaissance, was presiding over an influential "committee of inquiry" into the James Bay fiasco and speaking magisterially of "shame" over Quebec's treatment of its original people. That same day, the Montreal papers carried advance reports of a *grand spectacle* by popular entertainers for the James Bay natives. Two years after Bourassa's own *spectacle* in the Coliseum, the meaning of James Bay was beginning to reach people.

But it was late. Now the bulldozer gangs were preparing the site for LG-2. A dirt road snaked along La Grande's south bank seventy miles from Fort George to LG-2. More than 3,000 workers (an officially estimated fifty of them Indians) were pushing an all-weather road through the lake-stippled bush from Matagami to Fort George. Oil pollution was killing fish in the wild La Grande. In the two years it had taken to enter public awareness, the project was becoming a reality. It was very late.

If the public at large was slow to take fright, the economists were not. To them Bourassa appeared to be gambling wildly with billions in public money. Aside from the question of whether the project made sense at all, it obviously entailed a terrifying escalation in costs. As recently as 1970, Hydro-Quebec had harnessed Churchill Falls to produce 5,000 megawatts for just under $1 billion. In 1967, Hydro-Quebec had advanced a scheme to harness nine James Bay rivers to produce 10,000 megawatts and the cost of that had been estimated at $1.5 billion. In Bourassa's Coliseum extravaganza, he had talked about harnessing five major river systems and generating 14,000 megawatts—all at a development cost of $6 billion. One year later, announcing a start of the "northern" scheme, the premier claimed that channeling three rivers into La Grande would produce 8,000 megawatts at a cost of $5.8 billion. The cost of three rivers and 8,000 megawatts was to be roughly the same as five rivers and 14,000 megawatts! Questioned later, Bourassa conceded that the estimates could be on the low side and that costs could rise to $10 billion. Why, the economists and the opposition were asking, should a development that would produce less than twice as much power as Churchill Falls cost the province more than six times as much?

Another source of worry was Bourassa's erratic definition of the purpose of the project. At the Coliseum, he had boasted of solving New England's energy crisis, and it was assumed that the possibility of marketing large quantities of Quebec power in New York was one of the reasons for James Bay. Both Consolidated Edison and the New York Power Pool were contract customers of Hydro-Quebec and continued service to United States industry had certainly been part of the rationale for James Bay. But Bourassa depended upon Con Ed, owned by the Chase Manhattan Bank (Rockefeller), First National City Bank of New York and the Morgan interests, for access to the necessary investment funds. And the American utility was stalling him.

But in early 1972 Bourassa was making a pitch for financing from Ottawa. "The Canadian government through the Bank of Canada might find it interesting to finance this project," he said. "It is an asset for Quebec and can become an asset for Canada." Two months later, after a talk with Pierre Trudeau, the premier had veered back to foreign borrowing. Next, he emphasized that, without James Bay power, Quebec could face an energy shortage in 1978, a prophecy he later deferred to 1980. Oddest of all was the suggestion of a James Bay Development Corporation official that possibly the power generated at James Bay, which might ultimately double provincial capacity, could all be used in the immediate vicinity of underpopulated northwest Quebec, without any exports to the rest of the province!

Whether Quebec will need another 8,000 megawatts in 1980 is a highly debatable point. It was debatable, first of all, because the National Energy Board estimated that provincial demand would rise by five and a half or six percent per year, whereas Hydro-Quebec figured the growth would be seven to seven and a half percent. When these differing projections are compounded by seven years, they represent vastly different estimates of 1980 power needs, as the Superior Court hearings would dramatize. Bourassa, throughout, used Hydro's projections, now considered suspect. Hydro itself, of course, as the utility producing the electricity and promoting its sale, has some control over the demand curve. Yet it spurned conservationist policies, continued to encourage wasteful space-heating and a rate structure discounted to industrial corporations; it did nothing that might make James Bay appear less necessary.

In most jurisdictions dam-building is today considered a costly and outmoded means of power generation. Nuclear and thermal plants are delivering power at lower cost. But, when Hydro-Quebec's commissioners were considering James Bay, it is true that nuclear programs in both Canada and the United States were over budget and behind schedule. Hydro had convinced itself that Quebec's capacity had to be doubled from its 1971 capacity of 11,000 megawatts, to which Churchill Falls was adding 5,000, to a capacity of 26,000 megawatts by 1985.

James Bay power, for domestic use, cannot conceivably be cheap. When the northern rivers have been diverted into huge new reservoirs and a staircase of dams built down the 500-mile La Grande and the 700-mile transmission lines built to Montreal, that power is expected to reach the metropolis at a delivered cost of perhaps fourteen mills the kilowatt hour, a mill being one-tenth of a cent. This is almost three times the cost of power from Ontario Hydro's nuclear plant at Pickering delivered in Toronto and from Quebec-Hydro's own Churchill Falls installation delivered in Montreal. Even in 1980, Atomic Energy of Canada promises production units that will deliver at less than half the cost of the first output from James Bay. Hydro-Quebec faces an unenviable dilemma. It must escalate the price to consumers at twice the rate of past increases, or it must export power equivalent to three-quarters of La Grande's output to New York State on terms that might not be advantageous. The Massachusetts power economist Peter Slavin appraised Quebec's energy options in the spring of 1973. He concluded that any option, even thermal stations burning increasingly costly low-sulphur oil, would be more economic than James Bay power.

Does the James Bay power project, in short, make any sense at all?

Put that question to the former Liberal cabinet minister Eric Kierans, who is a quick, intuitive man, and he jerks up his hands, shrugs emphatically and answers: "It's madness." Put the same question to the Parti Québécois economist Jacques Parizeau, who is a man of more deliberative mien, and he pauses thoughtfully and answers: "It's madness." Kierans, of course, worries about the project's impact on the value of Canada's dollar and consequently upon our manufacturing industry, particularly if the Mackenzie Valley gas pipeline is undertaken at the same time as James Bay. Parizeau favours a chain of medium-capacity nuclear stations within easy reach of Montreal, a view endorsed by the authoritative nuclear specialist W. Paskievici.

Kierans' McGill colleague Kari Levitt worries about the future of manufacturing industry inside Quebec. Bourassa's opting for costly hydro power will make it vulnerable even to competition from within Canada. "Burdening the people of Quebec with high-cost power is a dangerous game," she told the Gilles Vigneault inquiry. "If this province loses the magnificent advantage of cheap power, there will be layoffs in manufacturing industries struggling under competition from both the U.S. and Ontario."

What she finds particularly omin us is the stalling of David Rockefeller in advancing James Bay capital and the delay of the related Consolidated Edison company in contracting for James Bay power. Why are they stalling? They could be waiting for a decline in nuclear production costs in the United States. If those costs were to drop to Ontario levels, Con Ed would be in a position to drive an exceedingly hard bargain with Hydro-Quebec.

In these circumstances, says Kari Levitt, Bourassa's frequent pilgrimages in search of foreign capital "could put us in a situation where some of the most powerful financial groups in the world will be able to dictate the terms on which they will lend us funds. Those terms could include high interest on the loan, plus a twenty-year contract for the delivery of electricity to Con Ed, plus guarantees that delivery would be on a non-interruptible basis."

She had glimpsed the same nightmare as the power economist Slavin: that, with the James Bay project committed beyond possible cancellation, Quebeckers could be pressured into subsidizing the export of their electricity at cost. In such an arrangement, all Quebec's consumers would be required to subsidize the corporations that light up New York, perhaps for a generation.

In the light of so many economic and social hazards, not to mention the widespread environmental havoc, one is forced to wonder how any sane provincial authority could plunge further into such a hapless undertaking. There can be no simple answer. But there are clues, discernible in the singular complexities of politics and power in contemporary Quebec. Whatever the ultimate cost, there are some who will profit from the adventure. There will be at least three levels of advantage for business in Quebec and its senior partners in the multinational corporations.

The first level is that of the Montreal construction and equipment companies now engaged in the construction and servicing of roads, bridges and airstrips. Firms of this type provide the campaign funds of the Liberal party and are susceptible to the patronage so skilfully managed by Paul Desrochers. It was upon the recommendation of such firms, it should be remembered, that Bourassa launched the project in the first place. In November, 1970, Hydro-Quebec assigned two Quebec firms of engineering consultants to report back on the feasibility of James Bay by the following March 1—in less than four months! Unsurprisingly, since both firms stood to pick up important contracts over a long period, they promptly reported precisely what Bourassa wanted to hear, full steam ahead! Hydro-Quebec, which in early 1971 was at least a year away from knowing the economic viability of development on the southern rivers (NBR) and knew virtually nothing about the northern ones, did propose serious long-term study. But Bourassa jumped the gun with his spectacular at the Coliseum.

Local contractors, then, potentially significant allies in ensuring the political future of the governing Liberals, would be the first beneficiaries. And, certainly, they would be able to spread some employment around, though Bourassa's initial boast of 125,000 jobs was remarkably downscaled to more modest estimates, settling at an expected construction peak ranging between 6,000 and 12,000. Once the hydro installation is in operation, it will be operated by a handful of white technicians.

The second beneficiary is the project management firm, Bechtel of San Francisco, now locked into contracts estimated at more than $250 million. From the standpoint of the huge international investment and mineral corporations with which Bechtel is interlocked, the presence of the American construction giant is a guarantee of management on sound multinational lines, with no more than a token bow towards local control (language of work on the project is, at least theoretically, French).

The third, and ultimately the important group of beneficiaries would be the international mineral corporations using the infrastructure so expensively laid down for James Bay and the American energy corporations importing the power. Some of these beneficiaries, of course, would be corporate relations of Bechtel. In the summer of 1973, as Bourassa moved anxiously towards a new election campaign, his speeches placed increasing emphasis on the mineral deposits of northwest Quebec.

The premier was in political trouble, haunted by the scandal shadowing murdered Pierre Laporte, impoverished by the impending departure of the most respected figure in his ministry, Claude Castonguay. Bourassa would find it necessary to inflate once again the economic promise of his development adventure. However costly La Grande power might be for the Montreal householder, it could provide cheap service for the extractive industries, as could the 500 miles of James Bay project roads. Iron and copper corporations had made many a reconnaissance of northwest Quebec in the fifties and sixties, withdrawing on the grounds that the necessary port, airstrip or highway services would prove too costly. Great Whale Iron Mines had talked of 400 million tons of iron ore concentrate, Duncan Range Iron Mines had claimed it could extract 5 million tons of iron ore annually for forty years. Nemiscau Mines, a subsidiary of International Nickel had copper claims in the region and Falconbridge Nickel had prospected there. There was talk of uranium deposits. It is not unrealistic to expect that the James Bay infrastructure, installed by dint of monumental provincial borrowing, will yet provide a bonanza for the great extractive corporations.

On May 22 and 23, 1973, Dr. J. Daniel Khazzoom blazed and flashed like a beacon of intellect from the witness stand in the Superior Court of Quebec. He was the last in a six-month parade of witnesses presented by the James Bay Task Force before Judge Albert Malouf and he was, in the words of task force organizer Dr. John Spence, "the most arrogant, testy, splendid and irrefutable witness" the judge had heard. For two days he turned the courtroom into an intellectual fireworks display and, when it was over, Hydro-Quebec's rationale for the James Bay project had been ripped to shreds.

Dr. Khazzoom was a forty-one-year-old economics professor at McGill, a scholar of international brilliance, and former chief econometrician for the Federal Power Commission of the United States. His speciality was to set up econometric models, the purpose of which he defined as "to quantify what the economist talks about in general qualitative terms." He had submitted Hydro-Quebec's projections for electricity consumption in the province up to 1985 to the test of an econometric model and he delivered his verdict at the start of his testimony.

"What," he was asked, "is your opinion of those projections?"

"I think they are exaggerated. I think they are out of line with anything that could be realistically expected."

For two days on the stand, Dr. Khazzoom displayed a vast erudition about all forms of electricity usage, the economics of power utilities and the mathematical structures of his science. Though he was exhaustively and sometimes repetitively cross-examined, he never flinched from his judgement that Hydro's projections were quite unreal.

194

For Dr. Khazzoom, the essential deficiency of the Hydro-Quebec projections was easily explained. What Hydro had done was project the growth rate of its sales in the 1960s "mechanically" into the future—as an unvarying upward curve. But the 1960s had been a decade of phenomenal growth in Hydro's sales because private electricity companies were nationalized in that decade. In the four years between 1960 and 1964, Hydro's share of the total electricity sold in the province doubled. Between 1960 and 1969, Hydro's share of the total surged from 30.8 percent to 67 percent. The increased sales reflected not increased consumption by Quebeckers but the expansion of the public utility at the expense of the former private electric companies!

Hydro's projections, if they were to have any value, insisted Dr. Khazzoom, would have to be based upon the growth of electricity sales in all of Quebec, and then they would have to be projected into the future in a more subtle fashion than as an unswerving line of constantly rising growth.

In fact, said Dr. Khazzoom, the rate of demand growth for all Quebec was 6.4 percent during the 1950s and 4.3 percent during the 1960s. That was roughly half the level of growth shown in the Hydro-Quebec projections.

Had Hydro projected accurately, it should also have considered means of using its productive capacity more effectively, through manipulation in the rate structure, and it should have considered alternative means of increasing capacity. "There are alternatives," he said, "that ought to be explored systematically before an investment of the magnitude of LG-2 should be undertaken. No well-managed business can afford to undertake an investment of this magnitude without exploring all possible alternatives available to it."

Perhaps the first clue that something was seriously amiss in the James Bay project came with the embarrassing exposure of Bourassa's near-farcical "environmental studies." Two months after his Coliseum announcement, a handful of civil servants in Ottawa and Quebec was designated a federal-provincial task force, given $30,000 and told to get together such published material as might appear relevant. Their briefing came from Hydro-Quebec's Andre Langlois. They were not to discuss whether or not there should be a project, he explained—that was already decided. They should just write about the environmental effects, and be quick about it. The group collected papers, held thirteen informal meetings and flew over the NBR rivers for three days as guests of Hydro-Quebec. By December their report was in print.

It was, inevitably, a flimsy document, particularly since critical passages and papers had been edited out. The emasculated published version was not taken seriously by the scientific community and prompted McGill biologist Dr. John Spence to "wonder what they did with the $30,000; I did as much analysis in three weeks' spare time at the university." Spence and his wife produced for the United Nations a serious study of the project's likely devastation. As for the federal-provincial task force, it made only one firm recommendation: that the headwaters of the northern Caniapiscau should never be diverted. Bourassa was to ignore that.

In fact, the first thorough, on-the-spot study of the northern region was to come only in 1972 under the impetus of Spence and his James Bay Task Force, combined with the work of Dr. Richard Salisbury's team of anthropologists. Spence also approached senior specialists across Canada and, by the time the Superior Court hearings opened in the winter of 1972, the first clear picture of what the project would do to the environment was beginning to emerge. The testimony of the scientists and native people parading before Judge Malouf would constitute the greatest body of knowledge ever assembled about the rivers and forests of northwest Quebec.

But the farce of federal-provincial studies that can change nothing continues. Ottawa and Quebec are currently spending a joint $4 million on "environmental impact studies," the first of which are due to be published in spring, 1974. By that time, according to the development corporation's construction schedule, three airports and the 450-mile road from Matagami will have been completed and construction will have started on the pivotal LG-2 dam. The studies now under way are what the corporation calls "inventory" and "baseline" work; serious study of environmental damage will not begin until 1974. By the time those results are in—in 1975 or 1976—they will be of no more than academic interest. If they are thoroughly done, they will be a record of devastation that has already taken place.

We are on the northern edge of the forested world. Flying north along the eastern shore of James Bay, the icy slash of river and lake punctuates the green of the boreal forest. But somewhere north of Fort George and south of Great Whale, the country changes, the forest thinning until it is tiny black patches of spruce that dot the whiteness of snow and shrubs—forest tundra. Farther north still, even the spruce patches thin out and then naked tundra stretches northeast to the tip of Ungava through an icy desert almost as big as Europe.

It is the edge of the forested world. The witness who made that point to Judge Malouf was Dr. Kenneth Hare, the bio-climatologist directing research for Environment Canada and a specialist in subarctic environments. What we know about such country, said Dr. Hare, is only "reconnaissance knowledge." One thing we do know is that life here is sparse and it is slow. Plants and animals grow slowly and there are few species. Here the chain of life is most fragile.

Dr. Hare described the region's 160,000 square miles of lichen, the rootless mossy carpet that northern mammals feed on when other plants lie dormant in winter. Lichens grow so slowly, said Dr. Hare, that it takes decades to produce a thick ground cover. And lichens, here, begin the chain of life. The mammals subsist on the lichen and the men subsist on the mammals.

The northern rivers project will flood 3,000 square miles, most of it the "wetland" country rimming rivers and lakes. It is the alders, willows and thickets of the wetlands, Dr. Hare explained, that are the habitat of the moose and the birds. When the wetlands are drowned by the project, "the new shoreline will be in contact with what is now dryland vegetation. You will, in time, get the establishment of a new kind of wetland vegetation. But the animals are not adaptable to such changes." They will die.

When Bourassa switched his project to the remoter, less visible north, he claimed it was for "ecological reasons." He did not acknowledge, perhaps, the marginality of life on the northern fringe, where a one-degree temperature change caused by the creation of reservoirs could mean the death of a species. Nor did he acknowledge that the northern scheme would spread the damage across the Ungava peninsula to the Eskimo settlement at Fort Chimo, 1,000 miles northeast of Montreal.

Under the northern scheme, half the flow of the Great Whale River, which empties into Hudson Bay, will be diverted south into La Grande. The Caniapiscau, which flows northeast to Ungava Bay, will be reduced forty percent to flush new reservoirs in the La Grande complex. South of La Grande, the Opinaca, a tributary of the Eastmain, will be dried up below new reservoirs. The overall effect, said Dr. Hare, will be to introduce more freshwater into James Bay and less into Ungava Bay, changing incalculably the water chemistry and the rhythm of ice breakup, of temperature and season in both of these regions.

On La Grande, said the Edmonton civil engineer Dr. Rolf Kellerhaus, "very spectacular erosion" will befall the plunging, 300-foot valley below the big dam at LG-2. Flows up to 100,000 cubic feet per second will spew sand, silt, clay, gravel and boulders into the debris-strewn river, its new shore a maze of dead trees. "Even rotting is a slow process in the north: the shores will be clogged for forty or fifty years." "Devastating fluctuations," said Ottawa biologist Melville Fenton, will prevent the re-establishment of stable vegetation. "The animals will be displaced and die."

At the beautiful place twenty miles upriver from Fort George that Indians call First Rapids and Hydro calls LG-1, Dr. John Spence counted one hundred fat, female whitefish moving to spawn in the shallows in August, 1972. LG-1 will dump fifty feet of spillway waters there. Whitefish, twelve percent of the diet of the Cree people of Fort George, will not spawn there again.

What the scientists who testified to Judge Malouf provided was a confirmation of the Indians' original perception of the James Bay project. It would destroy, as the Indians had suspected all along, the plants and animals, the chain of life, and the lifestyle of the Cree.

Sprawling Fort George at the mouth of La Grande still had a little sweetness in it in 1972. Tom Webb, the hotelkeeper, I noticed, attended Sunday evensong at St. Philip's Anglican mission before driving his kids to the movies in the immaculate, white-fenced compound of the French-speaking Roman Catholic mission at the other end of town. But Sunday was the only evening the helicopters were silent. The elders at St. Philip's worried about construction gangs, booze and whoring. Through the main village of the "coastal" Cree, around the suburban rows of the government houses and in the "inland" village, traditional home of the upstream trappers, there was a lack of ease.

Before this book went to press, that unease had been magnified by one hundred new pressures, many of them small and subtle. The summer of 1973 was remembered by the villagers for its poor fish run and much of the grumbling about the development corporation centred upon its habit of fouling the river with oil. Tom Webb's lodge was being expanded and, though there were many more white technicians in town, they confined most of their social life to the French-speaking compound around the hospital and the Roman Catholic mission. Josie Sam was still organizing opposition to the project and the villagers were still saying that it must not happen.

Philip Cox, who had been out on the trapline again during the winter of 1972–73, was saying that he would do the same in the winter of 1973–74. But he was now less sure. Cargoes of equipment landed at Fort George were being trucked along the dirt road to the LG-2 site, where 500 men at work on a diversion dam lived in tents and mobile homes on a site that would soon be a permanent village. Unusually persistent forest fires pocked the north bank in August, as if the wrath of God had fallen on the place, but jet planes could now land on the airport that had been levelled at the northern extremity of Cox's section. The trapper, though determined still, was less sure about the winter to come.

In Fort George I met a dozen women from the staff of the chidren's residence run by the federal government. They were capable, middle-aged matrons who held their jobs because they knew how to manage children; several were the wives of community leaders. It shocked me that they were so tense and afraid —afraid that the onrush of water from LG-2 would erode the village, that they would be ordered to move, that white men would take over the village. "If they destroy this place," said one, "we might as well die." Another said flatly: "No matter what they tell them, our children will never become white persons. We want to stay as we are."

That, in essence, was all the Cree had ever asked of the white man—to be allowed to stay as they were. But they would not be. And they knew that they would not.

Chapter Ten

Slaves of Waste

"Hydro believes the standard of living always goes up with the consumption of electricity. But I don't see Canada's living standard rising seven percent every year."

— George Bowman, Chairman, Manitoba Energy Council.

Back in the 1950s, the Bell Telephone Company in the U.S. made a discovery about growth. Company researchers analyzing the rate of increase in long-distance calls projected that rate into the future. Given the same growth rate and technology, they learned that by the 1970s they would need to employ all the women and girls in North America as long-distance telephone operators! Work on automated long-distance switching was consequently stepped up and today's computerized system began to take shape. In the face of approaching scarcity, Bell created a labour-saving technology.

Dr. Michael A. Goldberg, the University of British Columbia economist, uses the example of Bell to point up the fact that North America's hydro-electric industry, also facing approaching scarcity, has failed to produce an energy-saving technology.

It is easier, then, for a sophisticated society to reorganize its workforce than its pattern of energy consumption? Eighteenth-century Britain, after all, produced the steam engine, and consequently the Industrial Revolution, when confronted by a scarcity of wood fuels.

This is a daunting question for a layman to pose. When modern electric utilities advance a major project, they do it

200

with assurance and expertise, with an air of having studied all the questions and secured all the answers. Experienced engineers, economists and bureaucrats elaborate arguments to show their project is necessary and wise. The public, untutored on such technical matters, plays little part in making a decision. And the project goes through.

Then things go wrong. And it becomes difficult to maintain the belief that the project is the creation of some flawless act of supra-personal wisdom. Engineers, economists and bureaucrats, for all their authority, can obviously go terribly wrong. They must, after all, stumble through byways of fallible reasoning, sometimes making judgements that are erratic or subjective. Though they clearly feel their decisions flow from scientific principles, some of these principles have been adopted with the fixity of religious doctrines.

One such principle, or article of faith, was classically stated by Dr. Gordon Schrum, former chairman of British Columbia Hydro: "The progress and growth of our country, industrially and domestically, depends upon the increased use of electric power." The same idea, hackneyed by overuse, returns in the everyday assumption of power companies that "the standard of living rises with the consumption of energy." It would be illogical for followers of this faith to promote the saving of energy. They feel, without questioning their logic, that the faster we use our energy resources, the wealthier we shall be.

But suppose it isn't true? Dr. Goldberg put it in question with an ingenious series of graphs. The vertical side represented the dollar growth of the Gross National Product (total value of goods and services produced) per kilowatt hour consumed. The horizontal base represented increasing electricity consumption. Goldberg charted such graphs for British Columbia, Canada and the U.S.A. In B.C. and Canada, dollar growth per kilowatt hour scarcely changed while consumption doubled. In the U.S., the growth drastically declined. In a second sequence, Goldberg contrasted the GNP dollars produced by each kilowatt hour with the absolute per capita change in Gross National Product. In all three graphs, the GNP per capita soars between 1960 and 1970. In the U.S. and Canada the dollars per kilowatt hour line slumps throughout the decade; it stays roughly constant in B.C.

In the U.S., says Goldberg, the economic efficiency of the kilowatt consumed has been in an intermittent decline for more than a century. "Since 1850," he says, "periods of rapid economic and technological growth have been typified by increased efficiency in the use of energy, and periods of slackness have been typified by the increasing inefficiency with which we use our energy. While there does seem to be a definite relationship between the use of energy and growth, it seems to be a negative relationship. The more efficiently we use energy, the more rapidly we grow, which means we use relatively less energy."

If growth is compatible with energy conservation, the approach of most of the experts running Canadian utilities is a long way off base. Goldberg is not alone in suggesting this may be so. The Manitoba Energy Council's George Bowman suspects that electricity production and consumption is today a system running out of control. Its operation is the opposite of the classical free market, which contained built-in correctives. All the "feedback" a hydro company receives is information that will push it farther in the direction in which it's already moving. By generating new uses for power, by giving corporations price reductions on quantity and by building capacity in excess of needs to attract foreign investment capital, hydro utilities run beyond the control of either the market mechanism or the political governments.

Increases in capacity and discount prices serve to multiply demand. So do electrical space-heating, appliance advertising, all-night lighting and such gadgets as the electric toothbrush. If the tobacco industry pursued comparable promotional methods, it would buy advertisements to convince men that rubbing tobacco on their skin would give them "sex-appeal." Women would be told that "tobacco shampoos" would improve their hair.

The dynamo driving this binge in energy consumption is the process hydro men call "improving the load factor." The load factor is the ratio of average demand to peak demand or, in everyday terms, that part of capacity that is never put to use. No electric utility sells all the power it can produce. The daily load pattern is a series of peaks and valleys. From midnight to 6 A.M. is a valley. There is a swift ascent to a 9 A.M. peak, which levels off in a daylong plateau. At 6 P.M. the coincidence of industrial, commercial and domestic use pushes the load to its highest peak. At 7 P.M. it begins its decline into the valley of night.

Obviously, a more even pattern would be more efficient. The energy industry tries to even things out with rates encouraging the use of off-peak power. The rate structure of hydro companies is designed to sell cheap off-peak power to fill in the valleys. But the companies do not attempt to level the load by chopping off peaks! This logical extension is widely applied in Europe, where cheap off-peak rates are accompanied by stiff premiums on peak-hour use.

"A great deal can be achieved through such manipulation," says George Bowman, a veteran of the power business in Scotland. "In Britain, the rate structure is used to make the industry more efficient and more accountable for the capacity it uses. If we could level off our load curve by similar manipulation, we should be in the fortunate situation of having enough electricity to meet our needs." The Churchill River could be left in its natural course.

But, for most hydro engineers, rivers are simply "free goods." They do not enter the ledger of production costs. So the drive is to fill in the valleys without chopping off the peaks. The trouble is that there will soon be no more "free goods."

Alberta's Energy Resources Conservation Board recommended in 1973 that growth in the province's electric capacity must be based on its plentiful reserves of coal. The board's economists also want Alberta coal shipped east to Ontario Hydro. This, they argue, would be a more efficient use of Alberta's resources than piping more natural gas to Toronto. Better to use the gas in developing the petro-chemicals industry around Edmonton, or exporting it to increasingly profitable U.S. markets.

All this assumes the environment is a "free good." Ontario Hydro's conversion of the Hearn plant to natural gas halved Toronto's air pollution, believed to run around $200 per citizen per year in health costs and property damage. Those costs have not been reckoned in. At the producing end, the value of the beautiful Alberta foothills that are to be ripped up by strip-miners have not been reckoned in, either. It is not, in the end, the straightforward marketplace decision some economists think it is.

Canadians buy too much electricity and pay too little for it. The biggest wasters pay the lowest prices. Corporations that light up Toronto's night from ugly office towers get low discount rates. "The more the corporations use under the existing structure," George Bowman says, "the more the rest of us pay for it." The domestic user subsidizes the corporations, most of which are foreign-owned.

Electrical space heating, heavily advertised at the consumer's expense, is an extravagant use of power. Gas and oil water heaters in homes are sixty to eighty percent efficient. When the same source fuels are used by a generating station that will supply the home with electricity for heating, only thirty to forty percent of the original energy is ever put to work. An equal amount is dissipated in conversion and transmission.

Most Canadian hydro utilities have been provincially owned for decades, and their constitutions have emphasized the provision of cheap power. Their bosses, frequently engineers, have boasted of operating on strict business lines, with aggressive promotion and advertising, discounts for bulk purchase and incentives for off-peak use. Ad agencies sold electricity the same way they sold soap, detergents and hair shampoo. For years, hard-nosed hydro managements dismissed anti-pollution groups urging the conservation of energy and a recognition of the social costs of hydro generation as impractical kooks.

The energy crisis has changed all that. While the executives of Hydro-Quebec were still pleading the obsolete doctrines of the demand curve before Judge Albert Malouf in Quebec Superior Court, Ontario was planning to abandon the conventional wisdom of hydro utilities in a dramatic energy shakeup. Its author was Darcy McKeough, a vigorous and combative Tory politician who had resigned as Ontario's provincial treasurer after a conflict of interest involving property in his hometown of Chatham, and returned to work for Premier William Davis in the formulation of an energy policy. McKeough's assignment was to integrate the findings of Advisory Committee on Energy under Dr. John J. Deutsch with those of Task Force Hydro, an inquiry that had led to the reconstitution of Ontario Hydro as a crown corporation under ministerial control.

McKeough tendered his report June 1, 1973 and, within a week, Davis had set Ontario on a new course in energy policies that could influence provincial development for more than a decade and influence energy decisions across Canada. The Ontario premier announced a $3 billion program of nuclear expansion. He announced that Ontario would contest Alberta's new schedule of natural gas prices through the Supreme Court. He denounced the federal government for leaving Canadians at the mercy of profiteering oil corporations and promised the province a minister of Energy—McKeough.

As he placed his authority behind McKeough's heavily underscored message that "the era of cheap energy has ended," Davis made it clear that in Canada's most industrial province many of the attitudes of the past, many of the traditions of his party, his government and his bureaucracy at Queen's Park would have to end too. McKeough was suggesting controls on uranium exports to protect the nuclear program, a national electricity power grid, a hard look at the national oil policy, price regulation for oil, provincial investment in energy reserves, public hearings on hydro application for rate increases. Ontario, it was clear, was making a clean break from the past and was prepared to change many relationships to protect its energy needs of the future. His work invested with urgency by the inter-provincial quarrel over gas prices and Ottawa's apparent abdication of responsibility, McKeough had apparently sensed a historic moment, a moment in which a new start was both possible and necessary.

Thirty years earlier, his Tory predecessors under George Drew and Leslie Frost had been launching a phenomenal age of Ontario expansion that would be based on cheap hydro, fast deals, cutting a few corners and a liberal indulgence of the development ethic. The time for that, McKeough saw in the spring of 1973, had gone—new answers were needed and a lot of the mental baggage of that expansionist era, including the conventional wisdom of hydro chairmen, would have to be thrown out the window. In his emphasis on the need for efficiency in the use of energy—and he stressed that "the government . . . has an important role in clarifying the issues and providing leadership in terms of energy conservation"—McKeough was ready to pick the brains of those impractical kooks from the environmental movement; passages of his report would read like a rerun of one of the mustier releases from

Pollution Probe at the University of Toronto.

Stressing that the social and environmental costs of energy production would have to be reflected in prices, McKeough went on to relate conservation and efficiency in the use of energy to a wide range of public policy. The ideas, at this point, were no more than suggestions, but suggestions advanced under the most powerful sponsorship in the province.

Transit: The energy situation must give new impetus to Ontario policies designed to slow freeway construction and increase the use of public transportation in cities;

Trucks: A wholesale shift from the movement of goods by wasteful trucks to rail transport providing efficiency through economies of scale must be studied by the Transport Ministry;

Heating: Ontario Hydro and housing developers should end "builder promotions" encouraging wasteful electrical space heating of homes, and encourage better insulation that would reduce consumption of fuels;

Diffusion: Expensive, superior fuels should not be employed where inferior ones would do the job without environmental damage. Ways should be found to utilize energy wastes in the cooling of thermal plants and home heating systems;

Automobiles: The government should publicize the wasteful gas consumption of big cars and penalize owners of wasteful vehicles through a new system of license fees;

Daylight: Ontario Hydro alone could save 400 megawatts of capacity—the output of a small thermal plant—through the introduction of daylight saving time.

These and other measures, if followed up, would make a large impact on the pattern of energy use in Ontario's industry, commerce and urban transportation. But what serious students of the energy business such as Dr. Michael Goldberg and George Bowman would find most encouraging of all was that McKeough did not skirt around the crucial issue of the load curve. He made a frontal attack on the conventional wisdom of the hydro business. For the first time in any province the authoritative-sounding technical mythology that promotes Churchill diversions and James Bay projects was officially disavowed.

"Price structures," wrote McKeough, "should be designed to encourage economy of energy usage rather than to encourage increased consumption. Price policy should encourage and reward efficiency in the use of energy." His recommendation that modifications be made in the price structures of all energy forms could only mean that manipulation would begin to chop off the peaks in the load curve, as Bowman had suggested, and end the free ride enjoyed by corporate users at the expense of householders through the discount system. Noting "with approval" Ontario Hydro's recent withdrawal of load-building promotional advertising, McKeough also wanted private corporations and municipal utilities to avoid the encouragement of waste by ad campaigns and promotions. Dr. Michael Goldberg's thesis, in fact, had won substantial vindication.

If Ontario follows through with legislation, the official adoption of a conservation ethic will produce profound changes affecting utilities, corporations, business, consumers and the native peoples, changes established bureaucrats and company presidents will not like. It will arm people with realism against the corporate manipulators of scarcity. And, if we can avoid the emulation of U.S. blunders in such an important section of the domestic economy, it may enhance the prospect of Canadian independence, which could never be secured through an American value system of constantly rising consumption and growth. By refusing to be a wasteful society, Canadians would in fact become a different society. This, perhaps, was the kind of distinction implied by the Canadian philosopher George Grant when he wrote that "Canada should continue to be only if we could hold some alternative social vision to that of the great republic."

Chapter Eleven

Ottawa: The Careless Guardian

"It was established that American investment is eighty percent of the total foreign investment in Canada and that seventy-six percent of all companies in Canada with assets over $25 million are foreign owned. Fears were expressed that Canadian citizens might lose political as well as economic control of their own country; that they would be barred from the best jobs and the best land; that they would be run by absentee landlords; and that Canadian people and resources would be working for the enrichment of other peoples and other lands."

— Senate-Commons Committee on the Constitution, 1972.

"Unimposing." That is the measured understatement the Dalhousie Four professors apply to the performance of our central government in the great resources controversies of the last twenty years. It is not, in the light of the record, an uncharitable verdict.

Ottawa, for the fathers of Confederation as much as for millions of contemporary Canadians, has been considered the ultimate guardian of the nation's resource wealth and economic prosperity, of the integrity of the natural landscape, and of the wellbeing of all the people. Yet its guardianship, at best, has been "unimposing."

There are two aspects to this dereliction. The first is that when ill-considered resource projects have been launched on provincial initiatives, as so many have, the federal government has proved insufficiently protective of the nation's long-term interest, its environment and its native peoples. The second aspect is that, when huge developments have been organized under federal auspices, Ottawa has been prepared to serve as a promotional advance man and service contractor for giant foreign energy corporations.

In their brief to the Canadian Council of Resources and Environment Ministers, the Dalhousie professors had shown that most big energy projects had been "spurred by the burgeoning demands for primary resource inputs from the United States." The U.S. had become the beneficiary of provincial oversights about the true long-term value of the resources being exported and some of the unaccounted ecological costs of development—the environmental price of extracting resources had been exported by the U.S. to Canada.

The Dalhousie Four added this: "Conflict between the provincial and federal governments in terms of how to best utilize those resources has been an all too frequent characteristic In every case it would appear the strength of provincial constitutional claims over their resources, coupled with the federal government's undue caution, perhaps as a result of the series of Quebec federal-provincial jurisdictional crises, has led to a situation where the various provinces have enjoyed what amounted to a free rein to exploit nationally important resources as they saw fit."

Short-term parochialism in provincial capitals is serious enough, and Canadians have paid dearly for it. Careless guardianship in Ottawa, particularly in the context of the American energy crisis of the seventies, is clearly an even greater danger. The national geography and the contemporary pattern of exploitation being what they are, an increasing number of the targets of the resource developers will be those under federal jurisdiction. As the Energy Task Force under Dr. John J. Deutsch reported to the government of Ontario in the spring of 1973: "As the oil and gas production from the western sedimentary basin levels off in the mid-1970s and greater emphasis is placed on frontier resources, the centre of policy influence will swing from the provincial level to the federal level, those frontier resources being under federal jurisdiction and influence in one way and another."

Even before the frontier push, Ottawa held large formal

responsibilities for the guardianship of resources. Its National Energy Board was charged with the regulation of both inter-provincial and international trade in natural gas. Its national oil policy, which had helped spur the Alberta boom of the early sixties by providing an oil market as far east as the Ottawa Valley, had over the years fallen victim to the continent-wide price squeeze exerted by cartel companies controlling the pricing of both imported and western crude and petroleum, and was the subject of one of Ottawa's agonizingly protracted policy reviews. Its national power policy, introduced in 1963 to encourage the development of large-scale power sources at low cost, encouraged both interconnections between provincial hydro systems and the export of large blocks of power to the United States. Even exports of soon-to-be priceless uranium were not prohibited by its Atomic Energy Control Board, though Ottawa did move in 1970 to prevent the significant uranium reserves of Denison Mines falling under foreign control. The federal government also operated its own uranium mine and refinery and, as a partner of American corporations in Panarctic Oils Limited, served as an exploratory outrider for the cartel corporations at work in the Arctic Islands. Having noted the various federal interests in the energy field, the Deutsch report of 1973 noted that they indicated "not a single overall national energy policy—rather that there are a number of particular national policies relating to specific energy resources."

By 1973 that was a widely-heard complaint in Canada, a faithful echo of the unheeded protests of American resource economists in the squandered years of U.S. depletion. "How," asked Ontario's Darcy McKeough, "can we have a coherent, concise and clear industrial strategy for Canadian development when we lack one of the kingpins—a federal energy policy?" The only answer from Ottawa was that the matter, like most matters, was under review.

As foreign takeovers continued virtually unchecked and as larger numbers of Canadians realized the destructive consequences of the resources sellout, two broad conclusions were taking hold. One was that Ottawa was not using its powers to protect Canadian resources and the other was that, even if it had the will, Ottawa did not possess sufficient powers to undertake full protection.

210

The Dalhousie critique had shown quite vividly that, far from acting as a countervailing force to the promotion of provincial sellout, Ottawa was standing on the sidelines, a complaisant spectator.

It was, as we have seen, the Pearson government that ratified the Columbia River treaty, though it was a Canadian disaster. It was essentially W. A. C. Bennett's settlement, not a federal scheme, that the national leaders signed. The Dalhousie Four's conclusion was that the treaty "reflected British Columbia's expressed interests almost exclusively . . . in hindsight it is clear that not enough attention was paid to the future value of the resources at issue in the treaty." Yet Ottawa had an unquestioned right of veto; E. Davie Fulton and Paul Martin could, after making a hard-headed appraisal, have broken off negotiations with the United States. They chose the less controversial course of deciding that the treaty presented to Canada was better than no treaty at all. It is doubtful, in retrospect, if they knew what the treaty was really for. The hydro economist Larratt Higgins had long since concluded that "the Canadians were talking about a power treaty, whereas what the Americans wanted was flood control and water," and this was the later view of J. S. Cram's authoritative *Water: Canadian Needs and Resources.* "The Pacific Northwest," he wrote, "gets the big bulk of the water from the Columbia River—twenty-eight percent coming from Canada. The United States had that water in mind when it signed the Columbia River treaty, which, considering power alone, was a second best."

It was the National Energy Board that presided over the export of Alberta's best and most accessible natural gas at fire sale prices. It was not perhaps surprising that Alberta's Social Credit government, overawed by the overweening presence of the petroleum industry giants in the province should, as the Dalhousie Four put it, "opt in favour of a badly unrestrained 'export at any price now' policy." It is, surely, still difficult to credit that a national body armed with substantial regulatory power could have gone on licensing this fire sale until export commitments had rocketed more than one trillion cubic feet in excess of required reserves. Before that point, federal intervention would have been both constitutional and effective. Later, when Premier Peter Lougheed had come to power and doubled the price of natural gas to the industries of eastern Canada, it was natural enough for the Dalhousie Four to exclaim: "Why Canadians outside his province should have to subsidize the sub-optimal bargains made with the United States is something of a mystery." But it was then too late for Ottawa to intervene. Lougheed's drastic price revisions, however damaging to national manufacturing prospects, appeared to be within his constitutional right and were, in his view, "necessary"; if Ottawa had stopped the fire sale years before, the higher prices could never have been justified.

When the Alberta Social Credit government was flirting with the notion of water exports, Ottawa maintained a discreetly low profile. But, for years it pumped federal millions into a study of prairie river diversions that would make economic sense only if sales to the U.S. were involved. And it sponsored and paid for the high voltage direct current transmission system to Winnipeg from the Nelson river, an installation that was to help promote, under provincial auspices, the greatest river diversion in North American history on the Churchill.

The federal government's politically expedient tightrope walk to "neutrality" was not the least farcical touch in the James Bay extravaganza. Here Ottawa had ample scope for intervention—and knew it. In this case it could not even shelter under the constitutional complexities of the matter, since Michael J. Bird of the Department of the Environment's Policy and Planning Directorate had prepared a careful analysis of federal interests affected by the development, a report that was hushed up for several weeks in the summer of 1972. Once Bird's report had been received in the Department of Environment, Ottawa's inaction could no longer be attributed to ignorance.

There were, Bird reported, at least four grounds for federal intervention in the $6 billion James Bay hydro-electric development. Federal responsibilities for Indians and lands reserved for Indians and for migratory birds, navigation, coastal and inland fisheries were all affected by the scheme.

As a signatory to the Migratory Birds Convention of 1916, Canada had a treaty obligation to preserve the hundreds of thousands of Canada Geese that returned from their Texas wintering grounds along a flyway moving north along the east-ern shore of James Bay, where dams and diversions would soon swamp their feeding grounds. If the United States were so dis-posed, warned Bird, it could hold Canada liable for failure to take "suitable action" to preserve the geese. Given the energy crisis, and the American expectations of future Quebec power, that may seem a remote eventuality, but that consideration scarcely justifies the federal leadership in reneging on a treaty commitment and countenancing the possible decimation of the wild geese.

Under the Navigable Waters Act, Bird told his minister, construction of works on the Great Whale, La Grande and Eastmain rivers could proceed legally only after applications had been submitted to and approved by the federal minister of Transport. "Where the approval of the minister is not first obtained," said Bird, "the minister may require that the party responsible remove or alter such work, and should he fail to comply with the minister's order, the work may be destroyed." Ottawa's authority to prevent the massive destruction of white-fish and other species was, Bird found, equally clear: "Where the preservation of fisheries is threatened, as may occur in the James Bay hydro development, the federal government may intervene to protect the species." There was, he stressed, "no constitutional restraint . . . which prevents the federal govern-ment taking necessary action to preserve the fish population."

The effective restraints in Ottawa were not the Canadian constitution . . . but Canadian politics. Nowhere was this more apparent than in the federal government's looking-both-ways attitude to the issues affecting the 6,000 Cree Indians of north-west Quebec whose subsistence economy the project would destroy. Bird's constitutional report was unambiguous in sug-gesting that Ottawa had ample powers to save the Cree. There were at least four options: Ottawa could refer the James Bay Region Development Act to the courts to determine its consti-tutional validity; Ottawa could apply to the courts for a declara-tion of the usufructuary rights of the Indians and an injunction restraining the James Bay Development Corporation from ex-propriating land subject to Indian aboriginal title; Ottawa could move under the Indian Act to protect Indians inhabiting lands reserved for their use by Quebec under the Lands and Forests

Act of 1922; Ottawa could legislate for the protection of the Indian culture under Section 91 (24) and the federal general power of Section 91 of the British North America Act.

In fact, as we now know, Ottawa did none of these things. As Robert Bourassa ran up the grandiose corporate edifice for his "project of the century," it was not the mandarins in Ottawa but the Indians in the bush—Billy Diamond in Rupert House, Robert Kenatawat in Fort George, Philip Awashish in Mistassini—who were beginning to organize the enormous collective effort of Indian self-preservation. Repeatedly snubbed by Quebec officialdom, the Indians of Quebec Association would find important allies among the scientists of McGill University and in a superbly professional law firm on Notre Dame Street.

Ottawa was "neutral." It expressed sympathy, it advanced money, almost $300,000 of it for research it knew would contribute to the court fight—but it would not abandon its "neutral" stance; it failed to expose the socially destructive impact of the hydro scheme upon the life of the people for whom it was the supposed guardian. Perhaps Michael Bird's report provides one clue to the uncharacteristic federal "generosity" with funds for native peoples. "Should the federal government choose not to protect Indian interests," he had warned, "it may be liable for its failure to obtain compensation for the surrender of aboriginal rights in the region." And such a liability might cost it a good deal more than $300,000!

If the project were not to be stopped, Bird suggested, Ottawa has an option that could at least temper the devastation through effective environmental regulations. "In regards to the project itself," he wrote, "the federal government might legally declare it to be 'for the advantage of Canada', under Section 92 (10) (c) of the British North America Act. This would enable comprehensive environmental control of the entire region. An alternative means of control may be through the 'federal general power' of Section 91."

There were, in other words, half a dozen ways for Ottawa to move in defence of the James Bay Cree, through prohibitions or through the assumption of environmental controls. But, as he came to write the final paragraph of his report, Michael Bird must have glimpsed the inglorious realities of federal-provincial politics closing like shadows round his pigeonhole in the bureaucracy. For he then wrote: "Although it may not be politically expedient to unilaterally impose on the Quebec government such environmental controls as may be legally possible, it is suggested that the Dominion is in a position to urge both the Quebec government and the James Bay Development Corporation to study more closely the environmental effects of the projects before proceeding further." As Shaw's Earl of Warwick said of the arrangement to martyr Saint Joan, "political expediency, though occasionally erroneous, is always imperative!"

Most of what Bird had written about Ottawa's opportunities to stop, or civilize, the James Bay project was equally true for Manitoba's scheme to kill the Churchill River. But, there again, it was the threatened native community that was left to mount the legal fight for its life. It was not, in retrospect, a period that favoured serious federal interest in resource economics, native rights or the environment. It has been suggested that these topics simply bored the pre-election Trudeau cabinet. Ottawa then was preoccupied with asserting its political role in Quebec. The James Bay dispute emerged at a time when the Trudeau government was engaged in an exhausting eighteen-month campaign to convince Claude Castonguay, Quebec's minister of Social Affairs and the one universally respected member of the Bourassa regime, that it knew more about the social allowances required by Quebeckers than he did. "They've wasted years meddling in everything but the economy"—I recall a disenchanted Eric Kierans almost spitting out the words. "They worried more about getting federal signatures on pension cheques in Quebec than ever they did about resources policy."

If, as the Dalhousie scholars convincingly showed, successive Ottawa governments had failed to make good use of the powers they possessed, that is not to say that they unquestionably possessed sufficient powers. For thirty years, the process of foreign takeover has made sweeping inroads into that fragment of our economy that remains Canadian-owned. For at least three years, United States political pressure for a horse trade involving a commitment of Canadian energy resources has been growing markedly less genteel. And now the energy crisis brings an added tautness.

Against this backdrop, the constitutional report of a special committee of the Senate and Commons that dropped into Parliament's lap in the spring of 1972 might have been expected to cause a stir. For, given that the sellout process, the near-monopolist power of the energy corporations and the push for frontier resources add up to a grave threat to Confederation, the recommendations could have provided some needed national armor.

The report's first recommendation was for a new and distinctively Canadian constitution. Its second was for a "functional" federalism—one that would turn upside down the priorities that had so disgusted Kierans. The committee wanted social and cultural affairs to be determined by provinces—Castonguay, in other words, had been right—together with "a greater centralization in powers which have important economic effects at the national level." The committee had worked two years, held public meetings across Canada. When it listed the principal criticisms it had heard, the committee assigned priority to these:

"(1) The federal Parliament does not have sufficient power to manage and plan the economy.

(2) The federal Parliament does not have sufficient power to cope with large multinational corporations, international unions and the overwhelming influence and power of the United States of America."

So the parliamentarians under Senator Gildas Molgat and MP Mark MacGuigan emphasized a federalism capable of properly regulating the economy through structural, monetary and fiscal policies to attain national economic goals. This federal government would require exclusive jurisdiction over international and interprovincial trade and commerce, controls over wages, prices and profits, and concurrent power with provincial legislatures to regulate competition. "Many markets are dominated by a few major firms, and the degree to which a market economy exists in the classical sense has already been questioned . . . . The ability of provinces . . . to control effectively such large economic units is open to question"—as the 1968 McKenzie Commission had found with the four cartel corporations in Alberta. Federal paramountcy was needed to combat pollution, the committee found, and to "ensure that no province could become a pollution haven."

To control foreign ownership, the federal authority should have paramount powers, including those of nationalizing industries and expropriating land and resources threatened by takeover. "Witnesses pointed out," the committee reported, "that jurisdiction over land and resources is overwhelmingly provincial, while naturalization and aliens and citizenship are federal responsibilities. There is some uncertainty, however, as to how effectively the powers over aliens and citizenship could be used to control foreign corporations, investors and entrepreneurs operating in Canada. We therefore recommend that the power with respect to aliens be clarified . . . so that the federal Parliament would have, beyond any dispute, paramount power to deal with problems arising from foreign ownership." Unsurprisingly, the Trudeau ministry has shrunk from adopting any such policies. Though joint-chairman MacGuigan claims the report has had "enormous impact" on social questions, and it may be one reason why new health minister Marc Lalonde ended the "confrontation" tactics against Castonguay, Mac-Guigan concedes it has to date had no "discernible effect" on economic policy, and it would be less than realistic to expect this government to attempt the regulation of its friends and contributors in the international energy corporations.

But those corporations will have to be challenged, and it is conceivable that a concensus is developing. Recommendations of the constitutional committee and the Dalhousie Four strike an answering chord among indigenous businessmen who find themselves outside the charmed circle of the integrated energy corporations. Bruce F. Willson of Union Gas, for instance, a corporation president most of his life, is saying that "the 'market forces' theory of private enterprise obviously tends to break down when you deal with non-renewable resources. We need policies that will optimize the enterprise system and integrate it with the government controls now necessary in the nation's interest."

MacGuigan's committee appeared to be probing for that balance. Had that kind of federalism been at work in the economy, the resource blunders from the Columbia to James Bay might never have happened. Today, as projects get bigger and more irrecoverable, as the U.S. energy crisis exerts its relentless upward pressure on the costs of Canadian manufacturing and the cartel grip tightens round the frontier regions, the question of Canada's survival is more starkly posed: an effective federalism or none at all. The age of superabundance has gone. We do not have another expendable river to dam, another block of hydro or gasfield to export and, if the energy conglomerates sitting on our last frontiers succeed in shipping out the oil, the gas, the uranium and the minerals, there will be no remaining basis for an expansive Canadian industry. Outside the ranks of the Trudeau government, demands were rising for a new toughness and realism in resources policy.

At Hamilton's McMaster University, Walter Gordon, one of the founders of the Committee for an Independent Canada, demanded a crown corporation to control all oil and gas development in the far North. Control of frontier reserves by the cartel corporations, he warned, would, in the crisis atmosphere of the U.S. energy shortage, place American interests first in the major decisions of exploitation and marketing. The risk of a cartel "squeeze" against Canada, highly likely so long as the oil giants controlled all the sources of Canadian supply, would be reduced if the national oil policy were jettisoned and the TransCanada oil pipeline extended from Toronto through Montreal to the Maritimes—a vital first step towards national control of the petroleum market.

David Lewis, whose New Democratic Party had become the Parliamentary prop for the Trudeau regime, argued that a publicly-owned Canadian Petroleum Corporation involved in the exploration, production, transportation, refining, wholesaling and retailing of oil and natural gas could break the existing oil monopoly and establish effective competition.

At the provincial level, too, a new sense of urgency was widely apparent. Since provinces are the owners of resource deposits their part of any program of national reclamation would be a significant one. Ontario Premier William Davis, mindful perhaps of the dramatic intervention of his predecessor John Robarts to avert a Canadian constitutional shipwreck in the 1960s, had been pleading for months for some evidence of national policymaking towards resource extraction. Since it was not forthcoming, he took the lead himself in June, 1973.

Davis, and Energy Minister Darcy McKeough, were prepared for tough actions that might be necessary to protect

218

Ontario's interests. They were prepared to test their opposition to Alberta's arbitrary new gas prices before the Supreme Court. They were ready to look at provincial regulation of oil prices in the face of corporate squeeze plays, and they were talking about provincial investment in energy reserves. While their demands for tight control of uranium exports, a two-way oil pipeline between Ontario and eastern Canada and better regulation of electricity pricing were obviously made in the interests of Ontario's manufacturing industry, it could not be charged that their overall approach to the energy crisis was a narrow, sectional one. McKeough's June 1 statement, in fact, was strongly federalist in tone and content. Ontario knew the need for national planning to beat the crisis and, since Ottawa had offered no leadership, the province was putting its proposals on the table.

"Our resources lie next door to the appetites of the United States," wrote McKeough. "Canada, operating in the absence of the rudder of a clearly-articulated national energy policy, is not in a position to protect our domestic industry and users in terms of price, supply or, indeed, security of supply in the event of a severe supply crisis in the United States. Canada cannot gamble that the Middle East will never use the power implicit in its control of oil for international political purposes; a politically-inspired supply crisis in the United States must be considered a possibility."

In that situation, he declared, "the prudence of committing our Canadian resources of energy to the export market is questionable. In fact, should we be considering any further exports of primary sources of energy? Certainly we must not be hasty in bargaining away petroleum and gas resources that may be proven in our Arctic regions and the offshore sedimentary basins of the Atlantic region."

"We must not be hasty" . . . McKeough's words challenged the go-go pipeline promoters and their political friends in Ottawa. The statement would not be welcome reading for Energy Minister Donald Macdonald, whose role in the advocacy of the Mackenzie Valley pipeline had been compared by Eric Kierans to that of "an executive assistant to the president of Imperial Oil."

But the Ontario statement was not conceived to score easy debating points against Ottawa; its serious federalism precluded that. Achievement of such national goals as a Canada-wide power grid, controls on uranium exports and energy prices, and an oil pipeline to Montreal and the Maritimes, would obviously depend on a consensus between the federal and provincial governments. Though Ontario would sue Alberta to try to obtain protected gas prices, it would also support the demands of western premiers for economic freight rates, assist Alberta schemes for marketing coal in eastern Canada and provide funds for research into the possibilities of giant transport planes to move liquefied natural gas and crude oil out of the high Arctic. Ontario, too, was ahead of Ottawa in recognizing the potential of the Athabasca tar sands as a field of public investment. While insisting upon a national interest in the exploitation and pricing of Alberta's natural gas, said McKeough, "I am fully conceding that the resources of copper, nickel, uranium and other Ontario resources must first be made available to the people of Canada and only secondly be available to world markets." Ontario would recognize the obligations, as well as the benefits, of membership in a federal state.

Prophetically, almost eighteen months before McKeough's forceful statement, the Dalhousie Four had written: "Leadership in the national interest will have to derive from the provinces acting either independently or in concert, if history has any contemporary lessons to offer." Such leadership appeared to be forthcoming in Ontario. If it had not yet appeared in Manitoba, it was not because an effort had not been made. In a report to the NDP government there, which has not been adopted, the former Liberal cabinet minister Eric Kierans had made a considered proposal for the development of the province's northern mineral resources. Kierans' work was important for the whole resources field because of the obvious analogies between northern mining and petroleum exploitation in Canada's frontier regions. The mining business in Manitoba, like oil, had its own "major league," with four corporations—Inco, Falconbridge, Hudson's Bay and Sherritt Gordon—holding four-fifths of all mining claims, and thirty-six corporations controlling eighty-seven percent of the assets, eighty-six percent of the equity, eighty-four percent of the sales and eighty-six percent of the profits. Mining revealed the same pitiful corporate contributions in royalties and taxes, financing less than two percent of Manitoba's modest provincial expenditures. In metals, as in oil, the corporations push for ever-widening exploration because, as Kierans says, "their control of markets depends on their continued control of sources of supply." In metals, as in petroleum, Kierans found that "changing resource policies will . . . set the province on a collision course with the large corporation. No individual or institution can bear to lose privileges which it has long taken for granted and considers unalterable." And, in metals as in oil, a province's boasts of resource riches are idle "if the costs of bringing the resources to market are less than or simply equal to the value realized by their sale. There has been merely a consumption of the wealth and some activity during the process . . . . As the wealth is slowly eaten away, the landlords become poorer."

Traditionally, said Kierans, Canadian provinces have failed to realize that resource development could offer "reasonable returns" to the people whose resources are now enclosed for the use of large corporations. "In private hands, the activity and employment will last until the resources and wealth have disappeared. In public hands, the activity and employment will last just as long and, in addition, the new wealth will remain as the capital thus generated finances other economic and social objectives."

Kierans put it bluntly to the Schreyer government that, if it decided to maintain the status quo, "it should frankly say to the people . . . that it is unable, helpless, to challenge the power and control of the corporations." Schreyer did not do that. Nor apparently did he swallow Kierans' prescription for the mining and milling of new ore bodies through crown corporations, plus more realistic taxation on the entrenched corporations. The supposed consensus in Manitoba, to which Schreyer is uncommonly sensitive, may have been unprepared for a major change in mineral development. Today it is British Columbia that appears more likely to challenge the decades-long ripoff.

That does not mean the Kierans plan will not become an element in the burgeoning national debate on resources. Its reminder that provinces, as the owners of resources, can with planning and political toughness secure a significant return from their exploitation, is both relevant and timely, as is its canny forecast of the price to be paid—a "collision course with the large corporation." If, as the Alberta experience suggests, Canadians are no longer content to be mere "pricetakers" from the foreign corporations that enclose their wealth, such new approaches are needed now. If a concerned Canadian businessman such as Bruce F. Willson can say, albeit with reluctance, that "we may need some kind of socialism to preserve a Canadian economy," the nation, its energy supply severely threatened for the first time in history, may be turning away from resource development on the paternalistic formula of Gas-Arctic and Donald Macdonald.

The Dalhousie Report, written to dispel Canadian illusions about resources, implies the need for strong provincial leadership as well as a determined assertion of that "economic federalism" suggested by the committee on the constitution. That, surely, is the only combination capable of containing the acquisitive thrust of the energy corporations, managing Canadian resources and preserving a decent environment for the remnant of the fossil fuel age.

The crucial question is this: is the exploitation of our remaining reserves to be programmed to service sophisticated research and development and the industrial innovation that will carry a resilient Canadian economy into the post-petroleum age? Or will the foreign energy corporations be allowed to exploit the dwindling reserves at their pace, at their price, and to meet their global priorities?

Epilogue

Canada's energy resources, which belong to us all, have not been managed in the interest of Canadians for a very long time. In project after project, the interest of foreign resource corporations and local political promoters has been placed before the interest of the nation.

Resource conservationists understood this for years, but their reasoned criticisms were spurned by federal authority. Now government arrogance has been tempered by events, so that in the middle of September, 1973, Energy Minister Donald Macdonald, stricken by a lightning flash of revelation, was moved to exclaim: "How is it that we have so much oil in this country and yet we are importing so much, and importing at other people's prices?"

That remark, placed in its context of the oil-pricing controversy, was really a confession of the Trudeau government's bankruptcy in the management of energy resources. Energy ministers of the Trudeau years—first the histrionic Joe Greene and latterly Macdonald—had intermittently adopted nationalist postures. Then, invariably, they had retreated in obedience to the stultifying constraints imposed by their cabinet colleagues or the pressures exerted by the common front of federal authority and the energy corporations. Macdonald's outburst, a clue to long-repressed Canadian frustration created by the power of the petroleum industry, followed by only two months the publication by the minister of *An Energy Policy for Canada: Phase 1*, a rambling, 600-page policy statement that had been effectively neutered in the Trudeau cabinet. That statement, prepared under the cautious bureaucrat Gordon Murray MacNabb, once Ottawa's engineering adviser in the Columbia

River treaty, and Deputy Minister Jack Austin, a former mining company president, gave predictable support to the Mackenzie Valley pipeline and echoed piously the development priorities of the Liberal government. It suggested no immediate policy changes in Ottawa.

By September, as Macdonald's rhetorical question indicates, the policy statement was already out of date.

Between Dominion Day, when the do-nothing-now statement was published, and the middle of September, Macdonald had announced the regulation of oil exports to the United States, the abandonment of the national oil policy, which divides Canada into two distinct markets east and west of the Ottawa Valley line, and a two-price policy that would oblige American corporations to pay forty cents a barrel more than domestic consumers for Canadian oil. All these moves came in reaction to a racing crisis of supply and price—a crisis the Dominion Day statement had failed to anticipate and analyze. The Trudeau government acted only when it was forced to act. And the actions it took under pressure bared the worthlessness of its "policy statements" in the long years of languid neglect of demands for a coherent program of national energy management.

In the first half of 1973, the price of a gallon of gasoline at a Toronto service station had jumped five cents on four occasions. Each of those increases reflected an increase in the price of crude oil, which, before November, 1972, had been stable for two years. Those increases, we have shown, have nothing to do with the cost of producing oil, which is in decline in major oilfields. The increases were imposed upon the Canadian motorist by the great corporations of the international petroleum cartel (the big eight) and the counter-cartel of the producing nations in the Middle East and Venezuela (OPEC). Each time the producing nations squeeze a higher price out of the international corporations, which control the transportation, refining and marketing of petroleum in the Western world, the corporations squeeze a higher price out of the Canadian motorist.

Donald Macdonald, it must be said, *had* attempted to correct that abuse. The original draft of his July policy statement recommended a state corporation to negotiate directly with the oil-producing nations the price of Canadian oil imports. It was this part of the statement that was emasculated by the Trudeau cabinet—perhaps out of fraternal respect for its corporate partners in the adventure of northern development.

Until September, 1973, then, the prices of petroleum in Canada were controlled in one way or another by the giant oil corporations. If you lived west of the Ottawa Valley, you burned oil drilled in Alberta and the price you paid was dependent upon current prices in the Chicago market and upon the prices Imperial Oil, the Jersey Standard subsidiary, was prepared to pay for crude at its Canadian refineries. If you lived east of the Ottawa line, the price you paid reflected the prices charged by another Jersey subsidiary in Venezuela and the world corporation's carrying and refining charges. Wherever you lived in Canada, the giant corporations decided what you would pay for your heating oil and your gasoline. And, wherever you lived in Canada, you paid much more in 1973 because prices were soaring in the American market and the Middle East and Latin producers were demanding a much higher return. Macdonald, to his credit, had made an attempt to loosen this strangle hold upon Canadians. The shortsightedness of the Trudeau cabinet ensured that his first attempt failed.

But events would not wait for the Trudeau cabinet. A swift-changing world struggle for petroleum supplies and the profits of scarcity would not permit the months or years of "research," "studies" and "reviews" envisaged in the authorized version of the Macdonald energy statement.

The barrel of oil purchased by a Chicago refinery in September for $4.90 had $1.25 of 1973 increases built into its price. And Canada west of the Ottawa Valley was part of one market in petroleum with the United States. American industry, fearing widespread breakdown in the event of a cold winter in 1973–74, was prepared to pay more and more for petroleum products. Because of the "one continental market" beloved by Calgary oil executives, Canada was to be locked into the prices of scarcity—even though we were producing more oil than we were using. The clear emergence of that situation made a farce of the Trudeau cabinet's passive support of the outdated national oil policy. It made inevitable the extension of the Trans-Canada Pipeline to carry Alberta crude to the huge Montreal market, and the two-price policy Macdonald announced in mid-September.

The export of half the oil produced in Canada to the United States and the import of as much from the nations and corporations engaged in exploiting scarcity was clearly national nonsense. Even Macdonald could see it now. He said he would act to divorce Canadian prices from American prices, to create price stability in western Canada and then to extend that stability to Montreal.

Had such a policy been adopted ten years ago, Canadian manufacturing would today be insulated from runaway U.S. fuel prices. Had it been announced in the Dominion Day statement, federal leaders might have used it to persuade the provinces of the need for a new direction. By its belated reaction to a crisis, the Trudeau government appeared hasty and arbitrary to provincial governments and succeeded in outraging Alberta at least as much as the American State Department.

Ottawa's last-minute action was, predictably enough, of a band-aid nature. When he slapped what was in effect a forty-cents-a-barrel tax on oil exports, Macdonald "froze" Canadian oil prices for five months to give Canadian industry a "breathing space" from the winter escalation in fuel prices. But the minister anticipated that after January, 1974, when the freeze was lifted, the forty-cent gap between Canadian and U.S. prices for Alberta crude would soon narrow. The petroleum corporations would not, on their record, be slow in catching up to the prices in their base country, unless permanent controls were applied. Within a month, Imperial Oil was attempting to by-pass Macdonald's "freeze." Macdonald promised no permanent controls. And he had still produced no national energy policy that relates the development of one non-renewable resource to the development of all the others. Ottawa was still flying by the seat of its pants.

The quickly-discredited July statement revealed the awesome vulnerability of the Trudeau administration in its dealings with resource industry giants. Though the price strangle hold of the cartel was acknowledged as real, it was not condemned. *An Energy Policy for Canada* was less candid about the practices of the corporations than the U.S. Federal Trade Commission, which concluded a two-year study with the charge that

"The majors have used shortage . . . to attempt to debilitate, if not eradicate, the independent marketing sector." Nor did Macdonald propose the breaking down of the integrated petroleum giants into separate corporations engaged in production, or transportation, or refining, or marketing.

Nor was the statement frank on environmental issues. Though it sermonized about the $7 billion environmental costs of coming resource projects, it said nothing about the havoc already unleashed at James Bay, or the destruction of the Churchill River.

What may prove, in the long haul, more serious is that the policy statement reflected no philosophy of resources conservation. Unlike the strongly conservationist Ontario policy announced in midsummer, 1973, Ottawa's statement threw down no challenge to wastefulness by individuals and corporations. With an average annual per capita consumption equivalent to fifty-five barrels of oil, it noted, Canadians are the second heaviest users of energy in the world. And it implied that this rate of consumption was necessary—"to enjoy the lifestyle and activities they find satisfying." Macdonald did not call for transportation, housing, economic and conservation measures that would make possible a more rational pattern of energy consumption.

The Ontario statement, which had an element of leadership, refused to dignify conspicuous waste as a "Canadian way of life." The federal government, its older members associated with sellouts reaching back to the Columbia treaty, was apparently too committed to the development idea to draw any lessons from American experience. They saw exponentially-rising energy demands not as a way of life imposed upon the continent by monopolistic energy corporations, but as a "Canadian way of life." They could not see the imbalance of a corporate system producing private affluence and public poverty as the source of the energy crisis.

Macdonald's report threw no sharp focus on the question of economic rents or the fundamental distinction between rent and profit in resource exploitation. Rent, as Eric Kierans defines it, is a return for the use of the people's land and resources. Profit is the return on the use of capital and entrepreneurship. Considering 177 small metal mining operations in Manitoba as one firm, Kierans worked out that $163 million of their combined "profits" of $231 million could properly be categorized as rent: "a royalty tax on sales up to this level would not prevent the firm from operating."

Because population growth and the energy corporations are increasing the pressure to exploit the earth's fixed resources, Kierans now argues that "the rehabilitation of David Ricardo's rent theory is *the* essential element, *the* starting point for economic policy." One forecast, he points out, can be made with assurance: "Profits may rise or fall but rents can go nowhere but up." The rent theory provides a measurement with which Canadians might begin to regulate the disposition of their non-renewable resources. In Kierans' analysis: "Canadian resources policy has been a failure because we have given away the rents of our own wealth."

There is no comparable idea, no comparable coherence, in Macdonald's report. It does not stress what General McNaughton realized twenty years ago—that resource projects are worth considering only when they enhance the long-term per capita incomes of Canadians. It does not answer the more contemporary criticism of the Dalhousie scholars that sellouts are undertaken for short-term gain without regard to greater environmental and social losses over the long term. And, though it pays lip service to the relevance of rent theory, it does not postulate the receipt by Canadians of the economic rent of resource extraction as a pre-condition for major projects. Bland, cautious and uncreative, it is essentially a prescription for business as usual. That was the formula American governments tried. The result was the energy crisis.

Operating without the discipline of any philosophy of resources, of development and of the environment, recent Canadian governments have lurched from one sellout to another, patching up the damage here, attempting an eleventh hour rescue there. Action in defence of the national interest comes only at the point where further inaction would be politically indefensible.

For all that, the possibility exists that 1973 could prove historically decisive. It was the year in which the northern march of the energy corporations and the spill over of the American crisis made resource development a national controversy. Popular illusions were stripped away. People saw the Trudeau government, generally so lethargic in economic matters, forced to react on the nation's behalf against the gouging of the energy corporations. They read with incredulity the importunate bombast of Imperial Oil's W. O. Twaits, who attacked his old ally Macdonald for acting in the nation's interest and who represented Imperial Oil as too poor to be able to pay higher Alberta royalties. A rift was forced in the common front formed by Ottawa and the energy corporations in their mutual haste to "develop" the North.

There was, in the fall of 1973, a mounting counter-pressure against the oil cartel and its allies in the major political parties. Kierans' new popularization of the rent theory was winning converts. In British Columbia the David Barrett government was writing an important sequel to the dismal story of Westcoast Transmission so assiduously researched by Ian McDougall. The Barrett government proposed a crown agency to produce, market, process and carry natural gas. It promised to end the decades of British Columbian subsidization of American consumers through underpricing, now estimated to be costing Canadian producers and the provincial Treasury some $100 million a year. Westcoast was still exporting gas at prices twenty-six cents per thousand cubic feet below its value based on the prices of competing forms of energy. Significantly, Attorney-General Alex Macdonald gave this rationale for the nationalization move: "We want to recapture for the people of B.C. the kind of dividends that will result from natural gas rising to its true value on the market." Premier Barrett promised there would be no more giveaways, and suggested that ending the parasitism of the energy corporations could provide pensions that would enable B.C. workers to retire at age fifty-five.

But one could not pretend that Canadians were not beginning a dangerous time. On the eve of the crucial hearings on the Mackenzie pipeline proposal, the nation was still without an energy policy, even though Macdonald had at last agreed to demands from all ten provinces for a national conference on energy. Ottawa was embroiled in a struggle over petroleum policies with Alberta's Premier Lougheed. And federal export restrictions and pricing measures had obviously been too little and too late to make a serious impact in Washington. Undeterred by any consideration of Canadian priorities, the Nixon administration continued its push for the "secure" petroleum supplies that lay in the northern half of the continent.

American officialdom wanted quick approval for a Trans-Alaska oil pipeline from Prudhoe Bay, to be followed by a tanker route down the British Columbia coast. It wanted the Mackenzie pipeline to serve as a cheap "land bridge" for Prudhoe Bay gas. It also wanted the gas that lay under the Northwest Territories and Canadian Arctic Islands. American industry, as the University of British Columbia's Dr. John Helliwell had shown, stood to make a long-term saving of $10 billion through the purchase of Canada's northern gas. The Nixon regime would not lose sight of that.

And on the frontiers, the giant energy corporations, trailed by their camp followers in mineral exploitation, were already in command of the resources. As their grip tightened on the northern and underdeveloped regions of Canada, the possibility of an effective independence grew more remote. To introduce the needed programs of national resource management so long urged by Eric Kierans and the professors of the Dalhousie Law School, would demand at this juncture an awesome, even heroic effort. The Mackenzie pipeline decision could be the last chance to make it.

Bibliography

Advisory Committee to the Government of Ontario. *Energy in Ontario: The Outlook and Policy Implications*; December, 1972.

Bird, Michael J. *An Analysis of Federal Interests Affected by the Proposed James Bay Hydro Development*; Report to the Minister of the Environment, May, 1972.

Bocking, Richard C. *Canada's Water: For Sale?* James, Lewis & Samuel, 1972.

Burton, Thomas L. *Natural Resource Policy in Canada*; Mc-Clelland and Stewart, 1972.

Commons-Senate Special Joint Committee on the Constitution. *Final Report*, 1972.

Congress of the United States. Pubic Law 92-203; *An Act to provide for the settlement of certain land claims of Alaska Natives*; December 18, 1971.

Cumming, Peter A. "Our Land: Our People"; paper to the National Workshop convened by Canadian Arctic Resources Committee; May, 1972.

Diamond, Chief Billy. Testimony before the Superior Court of Quebec, December, 1972.

Energy Resources Conservation Board. *Report on Choices among Energy Resources for Generation of Electricity in Alberta*; April, 1973.

Energy, Mines & Resources, Department of. *An Energy Policy for Canada, Phase 1—Analysis*; July, 1973.

Federal Field Committee for Development Planning in Alaska. *Alaska Natives & The Land*; Report to U.S. Government; October, 1968.

Feit, Harvey A. "L'ethno-écologie des cris waswanipis, ou comment des chasseurs peuvent aménger leurs ressources"; Bulletin d'information, Recherches amérindiennes au quebec; December, 1971.

Finance, Department of. *A Northern Canadian Gas Pipeline: Evaluation of the Impact on the National Economy*; confidential report; October, 1972.

Fenton, Melville. Testimony before the Superior Court of Quebec, 1973.

Ganong, W. B. *Horizontal Integration of Energy Resources*; Report to Ontario Advisory Committee on Energy; March, 1972.

Gibbs, R. J., MacFarlane, D. W. & Knowles, H. J. "A Review of the National Energy Board Policies and Practices and Recent Hearings"; *Alberta Law Review*, 1971.

Glooschenko, Valanne. "The James Bay Power Project"; *Nature Canada*; January, 1972.

Goldberg, Michael A. "The Economics of Limiting Energy Use"; *Alternatives* magazine; Summer, 1972.

Government of Canada. *The National Energy Board Act*; February, 1971.

Hare, Kenneth. Testimony before the Superior Court of Quebec, 1973.

Higgins, Larratt. "McNaughton's Last Campaign"; paper to seminar on Canada-U.S. relations; January 30, 1967.

—————. "The Alienation of Canadian Resources," in Ian Lumsden, ed., *Close the 49th Parallel*, University of Toronto Press, 1970.

Hydro-Quebec. *Baie James: Rapport Intérimaire*; May, 1971.

Industry, Trade & Commerce, Department of. *Canada's Commercial Policy and Energy*; confidential report to National Energy Board; 1971.

Joint Federal-Provincial Task Force. *A Preliminary Study of the Environmental Impacts of The James Bay Development Project*; December 20, 1971.

Kellerhaus, Rolf. Testimony before the Superior Court of Quebec, 1973.

Khazzoom, J. Daniel. Testimony before the Superior Court of Quebec, 1973.

Kierans, Eric. "Canadian Resources Policy"; paper delivered to Canadian Economics Association; June, 1973.

————. *Report on Natural Resources Policy in Manitoba*; report to Government of Manitoba, 1973.

Krutilla, John V. *The Columbia River Treaty: The Economics of an International River Basin Development*; Johns Hopkins Press, 1967.

La Rusic, Ignatius. "La réaction des waswanipis à l'annonce du projet de la baie james"; Bulletin d'information, Recherches amérindiennes au quebec, December, 1971.

Lewis, David. *Louder Voices: The Corporate Welfare Bums*; James, Lewis & Samuel, 1972.

McDougall, Ian A. "The Churchill Diversion: Development of a Legal Framework for the Management of Canadian Water Resources"; paper prepared for Environment Canada, September, 1971.

————. "The Canadian National Energy Board: Economic 'Jurisprudence' in the National Interest or Symbolic Reassurance?" unpublished paper; May, 1972.

————. "The Development of International Law with respect to Trans-Boundary Water Resources: Cooperation for Mutual Advantage or Continentalism's Thin End of the Wedge?" article in *Osgoode Hall Law Journal*; November, 1971.

————. "The NEB: Let's give credit where credit is due"; article in *Canadian Forum*; July, 1973.

McDougall, Ian A., St. J. Macdonald, R., Johnston, Douglas, M., Harrison, Rowland J. H. "Economic Development with Environmental Security"; a brief to the Canadian Council of Resource and Environment Ministers, 1972.

McKeough, Darcy. Report on Energy to the Government of Ontario; June, 1973.

McKenzie, Kenneth A. Report of The Gasoline Marketing Enquiry Committee to the Government of Alberta; December, 1968.

Newbury, R. W. and Malaher, Gerald. *The Destruction of Manitoba's Last Great River*; Special Publication of Canadian Nature Federation; January, 1973.

North, F. K. "A Sane Look at Canada's Oil Resources"; address to Alberta Society of Petroleum Geologists, September 23, 1971.

————. "Oil and Gas Resources: Delusion or Deception?" article in Calgary *Herald*, November 28, 1972.

————. "A Commentary on The High Arctic"; paper to Mont Gabriel Seminar, September 12, 1972.

————. "Canada's Oil Reserves: Surplus or Shortage?" article in Ottawa *Journal*, February 14, 1973.

Parti Québécois. *Dossier: l'Affaire de la Baie James*, 1972.

Paskievici, W. "D'ici 1980, les centrales nucléaires seront devenues les plus économiques"; article in *Le Devoir*, April 13, 1972.

Pimlott, Douglas H. "The future of a river under an NDP government"; article in *Canadian Forum*, July, 1973.

Richardson, Boyce. *James Bay: The plot to drown the North Woods*; Clarke Irwin, 1972.

Ridgeway, James. *The Last Play: The Struggle to Monopolize the World's Energy Resources*; Clarke Irwin, 1973.

Roseman, Frank & Wilkinson, Bruce W. "Who Benefits? The Alberta energy price increases"; an analysis published in *Canadian Forum*, July, 1973.

Ryan, J. T. "One View of the Future of the Oil Industry in Alberta"; paper delivered October, 1971.

Saskatchewan-Nelson Basin Board. *Annual Report*, March 31, 1971.

Salisbury, Richard F., Fillon, Fernand; Rawji, Farida; Stewart, Donald A. *Development and James Bay: Social Implications of the proposals for the Hydroelectric scheme*; report prepared by Department of Anthropology at McGill for James Bay Development Corporation, June, 1972.

Schramm, Gunter. "Analyzing Opportunity Costs—The South Indian Lake Issue"; paper delivered to Canadian Institute of Forestry, October 7, 1970.

Sherman, Paddy. *Bennett*; McClelland & Stewart, 1966.

Slavin, Peter. "The Cost of Power"; paper delivered to James Bay Committee of Inquiry, April, 1973.

Spence, J. A. & Spence, G. C. *Ecological Considerations of the James Bay Project*; report prepared for UN Conference on Human Environment, April, 1972.

Stewart, Walter. "Water—The Sellout that could end Canada"; article in *Maclean's* magazine, March, 1970.

Sykes, Philip. "Manitoba: The Power of Positive Pragmatism"; Toronto *Star*, May, 1971.

—————. "James Bay Cree fight for the land they starved on"; Toronto *Star*, May, 1972.

—————. "Billion-dollar U.S. settlement raises Canadian native hopes"; Toronto *Star*, October, 1972.

—————. "Canada is losing the energy game"; Toronto *Star*, December, 1972.

Surette, Ralph; Davis, Bob; Zannis, Mark. "The International Wolf Pack moves in on the North"; article in *Last Post*, May, 1973.

Tanner, Adrian. "Existe-t-il des territoires de chasse?" Bulletin d'information, Recherches amérindiennes au quebec, December, 1971.

Thompson, Andrew & Crommelin, Michael. "Canada's petroleum leasing policy—a Cornucopia for whom?" article in *Canadian Forum*, July, 1973.

Union Gas Company. Submission to the Energy Resources Conservation Board hearings on Field Pricing of Natural Gas.

Waterfield, Donald. *Continental Waterboy—The Columbia River Controversy*; Clarke Irwin, 1970.

Waverman, Leonard. "National Policy and Natural Gas: The Costs of a Border"; article in *Canadian Journal of Economics*, August, 1972.

Wells, Eric. FOCUS report on Nelson River Power, Winnipeg; August, 1969.

Wilson, J. Tuzo. "Why Canada Should Guard Arctic Oil"; paper to Mont Gabriel Seminar, September, 1972, published in the Toronto *Globe & Mail*, October 17, 1972.